Collins

Social Studies for Jamaica

GRADE 9

Series Editor: **Farah Christian**

Collins

William Collins' dream of knowledge for all began with the publication of his first book in 1819. A self-educated mill worker, he not only enriched millions of lives, but also founded a flourishing publishing house. Today, staying true to this spirit, Collins books are packed with inspiration, innovation and practical expertise. They place you at the centre of a world of possibility and give you exactly what you need to explore it.

Collins. Freedom to teach.

Published by Collins
An imprint of HarperCollins*Publishers*
The News Building
1 London Bridge Street
London
SE1 9GF
UK

HarperCollins*Publishers*
Macken House
39/40 Mayor Street Upper
Dublin 1
D01 C9W8
Ireland

Browse the complete Collins Caribbean catalogue at
collins.co.uk/caribbeanschools

10 9 8 7 6 5 4 3

ISBN 978-0-00-841398-9

British Library Cataloguing in Publication Data
A catalogue record for this publication is available from the British Library.

The publishers gratefully acknowledge the permission granted to reproduce the copyright material in this book. Every effort has been made to trace copyright holders and to obtain their permission for the use of copyright material. The publishers will gladly receive any information enabling them to rectify any error or omission at the first opportunity. See page 300 for acknowledgements.

Series editor: Farah Christian
Author: Laura Pountney
Reviewers: Monique Campbell and Kayon Williams
Editorial consultancy: Oriel Square Limited
Publisher: Dr Elaine Higgleton
Product developer: Saaleh Patel
Development editors: Megan La Barre, Bruce Nicholson and Helen Cunningham
Copy editor: Lucy Hyde
Typesetter: Siliconchips Services Ltd UK and Jouve India Pvt. Ltd.
Mapping: Gordon MacGilp
Cover design: Kevin Robbins and Gordon MacGilp
Cover photo: LBSimms Photography/Shutterstock
Production controller: Lyndsey Rogers
Printed and bound in Great Britain by Bell and Bain Ltd, Glasgow

Contents

How to use this book

This page gives a summary of the exciting new ideas you will be learning about in the unit.

This is the topic covered in the unit, which links to the syllabus.

These lists at the end of a unit act as a checklist of the key ideas of the unit.

Learning objectives tell you what you will be learning about in the lesson.

Discussion features allow you to work in pairs, in a group or as a class to explore the topic further.

Try these questions to check your understanding of each topic. Green questions test recall; yellow questions require critical thinking and application of facts; and orange questions require higher order thinking, analysis and/or extended learning activities.

Activity features allow you to do practical activities related to the topic.

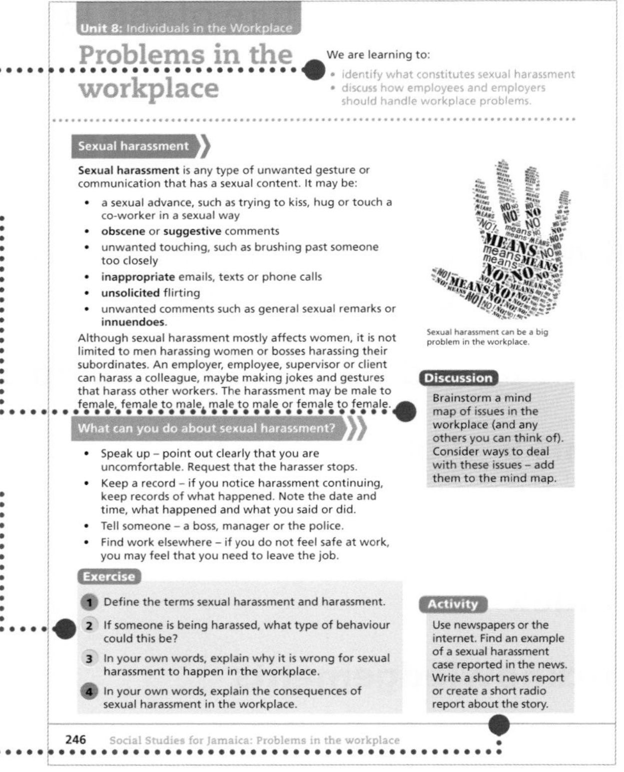

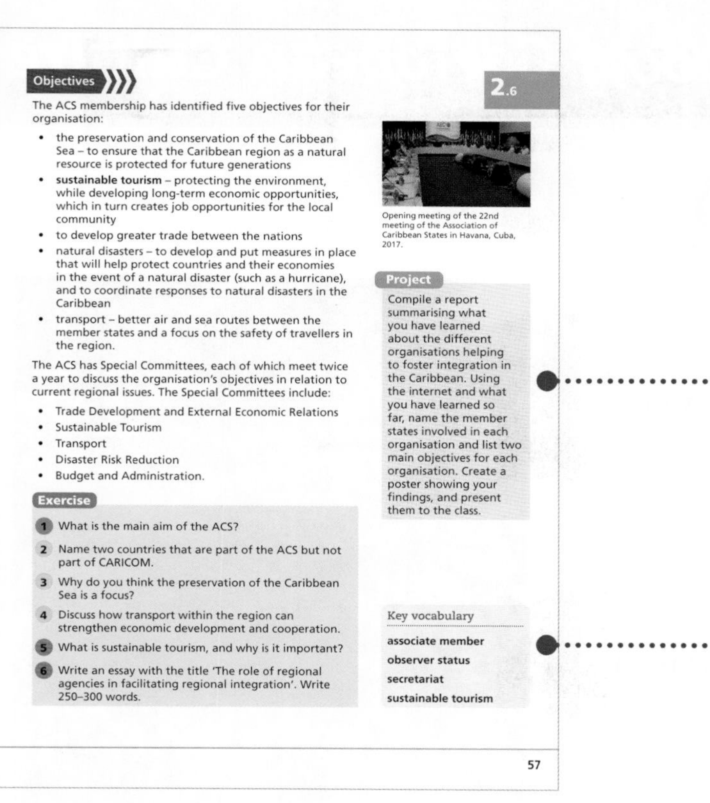

Objectives

2.6

The ACS membership has identified five objectives for their organisation:

- the preservation and conservation of the Caribbean Sea – to ensure that the Caribbean region as a natural resource is protected for future generations
- **sustainable tourism** – protecting the environment, while developing long-term economic opportunities, which in turn creates job opportunities for the local community
- to develop greater trade between the nations
- natural disasters – to develop and put measures in place that will help protect countries and their economies in the event of a natural disaster (such as a hurricane), and to coordinate responses to natural disasters in the Caribbean
- transport – better air and sea routes between the member states and a focus on the safety of travellers in the region.

The ACS has Special Committees, each of which meet twice a year to discuss the organisation's objectives in relation to current regional issues. The Special Committees include:

- Trade Development and External Economic Relations
- Sustainable Tourism
- Transport
- Disaster Risk Reduction
- Budget and Administration.

Opening meeting of the 22nd meeting of the Association of Caribbean States in Havana, Cuba, 2017.

Project

Compile a report summarising what you have learned about the different organisations helping to foster integration in the Caribbean. Using the internet and what you have learned so far, name the member states involved in each organisation and list two main objectives for each organisation. Create a poster showing your findings, and present them to the class.

Exercise

1. What is the main aim of the ACS?
2. Name two countries that are part of the ACS but not part of CARICOM.
3. Why do you think the preservation of the Caribbean Sea is a focus?
4. Discuss how transport within the region can strengthen economic development and cooperation.
5. What is sustainable tourism, and why is it important?
6. Write an essay with the title 'The role of regional agencies in facilitating regional integration'. Write 250–300 words.

Key vocabulary

associate member
observer status
secretariat
sustainable tourism

57

Project and Research features allow you to work on your own or in groups to explore the topic further and present your findings to your class or your teacher. Along with the Activity features, and higher order thinking questions, the Project and Research features reflect the STEM/STEAM principles embedded within the curriculum.

These are the most important new social studies words in the topic. Check their meanings in the Glossary at the end of the book.

These end-of-unit questions allow you and your teacher to check that you have understood the ideas in the unit by applying the skills and knowledge you have gained.

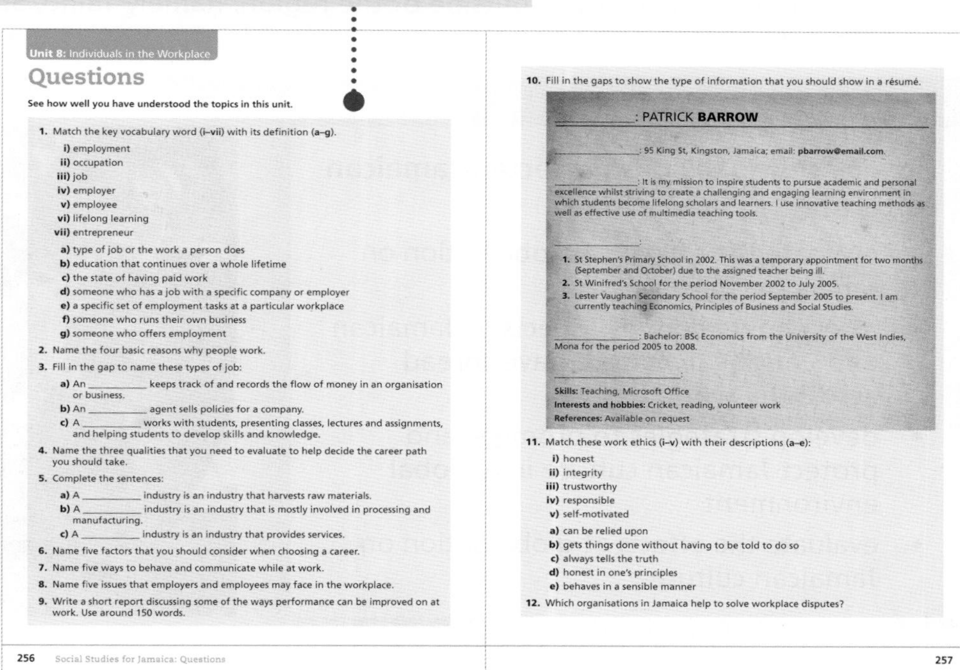

Unit 8: Individuals in the Workplace

Questions

See how well you have understood the topics in this unit.

1. Match the key vocabulary word (i–vii) with its definition (a–g).
   - **i)** employment
   - **ii)** occupation
   - **iii)** job
   - **iv)** employer
   - **v)** employee
   - **vi)** lifelong learning
   - **vii)** entrepreneur
   - **a)** type of job or the work a person does
   - **b)** education that continues over a whole lifetime
   - **c)** the state of having paid work
   - **d)** someone who has a job with a specific company or employer
   - **e)** a specific set of employment tasks at a particular workplace
   - **f)** someone who runs their own business
   - **g)** someone who offers employment
2. Name the four basic reasons why people work.
3. Fill in the gap to name these types of job:
   - **a)** An ___________ keeps track of and records the flow of money in an organisation or business.
   - **b)** An ___________ agent sells policies for a company.
   - **c)** A ___________ works with students, presenting classes, lectures and assignments, and helping students to develop skills and knowledge.
4. Name the three qualities that you need to evaluate to help decide the career path you should take.
5. Complete the sentences:
   - **a)** A ___________ industry is an industry that harvests raw materials.
   - **b)** A ___________ industry is an industry that is mostly involved in processing and manufacturing.
   - **c)** A ___________ industry is an industry that provides services.
6. Name five factors that you should consider when choosing a career.
7. Name five ways to behave and communicate while at work.
8. Name five issues that employers and employees may face in the workplace.
9. Write a short report discussing some of the ways performance can be improved on at work. Use around 150 words.

256 Social Studies for Jamaica: Questions

10. Fill in the gaps to show the type of information that you should show in a résumé.

_____________: PATRICK **BARROW**

_____________: 95 King St, Kingston, Jamaica; email: **pbarrow@email.com**.

_____________: It is my mission to inspire students to pursue academic and personal excellence whilst striving to create a challenging and engaging learning environment in which students become lifelong scholars and learners. I use innovative teaching methods as well as effective use of multimedia teaching tools.

_____________:

1. St Stephen's Primary School in 2002. This was a temporary appointment for two months (September and October) due to the assigned teacher being ill.
2. St Winifred's School for the period November 2002 to July 2005.
3. Lester Vaughan Secondary School for the period September 2005 to present. I am currently teaching Economics, Principles of Business and Social Studies.

_____________: Bachelor: BSc Economics from the University of the West Indies, Mona for the period 2005 to 2008.

_____________:

Skills: Teaching, Microsoft Office
Interests and hobbies: Cricket, reading, volunteer work
References: Available on request

11. Match these work ethics (i–v) with their descriptions (a–e):
    - **i)** honest
    - **ii)** integrity
    - **iii)** trustworthy
    - **iv)** responsible
    - **v)** self-motivated
    - **a)** can be relied upon
    - **b)** gets things done without having to be told to do so
    - **c)** always tells the truth
    - **d)** honest in one's principles
    - **e)** behaves in a sensible manner
12. Which organisations in Jamaica help to solve workplace disputes?

257

SOCIAL STUDIES

Unit 1: The Spread of Caribbean Culture

Objectives: You will be able to:

Key concepts in Caribbean culture

- understand culture, heritage, socialisation, tradition and preservation
- understand what cultural diffusion is
- explain diaspora.

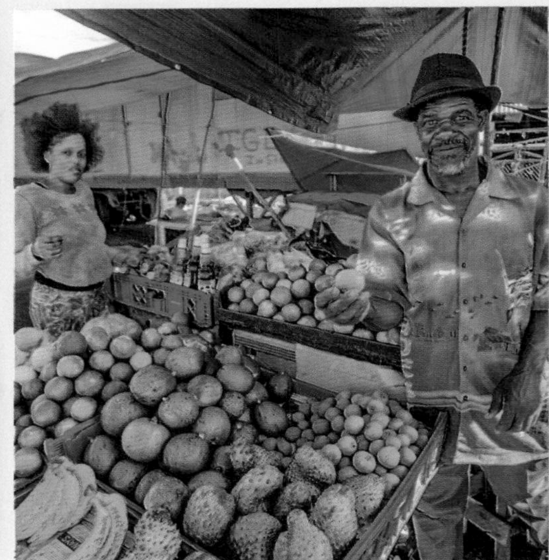

Subcultures in Jamaica

- develop a working defintion of the term subculture
- explore different subcultures in Jamaica and understand Rastafarianism.

How have different cultures influenced Jamaican culture?

- classify tangible and intangible aspects of Caribbean culture that have been assimilated from cultures outside of the region, namely Taino, Spanish, British and Maroon.

How has globalisation affected Jamaican culture?

- evaluate the effects of globalisation on Jamaican culture
- assess how and why aspects of Jamaican and Caribbean culture have spread across the world
- develop strategies to promote and protect Jamaican culture in a global environment
- evaluate the effects of globalisation on Jamaican culture.

How have sports and creative industries contributed to our national development?

- assess the contribution of the creative industries and sport to national development
- understand how sports have contributed to national development
  - Usain Bolt
  - Merlene Ottey
  - Courtney Walsh
- understand how creative industries have contributed to national development
  - Robert Nesta Marley
  - Louise Simone Bennett-Coverley
  - Edna Manley School of The Visual and Performing Arts.

Key concepts in Caribbean culture

We are learning to:

- recall key terms and concepts.

Culture, heritage, socialisation, tradition and preservation

As we saw from Grades 7 and 8, **culture** is the customs, beliefs, arts and technology of a nation or people. **Heritage** is the features that belong to the culture of a particular society which were created in the past and have a continuing historical importance to that society. Examples include customs, traditions or languages.

A **cultural background** includes things that a group of people share, such as their religion, language, music, traditions, customs, art and history. Our **cultural heritage** consists of the cultural traditions that we have inherited from past generations.

People learn their culture through the process of **socialisation**. This is where people internalise the norms and values of their culture. Socialisation begins from when we are born, throughout the rest of our lives.

The culture of people from the Caribbean is rich and **diverse**. People, for example, worship in different ways. Some people are Hindus, while others are Christian or Muslim. Most people speak English, but many also speak Chinese, Bhojpuri, Patois and Creole.

Some people eat rice, while others use cassava, cou cou or curry. Some listen to music played on the drums; others listen to music played on the sitar. Some celebrate Diwali, while others celebrate Eid al-Fitr or Christmas.

Almost all Caribbean countries have street festivals, for example, Carnival in Trinidad, Crop Over in Barbados, the Moonsplash Festival in Anguilla and the Reggae Sumfest in Jamaica.

CARIFESTA is a Caribbean-wide event whose aim is to celebrate the people of the region through music, drama, crafts, literature and dance.

Both local events, and region-wide events like CARIFESTA, help create our **national** and regional **identity**.

Flo Rida performing at Reggae Sumfest Jamaica in 2013.

Project

Make a presentation about the cultural backgrounds of the students in your class. First, brainstorm your ideas as a class and decide who will do what. Then, work in groups and do your research. Use a computer to make your presentation. Include photographs or illustrations as well as music.

Key vocabulary

cultural background
cultural heritage
culture
diverse
heritage
national identity
socialisation

Research

Carry out some research into the area where you live. Draw a map of your local area including the following:

1. Places of worship – noting the different religions
2. Restaurants – making a note of the different foods served, and from which cultural traditions
3. Food shops, including the range of foods they sell from different cultures.

Create a presentation of the various cultures represented in your local area. Map these out on a picture of the globe and present your findings back to your class.

Activity

Look at the following images and describe the different cultural heritage represented. Explain why each is important to the culture of Jamaica.

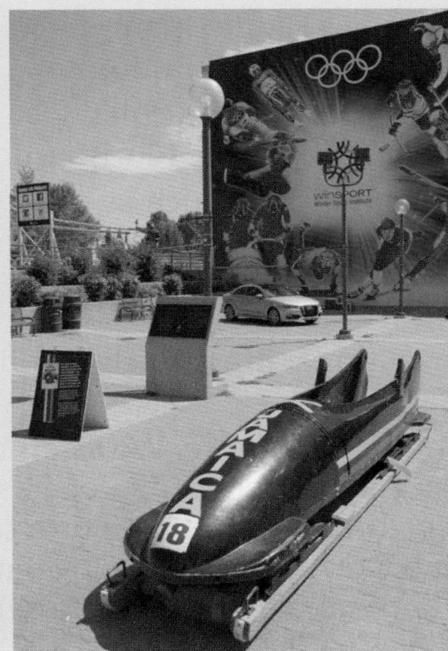

Exercise

1 In pairs, discuss, then write your own definitions of the terms:

a) multiculturalb **b)** ancestor **c)** cultural background
d) culture **e)** heritage **f)** cultural heritage.

2 What is your cultural background? You can begin by answering these questions:

a) Does your family have any distinct traditional practices? Describe them.
b) Does your family eat any special types of food or prepare meals in a distinct way?
c) Do you have religious beliefs? What are they?
d) Do you celebrate any particular festivals or events? Describe them.

3 Write a 300 word paragraph on the different cultures of Jamaica.

Characteristics of Caribbean culture

We are learning to:

- describe the characteristics (language, religions, traditions, festivals, history) of our cultural heritage.

Our cultural heritage

A **characteristic** is a typical or noticeable quality that someone or something has. For example, people in Jamaica speak many different **languages**, including English and Patois. Your country's cultural heritage today is made up of many different things:

Diwali is also known as the festival of lights.

- Different languages are spoken, such as English, French, Arabic, Chinese and Patois.
- There are different **religions**, such as Hindu, Islam, Catholic, Protestant, African traditional and Buddhism.
- There are different **traditions** and **festivals**, such as Hosay (Muslim), Diwali (Hindi) and Christmas (Christian).
- There are different types of **cuisine** (food), such as roti and curried mango (Indian), pelau (Spanish) dishes such as fried rice, sweet and sour chicken, and curried meat such as chicken or mutton.
- There are different types of traditional **dress**, such as Indian saris and African prints and head dresses.
- People in the Caribbean love **music** and dance. We listen to calypso, soca and rumba (all originating from Africa) reggae, dancehall, ska, mento and Jamaican folk music. The African influence in our culture can be seen in dance styles such as Kumina and Orisha. We also enjoy dances like the kuchipudi (Indian) or the lion and ribbon dances (Chinese).
- **Folklore** is also different. We hear and tell stories about Anansi (originally from Africa) and Papa Bois (from French Caribbean culture). We also have different **arts and crafts**.
- There are **historical sites** that are part of our Caribbean cultural heritage, such as the Blue and John Crow Mountains, as well as Bridgetown and its Garrison (Barbados) and the Brimstone Hill Fortress National Park (Saint Kitts and Nevis), all of which are UNESCO World Heritage Sites.

Research

Research how many different types of music and dance there are in Jamaica. Write 100 words on the topic.

Exercise

1. Give at least one example of cultural heritage that the Caribbean has inherited from each of these groups of people:

   a) Chinese **b)** Indian **c)** African **d)** Spanish.

2. What do you think cultural preservation means?

Project

Preserving our culture

Work in groups. You are going to create a wall display for a cultural or heritage day at your school. Each group will research and make a presentation about the contribution made by one group of immigrants to the culture of the Caribbean: the Amerindians, the Europeans, the Africans, the Chinese and the Syrians. In this wall display you will be describing how each group's culture is preserved in Jamaica today.

Your teacher will help you to choose one of the groups and will organise a field trip to a local museum and library to help you collect information.

Here are some suggestions about steps you could follow or things you could do:

- Discuss how you are going to go about this project. How will you collect information?
- Make a list of categories into which you can organise the information: languages, religion, traditions, music, cuisine (food), dress. Allocate one category to each person in the group.
- Collect information. Make notes as you work. If you find out something interesting about another category, pass on the information to the person in your group who is dealing with that category.
- Collect or draw pictures. Collect real items too (such as clothes or food) and make a display.
- Draft three paragraphs about each category.
- Make posters to display in your school. Check and edit your presentation.
- Combine the information you have collected into a table. Write the names of the people along the top of the table. Then write short notes about the cultural heritage in categories. For example:

Settlers	Amerindians	Europeans	
Languages		French,	
Religion			
Traditions			
Music			
Cuisine	cassava,		
Dress			

Discussion

In groups, discuss the contributions made by the settlers to our modern society. Collect photographs and make a collage to display all the characteristics discussed.

Key vocabulary

arts and crafts
characteristic
cuisine
dress
festival
folklore
historical sites
language
music
religion
tradition

What is cultural diffusion?

We are learning to:

- develop working definitions for the terms: cultural diffusion and diaspora
- assess how and why aspects of Jamaican and Caribbean culture has spread across the world.

Cultural diffusion is the spread of cultural beliefs and social activities from one group of people to another. Through cultural diffusion, people's horizons become broader and more culturally rich.

For example, more people in Jamaica today are applying the principles of feng shui (pronounced fung shway), an ancient Chinese practice in which we look at our living spaces and working environment and seek to strike a balance with the natural world. Applying these principles from a country halfway around the world has become a daily practice for many and it now forms part of their way of life. It is through cultural diffusion that celebrations such as Halloween and Thanksgiving are recognised in Jamaica, holidays that are North American in origin.

A visual representation of the elements of feng shui – fire, water, metal, wood and soil with the ying and yang symbol in the centre.

Cultural diffusion is largely influenced by migration, especially in cases where people emigrate permanently to settle in other countries. These individuals carry aspects of their culture which is shared with others in that culture. The mixing of world cultures through different ethnicities, religions, and nationalities interacting together has only increased with advanced communication, transportation, and technology. People living in Australia can communicate daily via social media with someone living in France. Improved transportation has led to increased travel across the globe, allowing more people to experience the other societies and cultures. This allows us to open our minds, and learn as much as we can from all over the Earth, and has resulted in cultural enrichment.

Examples of cultural diffusion

- In Japan, the One Love Jamaica Festival is an annual summer event that is held in Komazawa Olympic Park to celebrate reggae music and Jamaican culture.
- In Toronto, Canada, there is an annual Toronto Caribbean Festival which celebrates the food, music and languages of the Caribbean.
- In New York City's Chinatown you'll meet the largest concentration of Chinese people in the Western hemisphere. Here, you'll also find some of the most delicious and authentic Chinese cuisine in America.

- The spread of music throughout the world also illustrates cultural diffusion. For example, jazz started in the US as a blend of African and European musical traditions. Now, it's enjoyed across the globe, taking on many different variations within the genre.
- Japanese culture is rich and complex. The popularity of sushi around the world, a traditional Japanese dish, is a good example of the spread of Japanese culture and cuisine.
- The Notting Hill Carnival was first held in 1966 celebrating Caribbean culture and traditions in London. The carnival has since become the largest street festival in Europe, attracting hundreds of thousands to London, and continues to grow in popularity.

Discussion

Describe different cultures you see in your day-to-day life in Jamaica. How have they influenced your behaviour and tastes?

The Notting Hill Carnival in London celebrates Caribbean culture.

Diaspora

A **diaspora** is defined as the dispersion or spread of any people from their original homeland.

- A diaspora is a group of people who have been forced from or chosen to leave their homeland to settle in other lands.
- People of a diaspora typically preserve and celebrate the culture and traditions of their homeland.
- Diaspora may be created by voluntary emigration (leaving a place) or by force, as in the cases of wars, enslavement, or natural disasters.

Did you know...?

For 2000 years the term 'diaspora' was associated almost exclusively with Jewish history.

Examples of diaspora

Case study

The African Diaspora

- During the Transatlantic Slave Trade of the 16th to 19th centuries, as many as 12 million people in Western and Central Africa were taken captive and shipped to the Americas as enslaved people.
- Made up mainly of young men and women in their childbearing years, the African diaspora grew rapidly.
- These displaced people and their descendants greatly influenced the culture and social life in the American and other New World colonies, including Jamaica.
- Today, descendants of the African diaspora maintain and celebrate their shared culture and heritage in communities around the world. According to the US Census Bureau, nearly 46.5 million people of the African diaspora lived in the United States in 2017.

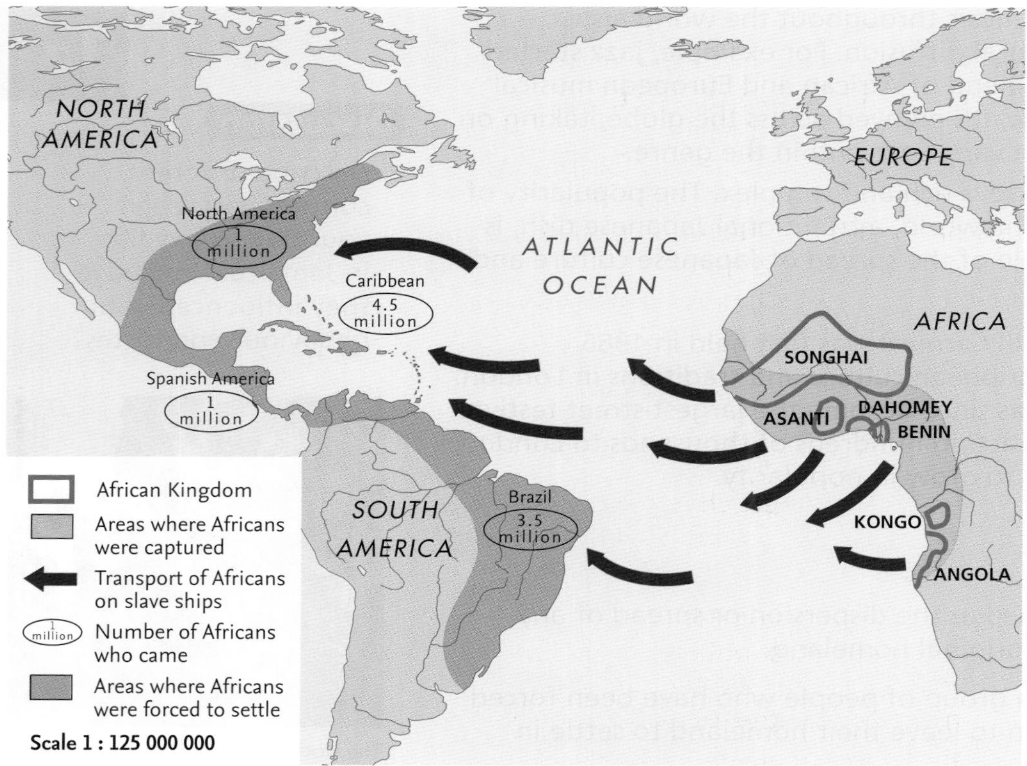

The Transatlantic Slave Trade routes.

Case study

The Caribbean Diaspora

- There is significant movement of people within the Caribbean, as well as beyond it. This group of people has come to be known as the Caribbean Diaspora.
- The Caribbean Diaspora can be found in different parts of the world but a large number, about 8 million, can be found in the United States alone. A large portion of the persons in this group are educated and highly-skilled professionals who make significant contributions to both the areas where they have settled, as well as the region itself.
- Those moving within the Caribbean invest in their new home country, through human capital or through financial investments. This is very important in helping to promote economic growth in the Caribbean region.

Jamaican Diaspora

Jamaicans can be found around the world, but the largest pools of Jamaicans, outside of Jamaica itself, exist in the United States, United Kingdom, Canada, other Caribbean islands, and all across the Caribbean coast of Central America, namely Panama, Costa Rica, Nicaragua, and Honduras. One of the largest and most famous Jamaican communities is in Brixton, South London. An estimated 4% of Londoners and 3.5% of people from Birmingham in England are of Jamaican heritage.

Brixton, South London has one of the largest Jamaican communities outside of Jamaica.

Why did people leave Jamaica?

There were several reasons why people chose to emigrate (leave) and settle in other countries. Some of the historical factors are listed below:

- employment opportunities abroad. For example, Jamaicans of various skill levels supplied labour internationally, especially during the two phases of the Panama Canal's construction in the 1880s and 1910s
- job opportunities aimed at Jamaicans in Britain in post-war reconstruction in the 1940s
- unemployment in Jamaica during the 1950s, and rising crime following the transition to independence in 1962 and slow economic growth also influenced increased Jamaican emigration
- immigration opportunities in Canada, the USA and Britain also helped, providing Jamaicans with a community of other Jamaicans to join.

Key vocabulary

cultural diffusion

diaspora

Exercise

1. What is meant by diaspora?
2. Why do diasporas occur? Explain in your own words.
3. Using the map on page 14, explain the main places that African enslaved people were taken to.
4. What were some of the reasons for Jamaicans to move to other parts of the world? Write a paragraph explaining the main reasons.

Research

Carry out research into a Jamaican diasporic group in another country. Find out:

1. How many Jamaican people are living there?
2. How does this group maintain its way of life?
3. What traditions are continued?
4. Why did Jamaican people choose to move there?

Subcultures in Jamaica

We are learning to:

- develop a working definition for the term subculture
- explore different subcultures in Jamaica.

A **subculture** is a group of people whose values and norms are in some way distinct from the main culture in a society. Subcultures sometimes help to enrich the culture by adding diversity. A main subculture found in Jamaica is Rastafarianism.

Emperor of Ethiopia, Haile Selassie, during a visit to Jamaica in April 1966.

Rastafarianism

Rastafarianism developed in Jamaica during the 1930s. This occurred when Ras Tafari was crowned Negus of Ethiopia, also known as the "King of Kings". This formal name was changed when he was coronated as Emperor Haile Selassie I. Selassie is regarded by many Rastafari as the Black Messiah, which means that he is regarded as someone who will save Black people from people who wish to oppress them. It also means that Selassie is seen as someone who will help make sure that Rastafari are reconnected with their land of origin, Africa. Today, Rastafarians make up around 5% of the Jamaican population.

Marcus Garvey, the important political leader, is said to have had a vision, or a prediction based on verse 31 of Psalm 68 of the Bible which says that "Princes shall come out of Egypt; Ethiopia shall soon stretch her hands out unto God". This prophecy is thought to mark the start of the Rastafari movement, with the word Rastafarian originating from Haile Selassie's name, which was 'Ras Tafari Makonnen'.

Here are some of the main beliefs and practices of Rastafarians:

- Many Rastafarians eat specific foods, and many are vegans or vegetarians. Food preferences are based on the idea of '**Ital**' which focuses on eating natural, rather than processed foods.
- '**Jah**' is the Rastafarian God.
- As well as the Bible being seen as an important, sacred text, Rastafarianism's main text is called the **Holy Piby**.
- Marijuana is used by some Rastafarians. It has a special role in Rastafari rituals such as **Reasoning** and **Nyabinghi**. These involve prayers, dancing and drumming.

Key vocabulary

dreadlocks

Holy Piby

Ital

Jah

Lion of Judah

martyr

Nyabinghi

Reasoning

subculture

What are the important symbols of the Rastafarian culture?

- **Dreadlocks** are one of the most well-known symbols of Rastafarianism and have a special meaning for this subculture. Dreadlocks are based on an idea in the Bible which states that hair should not be cut.
- Important symbolic colours for Rastafarians are red, gold and green. Red represents the blood of the **martyrs** (people willing to give themselves in the Black struggle for liberation), gold, which stands for the wealth of their African homeland and green which represents the natural beauty of Ethiopia.
- Another important symbol of Rastafarianism is the **Lion of Judah** which is seen to represent Haile Selassie as the King of Kings of Africa, who is both strong and proud.

Dreadlocks are a well-known symbol of Rastafarian culture.

Each colour of the flag represents a particular characteristic.

Why is Marijuana smoking part of Rastafarian culture?

- Not all Rastafarians smoke Marijuana. Those who do, do so to meditate and discuss religious ideas in a group.
- Smoking marijuana is not something Rastafarians are expected to do, it is optional.
- It is claimed that smoking Marijuana for some helps them to feel at one with nature.

Smoking marijuana is a custom for some Rastafarians.

Did you know...?

The word Ital comes from the English word "vital" with the initial syllable replaced by the letter "i" to signify unity with nature.

Rastafarian music

- Rastafari culture is where the roots of contemporary **gospel music** came from, so although it is not unique to the Rastafarian culture, it is a part of it.
- **Reggae** is a type of music that has actually only become associated with Rastafarianism within the last 30–40 years. It originated in the 1960s and emerged from Ska, the music form that came before it.
- Some forms of the music consist of the rhythms of Nyabinghi, as well as some other forms of African music.
- Through the famous Rastafarian Bob Marley, awareness of the religion and culture of the Jamaican Rastafarian people increased and spread globally.

Rastafarian music includes the rhythms of Nyabinghi.

Rastafarian music has roots in African traditions.

Rastafarian language

- Language is another important part of being Rastafarian.
- The Rastafarian language is known as Patois or **Patwa**.
- This language was developed in order for enslaved Africans to maintain and protect their original languages, while at the same time having to speak English.
- This means that the rhythm of the language sounds African and yet has English parts to it.
- Some of the words and phrases are changed to be more positive than the original English translation, for example:

dedicated	livicated (to focus on the living and not the 'dead')
understand	overstand ('under' denotes below).

Exercise

1. What percentage of Jamaicans are Rastafarian?
2. What is a custom? Explain, using your own words.
3. Write a six paragraph essay explaining the customs and traditions of Rastafarians.

Project

Visit a Rastafarian village and observe their average day's activities. You may also prepare a class interview sheet and interview one of the Rastafarians.

Research

Carry out some research into the influence of Rastafarianism on Jamaica's culture and society in general. Consider the following:

i) food
ii) music
iii) symbols

Case study

Maroons

Another important subculture in Jamaica are known as the Maroons. When the British took Jamaica from Spain in 1655, the African enslaved people on the Spanish owned plantations took the opportunity to escape to the mountainous interior of the island. They formed independent communities and became known as Maroons. Their numbers grew as rebel enslaved people escaped to join them. After some fighting between the Maroons and the British, treaties were made which led to more peace. The Maroons had a considerable legacy including:

- Nanny of the Maroons, a leader of the community of Maroons, who is an iconic figure in Jamaican history and whose legacy has been celebrated in poems, portraits, and currency.
- Accompong is a historical Maroon village located in the hills of St Elizabeth Parish. It is located in Cockpit Country, where Jamaican Maroons and indigenous Taíno established a fortified stronghold in the hilly terrain in the 17th century.
- The Accompong Maroon Festival is a cultural celebration that commemorates over 200 years since the signing of the peace treaty between the Maroons and the British. The festival marks the victory of the First Maroon War against the British in which they fought for their freedom, led by their late hero Cudjoe.

Nanny of the Maroons is found on currency in Jamaica.

An inhabitant of the historical Maroon village of Accompong.

The Accompong Maroon Festival.

Research

Carry out research into a Jamaican subculture of your choice. Find out:

a) what food traditions they have
b) what ways of life they practice
c) what religion they practice
d) what celebrations they have.

Key vocabulary

gospel music
Patwa
Reggae

How have different cultures influenced Jamaican culture?

We are learning to:

- classify tangible and intangible aspects of Caribbean culture that have been assimilated from cultures outside of the region.

There have been many influences on Jamaican culture based on the history of the country, immigration and globalisation (the process by which the world is becoming more connected).

Taino

The **Taino** are the earliest known inhabitants of Jamaica. They have contributed to Jamaican culture through:

- rock carvings (petroglyphs) and rock paintings (pictographs)
- they are featured on the Jamaican Coat of Arms
- Taino Day – seeks to commemorate the life and legacy of Jamaica's first inhabitants, who were formally referred to as the Arawaks. The day involves remembering Taino culture, how they lived and their legacy.
- bammy is a traditional Jamaican cassava flatbread descended from the simple flatbread eaten by the Tainos
- thatch roof housing, and the pitch-style roof built to withstand hurricanes
- naming of the island – Xaymaca was the Taíno name given to the island, meaning "land abounding with springs", which later evolved into Jamaica which means the land of wood and water.

An example of a Taino rock carving.

Discussion

Think back to your work from Grades 7 and 8 about which groups have settled in Jamaica. Discuss how these groups influence Jamaica today.

Research

Carry out some research into other Taino influences on Jamaican life today, such as the use of Taino words as part of our language and the names of places. Create a PowerPoint presentation about this for the rest of your group. Include images and videos in your presentation.

Spanish

Christopher Columbus arrived in Jamaica in 1494 and claimed the island for Spain.

The Spanish **legacy** includes:

- the introduction of many crops such as sugar cane, bananas and citrus
- the introduction of most domesticated animals such as pigs, horses, goats, cats, dogs and chickens
- the first town the Spanish built was called New Seville or Sevilla la Nueva. The towns that were established by the Spaniards developed into little more than **settlements**. The only town that was truly developed was Spanish Town, which was the old capital of Jamaica, then called St Jago de la Vega. It was the centre of government and trade and had many churches and convents
- Spanish style architecture: for example, plantation houses like Halse Hall in Clarendon, for instance, is a huge, two-storey house with thick walls that doubled as a defence.

Unfortunately the Spanish also brought diseases and illnesses which killed a lot of Taino people, who were not immune from these diseases, including smallpox.

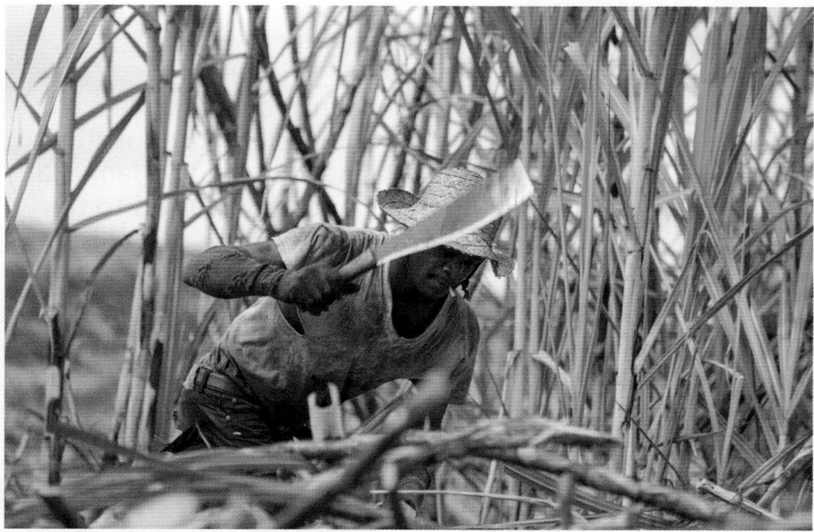

A worker harvesting sugar cane in St Elizabeth, Jamaica.

British

In 1665, the British captured Jamaica from the Spanish and ruled the island until 1962. The British left the following legacy:

- the English language, which is the official language of the country, despite the use of Patois as the main language by most people in their daily lives
- parliamentary form of government called the Westminster model
- an established legal and judicial system; at independence, this led to the formation of a constitution
- an established system of education modelled on what existed in Britain at the time
- British architecture, for example Falmouth Court House
- not all of the legacy is positive, as the British maintained the system of enslavement for more than 200 years and enslaved many West Africans.

Rodney's Memorial is an example of British architecture, located in Spanish Town, Jamaica.

Research

Carry out an investigation into the architecture of the buildings in your local area. What cultural traditions do they represent? Take pictures and create a presentation for the rest of your class.

African

Over 90% of the Jamaican population is made up of individuals of African descent.

- The first Africans arrived in Jamaica in 1513, as enslaved servants to the Spanish settlers.
- These Africans were freed by the Spanish when the English captured the island in 1655. They fled straight away to the mountains where they fought to continue their freedom and became the first Maroons.
- When sugar plantations were established, there was a shortage of labour. This problem led to the large scale importation of enslaved Africans.
- The slave trade was abolished or ended in 1807. However, this did not mean that people of African origin no longer came to Jamaica. In fact many people of African descent came to Jamaica as free labourers following the 1807 abolition.

Activity

Carry out some research into other groups that have moved to Jamaica and contributed to the cultural life of the island today. Create a wall display highlighting their contribution, with images, facts and information.

Ruins of a sugar mill in Lucea, Hanover Parish.

Case study

Taino Day

Thursday 5 May, 2011

The Jamaica National Heritage Trust (JNHT) today mark's Taino Day with a public lecture at the Institute of Jamaica Lecture Room, 12–16 East Street.

Taino Day started in 2006, with the aim of increasing public awareness of the contribution of the Tainos to Jamaica. This year, Taino Day will be held under the theme 'Tracing Our Taino Ancestry'.

The Jamaica National Heritage Trust has asked educational institutions across the island to pause for a moment to remember the Tainos, the earliest known inhabitants of Jamaica. In the past, the role of the Tainos would often get left out of national celebrations. There will also be lectures and displays in selected schools.

There is also an exhibition of Taino artefacts by the museums division of the Institute of Jamaica. The aim is that it will introduce Jamaicans to some of the material cultural heritage left behind by the Tainos. Members of the public can attend and view the exhibition.

The Tainos arrived in Jamaica between 650 AD and 900 AD, and lived in Jamaica for hundreds of years before the arrival of the earliest Europeans, the Spanish. When Columbus landed in Jamaica, in 1494, there was an estimated Taino population of approximately 600 000. The Tainos lived mostly in the plains, near rivers and by the sea in places such as White Marl, St Catherine, Seville, St Ann, Jacks Hill, St Andrew, and Botany Bay, St Ann. The Jamaica National Heritage Trust has a wide collection of Taino artefacts unearthed during archaeological excavations of these sites.

Adapted from: The Jamaican Gleaner, and my-island-jamaica.com.

Questions

1. What is the purpose of Taino Day in Jamaica?
2. Why do you think it is important to remember the Tainos?
3. Write a short text called *What did the Tainos contribute to Jamaica?* Visit the My-Island-Jamaica website and search for 'Tainos in Jamaica' to help with you answer.

Exercise

1. Describe the contribution made to life in Jamaica by Taino, Spanish, British and African cultures, and classify these contributions as tangible or intangible.
2. Why is it important to remember the cultural practices of different groups who have lived in Jamaica?
3. Carry out some research into one of the following:
   - farming methods used
   - flora and fauna introduced
   - architecture
   - food and cooking practices

   by one of the groups discussed above. Consider the influence this has had on your life in Jamaica today.

An example of Tainos carving.

Key vocabulary

legacy

settlement

Taíno

How has globalisation affected Jamaican culture?

We are learning to:

- evaluate the effects of globalisation on the Jamaican culture
- assess how and why aspects of Jamaican and Caribbean culture has spread across the world.

Globalisation, the process whereby the world is becoming more connected through increased travel and communication, is having several important effects on Jamaica. In this section we explore the way in which globalisation is affecting Jamaican culture.

The effects of globalisation on Jamaica's culture

At the most basic level, globalisation, particularly access to technology, has caused or influenced changes in the ways in which many of our people dress, eat, think, trade and communicate. According to one academic, an example would be the way we have begun to celebrate events, such as Halloween. At the same time, globalisation has meant that Jamaican culture is being spread around the world too.

For example, Jamaican music's influence on popular culture in Japan is remarkable. Are Jamaicans better off for being exposed to global culture? The answer is not a simple 'yes' or 'no'. It is much more complex than that. Globalisation has allowed people to learn more about our culture but it has also exposed us more to the culture of others. This has caused the Jamaican culture to become even more rich and diverse but, in some ways, aspects of the culture may be eroding as well.

Cultural icons such as Miss Lou and Dr Olive Lewin have passed away, but many argue that we must not only build on their legacies but should also remember what they and other cultural heroes did in their time, and what they represented. This has led many in government to call for more effort to preserve our traditions and present the positive, Jamaican, traditional values we see as part of our society, to our people.

Globalisation is the world becoming more connected.

Key vocabulary

apartheid
globalisation
repatriation
Ska

Recent influences on Jamaica's culture

North America and Europe have had considerable influence on Jamaica. For example:

- Foods, for example fast foods, have become much more common in Jamaica.
- Various forms of music have influenced Jamaican culture, for example, in terms of music, jazz, pop, rock and classical music have become more common in Jamaica. These musical traditions come from North America, Europe and beyond.
- Fashion is now widely influenced by North America, with many people wearing modern designs of clothing rather than traditional Jamaican clothing.

Music traditions reflect global influences.

Fashion in Jamaica is influenced by North America and Europe.

Research

1. Carry out some research into the influences of North America on Jamaican culture in detail in one of the following areas:
   - **a)** clothing
   - **b)** dance
   - **c)** food
   - **d)** music.
2. Make a list of the positive and negative effects of the influence in this particular area of life.
3. What strategies might be developed in order to preserve Jamaican culture in this area of life? Make a list of suggestions.

Exercise

1. Explain the term 'globalisation' in your own words.
2. What does an 'academic' do for a job?
3. Create a table with two columns. On one side, write a list of the Jamaican traditions and cultural practices which have been promoted and strengthened by globalisation, in Jamaica and around the world. In the other column write down a list of all the ways that global cultures have affected and influenced Jamaica.

Discussion

Explain what is meant by the following quote. Do you agree with this? Discuss in a group.

"Use the media to tell the important stories about our history, our development, our communities, our people. We have to tell our stories or they will die with generations past."

Project

Create a model or display board that represents your definition of globalisation and illustrates the impact it has had on Jamaica's culture.

What aspects of Jamaican culture have spread across the world?

There are many ways in which Jamaican culture has spread around the world and has influenced both and cultural and social changes in different places. Here are some examples:

Ways Jamaican culture has spread around the world

1. Influenced the Global Civil Rights Movement. Jamaica has contributed to the civil rights movements taking place across the world from the early 1960s onwards through the ideas of Jamaican national hero, Marcus Garvey, a Black activist who preached about Black racial identity.

2. Introduced new forms of music – Reggae & **Ska**: Originating in Jamaica in the early 1960s, Reggae is noted for its message of love, equality and justice. Thanks to its most iconic icon, Bob Marley, Reggae became popular around the world.

3. Jamaica played an important role in opposing **apartheid** in South Africa. Apartheid was a system of racial division. Through protests and petitions and songs, Jamaica kept the anti-apartheid issue on the global agenda and forced action by other nations.

4. The development of music, dance and language subcultures in places like the UK and Japan as a result of Jamaican influence.

5. Introduced a new religion – Rastafarianism. Developed in Jamaica in the 1930s, Rastafarians revere the late emperor of Ethiopia, Haile Selassie, support **repatriation** (returning) to Africa, the home of their ancestors and racial pride and identity. The followers now number in the thousands around the world.

6. Food traditions and exports from Jamaica such as Blue Mountain Coffee, Red Stripe Beer and Jerk Spice have been fully established worldwide, with Jamaican meat pies, or patties, growing in popularity.

Blue Mountain Coffee.

Red Stripe Beer.

Exercise

1. In your own words, summarise the positive aspects of Jamaican culture that are being spread throughout the world.
2. Think about which other cultures you are aware of through music and food. How has globalisation made this possible?
3. Write a short essay on the influence of Jamaican culture in other parts of the world, giving examples.

Case study

Reggae music

International Reggae Day is an annual event held (first held in 1996) in Kingston and is dedicated to celebrating the style of music that today is in every part of the world. Reggae as a form of music began in the 1960s, but had its origins in mento (Jamaican folk music) from the 1940s and 1950s.

The popularity of mento (a style of Jamaican folk music) began to fade as more Jamaicans became influenced by R&B music from the USA, and when dances started to become popular with the advent of the new mobile sound systems. Soon, the sound men who ran the sound systems began to record their own music, instead of playing the imported soul music.

From this, recording studios were set up and after 1962, when Jamaica became independent, ska music began to increase in its popularity. Ska music then gave way to rocksteady, but a turning point was in 1966 when Emperor Haile Selassie I of Ethiopia visited Jamaica. This was an important moment for those who followed the Rastafari movement. From this movement, roots reggae music began to develop and along with its social message of protest and revolution, it began to become the main musical form in Jamaica.

Toots Hibbert, the lead singer of Toots and the Maytals, one of Jamaica's greatest reggae groups.

Bob Marley had been performing in his group Bob Marley and the Wailers since the early 1960s, but when he converted to Rastafarianism in the late 1960s, his musical style started to reflect the roots of reggae. From the late 1960s to his death in 1981, he became one of the most famous musicians in the world, having sold more than 75 million records.

Other well-known Jamaican reggae singers and groups include Horace Andy, Tommy McCook, Dennis Brown, Jimmy Cliff, Toots and the Maytals, Israel Vibration, Prince Buster and Lee Perry. Producers such as King Tubby, Clement Coxsone Dodd and Bunny Lee were also important to the growth of Jamaican reggae music.

The film The Harder They Come, 1972, is most famous for its reggae soundtrack which is said to have brought reggae to the world.

The impact of reggae music on the world has been huge. Not just was it important as a musical style, as it influenced huge changes in musical culture all over the world, but it was important for its social message of justice and equal rights. At the heart of reggae is the 'One Love' philosophy first used by Marcus Garvey, another Jamaican great.

Questions

1. In your own words, explain why reggae has had such a global impact, both culturally and politically.
2. Explain the link between Rastafarianism and reggae music.
3. Research International Reggae Day and why it was established.

How can we protect Jamaican culture in a globalised world?

We are learning to:

- develop strategies to promote and protect Jamaican culture in a global environment
- evaluate the effects of globalisation on Jamaican culture.

There are ways in which the Jamaican government are seeking to protect Jamaican culture in a world that is increasingly filled with information about other cultures through the internet and increased travel.

There are real concerns that Jamaican brands and symbols are being used by others in ways which do not always enable Jamaican people to control their image and culture. This led to the creation of the Jamaica Intellectual Property Office, which oversees **trademarks, patents** and **copyrights**. This ensures that the Jamaican 'brand' with its symbols and icons are not misused, or used for profit for non-Jamaican companies or individuals.

For example, the Jamaican government introduced a National Branding Committee. Its aims might include researching whether the word 'jerk', meaning both the seasoning and a specific way of cooking chicken and pork, can be protected as a specific Jamaican practice.

Another example of the need to protect the Jamaican culture and image is through the work of the Jamaican athlete, Usain Bolt, who has worked hard to protect his image. He registered several trademarks, including his famous lightning bolt stance, after winning a gold medal in the Olympics in China. He has trademarks in Jamaica, the US and several other countries.

An example of a Jamaican brand.

Usain Bolt's trademarked Lightning Bolt stance.

Exercise

1. Look up the words **a)** trademark, **b)** patent **c)** copyright. Explain what they mean, giving examples.
2. Think of another Jamaican symbol in need of protection, explaining how it might be misused.
3. Carry out research into examples of the current work of the National Branding Committee, and write a 200 word report on your findings.

The Institute of Jamaica (IOJ) and the Jamaica National Heritage Trust (JNHT)

As part of efforts to promote Jamaica's heritage, both organisations are involved in protecting tangible and intangible cultural elements that are a significant part of Jamaica's history.

Curators (people who work in museums) make sure that promoting cultural awareness is one of the organisation's main priorities.

The role of curators is also to educate Jamaicans on how to preserve their heritage through public education, for example, going into schools and showing the artefacts to students. This is to teach young people about their culture and what we have inherited from all the persons who make up Jamaica.

The Institute of Jamaica has introduced several initiatives which are focused on retaining and preserving Jamaican culture; for example, the Moveable Property Culture Programme, which allows citizens to be educated about Jamaica's heritage by going into communities to give presentations. The Institute of Jamaica works with schools to promote cultural awareness among young people.

The nine divisions of the Institute of Jamaica are summarised in the spidergram below:

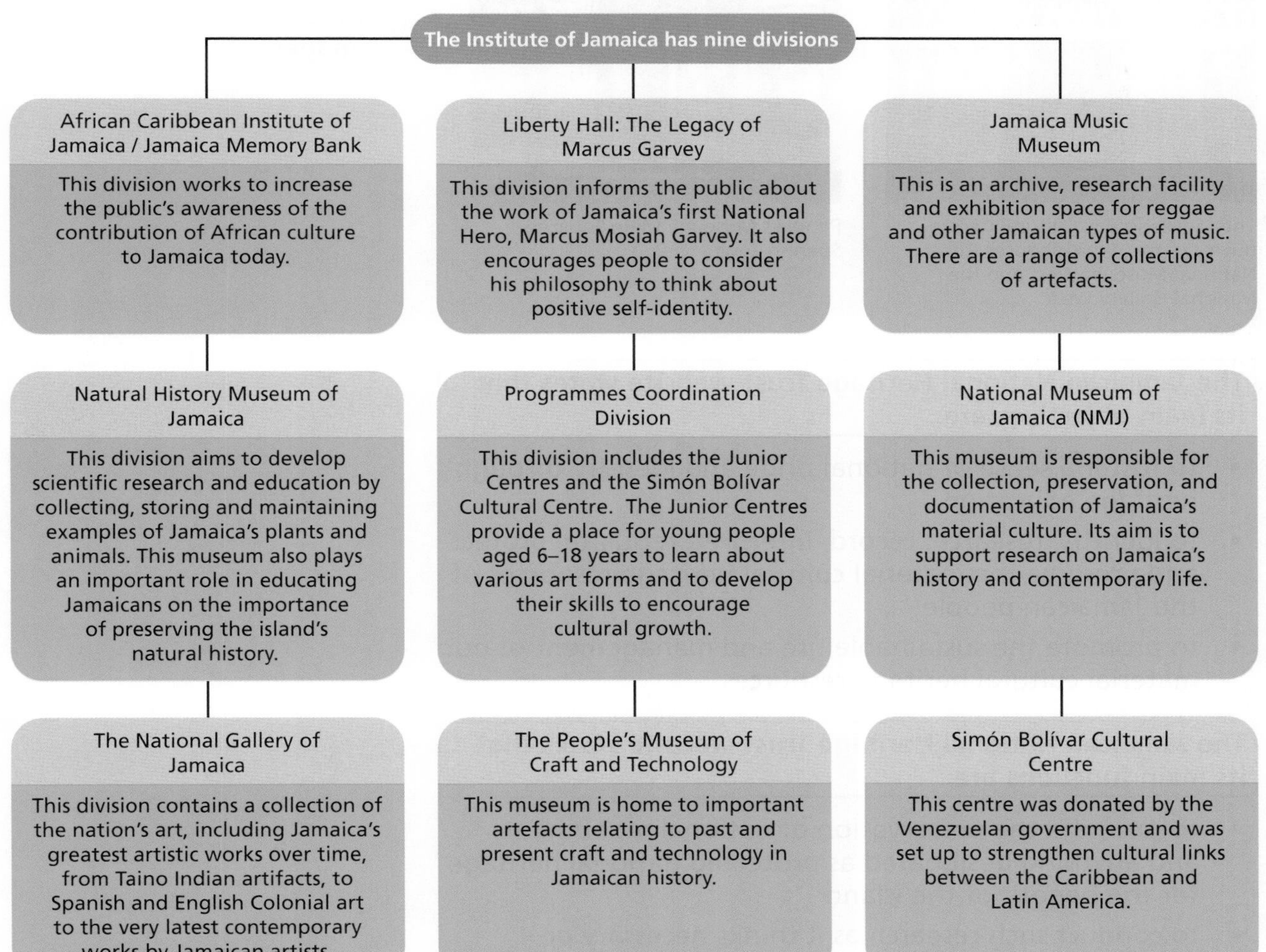

The Institute of Jamaica has nine divisions
African Caribbean Institute of Jamaica / Jamaica Memory Bank
This division works to increase the public's awareness of the contribution of African culture to Jamaica today.
Liberty Hall: The Legacy of Marcus Garvey
This division informs the public about the work of Jamaica's first National Hero, Marcus Mosiah Garvey. It also encourages people to consider his philosophy to think about positive self-identity.
Jamaica Music Museum
This is an archive, research facility and exhibition space for reggae and other Jamaican types of music. There are a range of collections of artefacts.
Natural History Museum of Jamaica
This division aims to develop scientific research and education by collecting, storing and maintaining examples of Jamaica's plants and animals. This museum also plays an important role in educating Jamaicans on the importance of preserving the island's natural history.
Programmes Coordination Division
This division includes the Junior Centres and the Simón Bolívar Cultural Centre. The Junior Centres provide a place for young people aged 6–18 years to learn about various art forms and to develop their skills to encourage cultural growth.
National Museum of Jamaica (NMJ)
This museum is responsible for the collection, preservation, and documentation of Jamaica's material culture. Its aim is to support research on Jamaica's history and contemporary life.
The National Gallery of Jamaica
This division contains a collection of the nation's art, including Jamaica's greatest artistic works over time, from Taino Indian artifacts, to Spanish and English Colonial art to the very latest contemporary works by Jamaican artists.
The People's Museum of Craft and Technology
This museum is home to important artefacts relating to past and present craft and technology in Jamaican history.
Simón Bolívar Cultural Centre
This centre was donated by the Venezuelan government and was set up to strengthen cultural links between the Caribbean and Latin America.

Jamaica National Heritage Trust

According to The Jamaica National Heritage Trust, the mission of the organisation is, "to inspire a sense of national pride through the promotion, preservation, and development of our material cultural heritage, utilising a highly motivated and qualified team in conjunction with all our partners". The vision of the organisation is to be the primary organisation that actively promotes and sustains Jamaica's rich heritage.

Research

Visit one of the places shown in the pictures to the left and on the next page. Make notes as you look at the displays and consider the role of the organisation in promoting and protecting Jamaican culture. Include three specific examples of displays. Produce a PowerPoint presentation and present it to your class, using facts and images.

The Montego Bay Cultural Centre (Civic Centre), which houses the National Museum West and the National Gallery West.

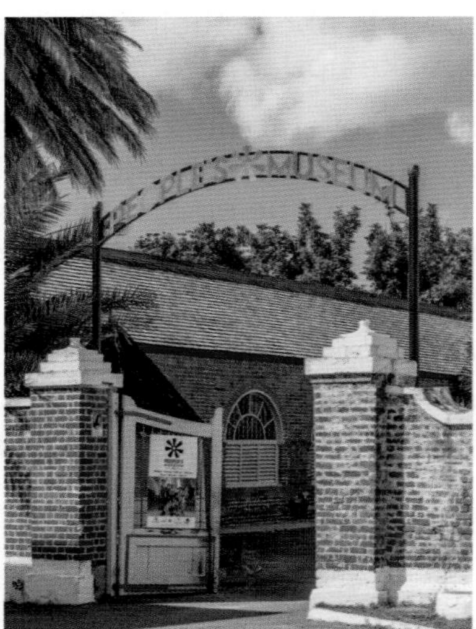

People's Museum, Main Square, Spanish Town.

The Jamaican National Heritage Trust website states that its main objectives are:

- to foster a sense of national pride and identity through heritage education
- to identify, research, record, interpret, regulate, protect and preserve the material cultural heritage resources of the Jamaican people
- to promote the sustainable use and management of our material cultural heritage resources.

The Jamaican National Heritage Trust website states that its main functions are:

- to promote the preservation of national monuments and anything designated as protected national heritage for the benefit of the island
- to conduct such research as it thinks necessary or desirable for the purposes of the performance of its functions under the Jamaica National Heritage Act

- to carry out such development as it considers necessary for the preservation of any national monuments or anything designated as protected national heritage
- to record any precious objects or works of art to be preserved and to identify and record any species of plant or animal life to be protected.

Source: jnht.com/mission_function.php

National Gallery of Jamaica, Downtown Kingston.

Bob Marley Museum, Kingston.

Institute of Jamaica, Kingston.

Devon House, designated as a National Monument by the Jamaica National Heritage Trust in 1990.

Exercise

1. Explain the role of the Institute of Jamaica (IOJ) and the Jamaica National Heritage Trust (JNHT).
2. Explain, using your own words, what is meant by

   a) an artefact **b)** material culture **c)** a curator.
3. Write a six-paragraph essay explaining why each organisation is necessary to promote and protect Jamaican culture, using examples of the various museums and the role they play in Jamaica.

Other strategies to promote Jamaican culture in a global context

As well as government-led organisations specifically focussing on the protection and promotion of Jamaican culture, there are other forms of government and non-governmental work being carried out, for example:

Supporting cultural ambassadors

On National Heroes Day, the third Monday in October, we recognise the work of people who promote Jamaican culture in different parts of the world. For example, in 2009 Norma E. Darby, who is the Director of the Jamaica Folk Revue, a Miami-based cultural group, received national honours from the Governor-General, for service to Jamaica, and its diaspora, in the field of the cultural arts.

More recently, in 2020, Hazelle P. Rogers was awarded for exceptional service to the Jamaican and the Caribbean Diaspora in the United States of America through State and Legislative Representation in Florida, USA.

National Heroes Day is a day which celebrates the island's national heroes, who shed blood, sweat and tears so the people of Jamaica today can enjoy the freedom that they have.

The first National Heroes Day was held on 20 October 1969, when the life of Marcus Garvey was celebrated.
Some of the other national heroes given this honour are:

- Norman Washington Manley
- Sir Alexander Bustamante
- Nanny of the Maroons
- Paul Bogle
- George William Gordon
- Samuel Sharpe.

To celebrate the day there is a service to commemorate the national heroes, as well as concerts and flag raising ceremonies. There are also additional award ceremonies to honour those in the community who have recently made outstanding service to Jamaica.

Discussion

How do you learn about Jamaican culture at school? Give some examples of what you have learnt about important artefacts. Discuss why it is important for you to learn about these.

Jamaica's Olympic medallists Usain Bolt and Veronica Campbell Brown attend a ceremony at the National Heroes Monument in Kingston 15 October, 2012.

Use of mainstream and social media, cable network stations

Today, there are many forms of media which help promote and protect Jamaican culture and traditions. For example, the Jamaica Travel Channel. The internet is a rich source of information on Jamaica, including websites such as:

- The Jamaica Information Service
- Visit Jamaica

Jamaican embassies overseas

An **embassy** is part of the government of a country which is generally found in the capital city in another country. Run by its country of origin, through the work of an **ambassador** and a team of others, it offers a full range of services, including helping people with citizenship and travel issues. However, another role of an embassy is to promote the culture and traditions of its country in a positive way including:

- promoting tourism, providing travel information
- acting to promote trade between Jamaica and other countries
- helping to promote cultural exchanges between Jamaica and other countries
- helping support international sporting events, to ensure that Jamaica is represented.

The Jamaican Embassy in the USA.

Participation in global events (e.g, sports, conferences)

An important way of promoting and maintaining the culture and identity of Jamaica today is through attendance of global sporting or cultural events. This includes Jamaicans participating in conferences and meetings. Examples include:

- The Olympics
- The UNESCO Youth Forum
- FIFA World Cup.

Activity

Make a list of other websites and TV channels that provide information about Jamaica. Discuss how each promotes Jamaican national identity.

Exercise

1. Write a list of the different ways that the government and non-governmental organisations promote and preserve Jamaican culture.
2. Look up the word 'ambassador' and explain what it means, using your own words.
3. Carry out research on another Jamaican who has received a National Honours Award for service to Jamaica. Create a factsheet explaining their contribution.

Key vocabulary

ambassador
copyright
curator
embassy
patent
trademark

How have creative industries and sport contributed to our national development?

We are learning to:

- assess the contribution of the creative industries and sport to national development.

Jamaica has a rich sporting and creative history. In this section we explore the contribution of talented Jamaicans and Jamaican-run organisations that have increased the profile of Jamaica around the world and the spread of Jamaica's culture. These events and activities have played an important part in developing and maintaining Jamaica's national identity by:

- allowing Jamaica a globally recognised identity
- providing role models to other Jamaicans to inspire them
- celebrating the qualities of Jamaican culture, to ensure that these are recognised and valued globally.

Discussion

Why is it important that Jamaica produces globally renowned creative and sporting people? Discuss who or what, for you, is important in both sport and in the creative industries, explaining why.

The contribution of sport to national development

Profile

Usain Bolt

Usain St Leo Bolt (born 21 August 1986) is a Jamaican former sprinter. He is a world record holder in the 100 metres, 200 metres and 4 × 100 metres relay. Many people consider him to be the greatest sprinter of all time.

Bolt has won eight Olympic gold medals. He is the only sprinter to win Olympic 100m and 200m titles at three Olympic games (2008, 2012 and 2016). He also has two 4 × 100m relay gold medals. He is possibly most well known for winning two sprint races in world record times at the 2008 Beijing Olympics.

As well as this, Bolt is an eleven-time World Champion. He won the 100m, 200m and 4 x 100m relay gold medals from 2009 to 2015, except for a 100m false start in 2011. Bolt is the first athlete to win four World Championship titles in the 200m and is the joint-most

Usain Bolt, the former sprinter.

successful in the 100m with three titles. Bolt is therefore known as the most successful athlete of the World Championships.

Bolt improved upon his second 100m world record of 9.69 with 9.58 seconds in 2009 which is recorded as the biggest improvement since the start of electronic timing. He has twice broken the 200 metres world record, setting 19.30 in 2008 and 19.19 in 2009. He has been part of three 4 × 100m relay world records, for Jamaica with the current record being 36.84 seconds set in 2012. Bolt's most successful event is the 200m, with three Olympic and four World titles.

Bolt became known in the media as "Lightning Bolt", and his awards include the IAAF World Athlete of the Year, Track & Field Athlete of the Year, BBC Overseas Sports Personality of the Year (three times) and Laureus World Sportsman of the Year (four times). Bolt retired after the 2017 World Championships.

Did you know...?

Usain Bolt is 6 foot 5 inches tall.

Profile

Merlene Ottey

Merlene Joyce Ottey (born 10 May 1960) is a Jamaican former track and field sprinter. She first represented Jamaica in 1978, and carried on for 24 years. She is the current world indoor record holder for 200 metres with 21.87 seconds, set in 1993.

Ottey had the longest career as a top level international sprinter appearing at the Pan Am games in 1979 as a 19-year-old. A nine-time Olympic medallist, she holds the record for the most Olympic appearances (seven) of any track and field athlete. Ottey won three silver and six bronze medals. She won 14 World Championship medals, and holds the record for most medals in individual events with 10. Her achievements over many years led to her being known as the "Queen of the Track".

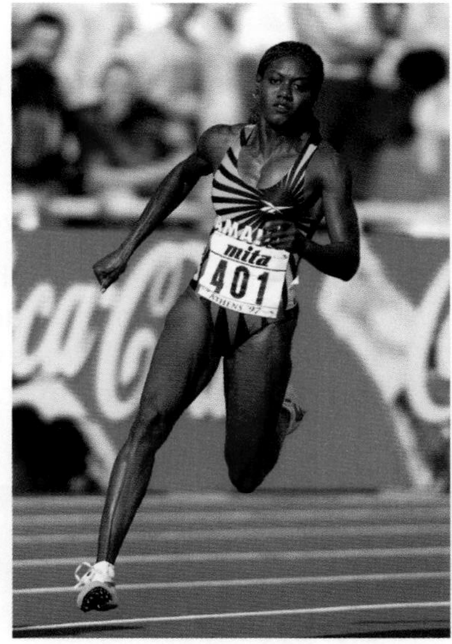

Merlene Joyce Ottey, former track and field sprinter.

Discussion

Have a classroom discussion about the contributions to national development made by sports heroes and people from the creative fields.

Profile

Courtney Walsh

Courtney Andrew Walsh (born 30 October 1962) is a former Jamaican cricketer who represented the West Indies from 1984 to 2001. He captained the West Indies team in 22 Test matches. He is a fast bowler, and became famous for an exceptionally successful opening bowling partnership with his West Indian teammate Curtly Ambrose.

Walsh played 132 Tests and 205 One Day Internationals for the West Indies, taking 519 and 227 wickets in each. He held the record of most Test wickets from 2000. He was the first bowler to reach 500 wickets in Test cricket. Walsh was named one of the Wisden Cricketers of the Year in 1987, and then a year later, one of the West Indian Cricket Cricketers of the Year. In October 2010, he was inducted into the International Cricket Council Hall of Fame.

Courtney Walsh, the former Jamaican cricketer.

Exercise

1. How did each of these three sports people help raise awareness of Jamaica through their achievements?
2. How important do you think sporting heroes are in being role models for younger generations?
3. Carry out some research on another famous sports person from Jamaica, and create a 3-minute PowerPoint on them, explaining how they have promoted Jamaica in some way.

Activity

Find out what award each of these three sports people were given by the Jamaican Government.

The contribution of creative industries to national identity

The creative industries refer to the field of the arts, which includes fine art, sculpture, music, writing, dance and other individual and group projects that involve skills. Talent and hard work.

Profile

Robert Nesta Marley (6 February 1945 – 11 May 1981)

Robert Nesta Marley, known as Bob Marley, was a Jamaican singer, songwriter and musician. Considered one of the pioneers of reggae, his musical career was distinctive because he fused elements of reggae, ska, and rocksteady, as well as being known for his distinctive vocal and song-writing style.

Marley's contributions to music increased the popularity and visibility of Jamaican music all over the world, and made him a global figure in popular culture. Marley became known as a Rastafari icon. He is also seen by many as a global symbol of Jamaican music and culture and identity.

Marley was born in Nine Mile in Jamaica. He began his professional musical career in 1963, after forming the group, Bob Marley and the Wailers. The group released its debut studio album The Wailing Wailers in 1965, which contained the popular single 'One Love/People Get Ready'. The Wailers released eleven further albums. Marley moved to London where he continued to grow in popularity.

The group became an international success after the release of the albums Catch a Fire and Burnin' (both 1973), and they began to go on tour around the world. Marley went on to release his solo material under the band's name, in 1974. His debut studio album Natty Dread (1974) followed by Rastaman Vibration (1976) were very popular. During his time in London Marley recorded the album Exodus (1977); it incorporated elements of blues, soul, and British rock, and was very successful, securing Marley's position as a top global artist.

In 1977, Marley became ill and was diagnosed with skin cancer, which led to his death in 1981. His fans around the world were devastated, and he received a state funeral in Jamaica. To get a sense of his importance, both in Jamaica and beyond, his greatest hits album Legend was released in 1984, and became the best-selling reggae album of all time. Marley is also one of the best-selling music artists of all time, with estimated sales of more than 75 million records worldwide. He was posthumously honoured by Jamaica soon after his death with an Order of Merit.

Bob Marley performing.

Discussion

Why do you think that Bob Marley remains so famous even after his death?

Profile

Louise Simone Bennett-Coverley (7 September 1919 – 26 July 2006)

An extract from Dry-Foot Bwoy

Wha wrong wid Mary dry-foot bwoy?
Dem gal got him fi mock,
An when me meet him tarra night
De bwoy gi me a shock!
Me tell him seh him auntie an
Him cousin dem sen howdy
An ask him how him getting awn.
Him seh, 'Oh, jolley, jolley!'

Known also as 'Miss Lou', Louise Bennett was a Jamaican poet, folklorist, writer, and educator. She was known for writing and performing her poems in Jamaican Patois. Bennett worked to preserve the practice of presenting poetry, folk songs and stories in patois, making sure that the local language of Jamaican was seen as an important.

Bennett was born in North Street in Kingston. She attended elementary school at Ebenezer and Calabar, and went on to St Simon's College and Excelsior College in Kingston. In 1943, she enrolled at Friends College in Highgate, St Mary where she studied Jamaican folklore. In the same year her poetry was first published in the Sunday Gleaner. In 1945, Bennett became the first Black student to study at London's Royal Academy of Dramatic Art (RADA) after being awarded a scholarship from the British Council.

After graduating from RADA, Bennett performed her poetry and folk songs with a number of different theatre companies as well as presenting radio shows in the UK promoting Jamaican culture and literature. Bennett worked for the Jamaica Social Welfare Commission from 1955 to 1959, as well as teaching folklore and drama at the University of the West Indies.

Bennett authored several books and poetry in Jamaican Patois, and worked hard to help it become recognised as a 'nation language'. From 1965 to 1982 she produced Miss Lou's Views, a series of radio **monologues** and in

Louise Simone Bennett-Coverley.

Research

Read the poem in full. Find out about the meaning of Dry-Foot Bwoy.

Key vocabulary

monologue

1970 started hosting the children's television programme Ring Ding. This programme continued until 1982. Bennett strongly believed "that 'de pickney-dem learn de sinting dat belong to dem" (that the children learn about their heritage). The programme involved children from across Jamaica sharing their artistic talents on-air. As well as her television appearances, Bennett appeared in various films, including Calypso (1958) and Club Paradise (1986).

Bennett lived in America for the last few years of her life, but a funeral was held in Kingston at the Coke Methodist Church followed by her burial in the cultural icons section of the country's National Heroes Park.

Research

Find out more about Bennett's poetry. What were the messages and themes of her poetry? How does Bennett's work demonstrate the qualities of Jamaican people and culture?

Activity

Carry out research into one of the following people or organisations listed below, explaining:

a) the contribution made to Jamaica's development

b) how each developed, and their legacy today

c) how this/they have promoted Jamaican culture globally.

- Ronald Williams
- Professor Rex Nettleford
- The Creative Production and Training Centre
- University of the West Indies
- JCDC

Exercise

1. Explain the contribution made by each creative person above, in your own words, to the development of Jamaica.
2. How did the government of Jamaica award each of the individuals mentioned above?
3. Write a paragraph on importance of Jamaican role models in the creative fields.

Questions

See how well you have understood the topics in this unit.

1. Explain what is meant by cultural heritage and preservation.
2. A __________ is where people of a particular ethnic group are scattered across a wide geographical area.
   - **a)** migrant
   - **b)** citizen
   - **c)** diaspora
   - **d)** artefact
3. Globalisation refers to the way that the world has:
   - **a)** become a larger place
   - **b)** become a more connected place
   - **c)** stayed the same
   - **d)** will change at some point.
4. The following people have had a significant impact on Jamaica's development, in which field?
   - **a)** Bob Marley
   - **b)** Usain Bolt
   - **c)** Miss Lou
5. A/An ________ is an object with specific cultural meaning.
   - **a)** subject
   - **b)** curator
   - **c)** artefact
   - **d)** museum
6. Correct this statement: The Institute of Jamaica (IOJ) and the Jamaica National Heritage Trust (JNHT) work hard to ensure that people take care of the natural environment.
7. True or false: A subculture is a smaller group within a larger group, who share some cultural characteristics.

8. Describe three characteristics of Jamaican culture that have spread around the world.
9. Explain three ways that Jamaican life has been influenced by other cultures.
10. Explain how advances in technology and increased globalisation have affected Jamaica's culture.
11. What is a curator?
12. Describe some of the characteristics of Rastafarians as a subculture.
13. Give examples of how the following groups influence Jamaican culture today:
    a) Taino
    b) Spanish
    c) English
    d) Africans.
14. Write a paragraph on a Jamaican you believe has had a powerful influence on how Jamaica is seen in the world today.
15. What legacy was left by Louise Bennett-Coverley?
16. What are some values associated with Jamaican culture, that are being spread throughout the world?

Grade 9 Unit 1 Summary

Key concepts in Caribbean culture

In this chapter, you have learned about:

- Culture, heritage, socialisation, tradition and preservation
- What is meant by cultural background and cultural heritage
- The role of socialisation in passing cultural background and heritage on to citizens
- The main characteristics of Caribbean culture
- What cultural diffusion is and examples of how it occurs
- The roles of African, Caribbean and Jamaican diaspora in cultural diffusion
- The reasons Jamaican emigrate to settle in other countries
- The features of subcultures such as Rastafarianism and Marronage.

The influence of other cultures on Jamaica

In this chapter, you have learned about:

- The influence of the Tainos on Jamaican culture
- The effects of the Spanish and the British on the culture of Jamaica
- The impact of African cultures on Jamaican culture.

How Jamaican culture has been impacted by globalisation, sports and creative industries

In this chapter, you have learned about:

- How globalisation affects Jamaican culture
- Evidence of recent influences on Jamaica's culture
- Aspects of Jamaican culture that have spread across the globe
- Developing strategies to protect Jamaican culture in a globalised world
- The roles of the Institute of Jamaica and the Jamaica National Heritage Trust in protecting Jamaican culture and heritage
- Promoting Jamaican culture through cultural ambassadors, mainstream and social media, Jamaican embassies, and participation in global events
- How sports contribute to national development
- The contribution of creative industries to national identity.

Checking your progress

To make good progress in understanding spread of Jamaican culture, check that you understand these ideas.

- ☐ Explain and use correctly the term *culture* and *heritage*.
- ☐ Describe how technological advances are ensuring globalisation occurring.
- ☐ Explain the contribution of different sports people as well as people from the creative industries.

- ☐ Explain and use correctly the term *cultural diffusion* and *diaspora*.
- ☐ Name examples of diasporic groups around the world.
- ☐ Explain how Jamaican culture has spread around the world.

- ☐ Explain and use correctly the term *subculture*.
- ☐ Name examples of subcultures in Jamaica.
- ☐ Describe the characteristics of Rastafarian subculture.

- ☐ Explain and use correctly the term *globalisation*.
- ☐ Describe the ways in which other cultures have influenced Jamaica.
- ☐ Explain the functions of agencies that promote Jamaican culture.

SOCIAL STUDIES

Unit 2: The Caribbean Individual and Regional Integration

Objectives: You will be able to: 

Regional integration

- define relevant terms and concepts: multilateral agreement, regional integration, bilateral agreement, cooperation, dependence, economy, interdependence, region.

The West Indian Federation, CARIFTA, CARICOM, CSME, OECS and Association of Caribbean States

- describe the Caribbean integration process from the 1950s to the present
- outline the objectives and membership of institutions/bodies which form part of the integration process.

Sport, education, medicine, culture and disaster preparedness

- identify non-political areas of cooperation within the Caribbean region
- assess the role of regional agencies in facilitating the integration process.

The Caribbean Court of Justice

- identify non-political areas of cooperation within the Caribbean region: justice and law enforcement
- assess the role of regional agencies in facilitating the integration process.

Regional integration and cooperation, and obstacles

- analyse ways in which the individual, businesses and countries benefit from and deepen regional integration
- discuss some of the obstacles and barriers to regional integration.

Regional integration

We are learning to:

- define relevant terms and concepts: multilateral agreement, regional integration, bilateral agreement, cooperation, dependence, economy, interdependence, region.

Regional integration is when countries in a region cooperate and work together towards common goals. This has been a priority since the 1950s, when the first attempts were made by Caribbean states to work cooperatively towards common goals. This came about because states wanted to be less dependent on former colonial powers.

Carnival is an event where people from different cultural backgrounds can come together.

Integration

To **integrate** means to bring together ideas and people so that they work together or become part of the same group. The aim of integration is to give members equal status in a group and to share the advantages and strengths that the group brings. There are several types of integration:

- **Social integration** happens when people of different cultural backgrounds learn tolerance and respect for each other.
- **Racial integration** is when people of different races are treated equally so they can live and work together.
- **Economic integration** is achieved when two or more states in a geographic area set common economic goals and reduce the barriers to trade between them. This complements a country's own economy, which is made up of businesses that provide goods and services to meet people's needs.
- **Political integration** happens when countries work together on economic and social issues and policies.

Discussion

Work in groups and discuss how interdependence can help the states in the Caribbean to develop.

Project

Do your own research in groups. Take one of the terms explained on these pages, and find out more about the term. Then look in newspapers and find examples of events that illustrate what it means.

Cooperation

Cooperation means working together and helping each other to achieve common goals. For example, we need to cooperate with our neighbours and other members of our community. If there is a problem in a community and everyone cooperates fully, the problem can be solved.

Exercise

1. In your own words, define regional integration.
2. Explain the difference between economic and political integration.
3. Why do you think social integration is important in Caribbean countries?

Dependence

To depend on something is to rely on or be controlled by it. **Dependence** on other people has many disadvantages, because it means you are not free to do as you wish.

During colonial times, Caribbean countries were dependent on their colonial masters (for example, the United Kingdom) and were forced to live by the social and economic laws and rules of their colonisers.

Colonies had little or no control over their own laws or the economic and social development of their own countries.

From the 1950s onwards, Caribbean states tried to lessen their dependence on their colonial rulers in order to strengthen their economies.

In the 1960s, when many Caribbean states gained independence, foreigners still owned much of the good farming land and also many of the businesses. The profits from these economic activities were not used to develop the Caribbean countries.

Countries began to establish what are called **bilateral agreements** – agreements where two countries help each other – and **treaties** to help develop the **region** as a whole.

US President Barack Obama takes part in a meeting with Caribbean Community (CARICOM) leaders at the University of the West Indies (Kingston) on 9 April 2015.

Interdependence

Countries that help each other or rely on each other are **interdependent**. The leaders of states in the Caribbean saw **interdependence** as the way forward and as a means of strengthening the development of states in the region.

This interdependence started in the 1950s with the **West Indian Federation** and continues today through organisations like CARICOM and the **Association of Caribbean States** (ACS).

Key vocabulary

Association of Caribbean States

bilateral agreement

cooperation

dependence

economic integration

integrate

interdependent/ interdependence

political integration

racial integration

regional integration

region

social integration

treaty

West Indian Federation

Exercise

4 In your own words, define the terms 'dependence' and 'interdependence'.

5 Explain, using your own words, what it means to be a colony of another state.

6 In what way were the Caribbean colonies once dependent on the United Kingdom?

The West Indian Federation

We are learning to:

- define relevant terms and concepts: multilateral agreement, multinational corporation
- describe the Caribbean integration process from the 1950s to the present: West Indian Federation
- outline the objectives and membership of institutions/bodies which form part of the integration process: West Indian Federation.

West Indian Federation

The first significant attempt at integration by Caribbean states took place in 1958, when 10 Caribbean countries, who were all still British colonies at the time, formed the West Indian Federation as an attempt at a political union.

The West Indian Federation was the first example in the region of an organisation that was based on **multilateral agreement**. A multilateral agreement usually refers to agreements between more than one country or **multinational corporation** (a large organisation that has business interests in more than one country). The West Indian Federation is an example of a **multilateral** agreement.

The flag of the West Indian Federation.

Did you know...?

The following states were members of the Federation:

- Antigua and Barbuda
- Barbados
- Dominica
- Grenada
- Jamaica
- Montserrat
- St Kitts-Nevis-Anguilla
- St Vincent and the Grenadines
- St Lucia
- Trinidad and Tobago

Objectives and membership of the West Indian Federation

At the time of its formation in 1958, the membership of the West Indian Federation was:

- Antigua and Barbuda
- Barbados
- Dominica
- Jamaica
- Grenada
- St Kitts-Nevis-Anguilla
- Montserrat
- St Lucia
- St Vincent and the Grenadines
- Trinidad and Tobago.

The main aim of the Federation was to reduce dependence on (and ultimately to achieve independence from) Britain. The advantages of being part of the Federation included planning development, improving the education system and establishing regional customs.

Exercise

1. When was the West Indian Federation set up?
2. Name the members of the West Indian Federation.
3. Write a paragraph explaining the benefits of creating a federation.

The Federation is disbanded

The West Indian Federation lasted until 1962. The Federation was **disbanded** when Jamaica and Trinidad and Tobago decided to leave it. There were a number of reasons for this:

- Trinidad and Tobago and Jamaica were the biggest countries in the Federation and they were expected to bear most of its costs. This was considered to be unfair.
- The smaller countries feared that the more powerful countries would dominate the Federation.
- There was disagreement as to where the capital of the Federation should be.
- Jamaica objected to the colonial status of the Federation and felt that it was holding back independence from Britain.
- The most respected leaders of the time preferred to stay on as leaders in their own country, rather than lead the Federation.
- In September 1961, Jamaica held a **referendum** in which the people of Jamaica elected to pull out of the Federation. This led to the withdrawal of Trinidad and Tobago as well, after Dr Eric Williams famously said in a speech that 'One from ten leaves zero.'

Activity

Do you think countries can get cheaper imports by working together? How would this work?

Exercise

4 Outline the reasons why the West Indian Federation disbanded.

5 Your teacher will play you the calypso 'Federation', by Mighty Sparrow. Listen carefully to the lyrics and then discuss these questions.

a) Why, in the opinion of Mighty Sparrow, did Jamaica want to pull out of the Federation?

b) What reasons did Mighty Sparrow give for the collapse of the Federation?

c) What is Mighty Sparrow's opinion of the Federation? Was it a good thing or not?

d) Do you think Trinidad and Tobago was to blame in any way?

6 Compile a timeline of the key dates of the history of the West Indian Federation.

Key vocabulary

disbanded
multilateral agreement
multilateral
multinational company/ corporation
referendum

CARIFTA

We are learning to:

- define relevant terms and concepts: free trade, liberalisation
- describe the Caribbean integration process from the 1950s to the present: CARIFTA
- outline the objectives and membership of institutions/bodies which form part of the integration process: CARIFTA.

CARIFTA

The next attempt at integration occurred when the **Caribbean Free Trade Association (CARIFTA)** was formed in 1965 with the signing of the Dickenson Bay Agreement. This was a much more successful attempt, which later led to the formation of CARICOM – an organisation that is still very active today.

The 2019 CARIFTA games were held in the Cayman Islands.

Membership of CARIFTA

The idea of a **free trade** region was first discussed at meetings between the leaders of Trinidad and Tobago, Guyana (then called British Guiana), Antigua and Barbuda and Barbados – the original members of CARIFTA.

The Prime Minister of Trinidad and Tobago convened this meeting in 1963 after announcing that the country intended to pull out of the West Indian Federation. As a result of these discussions a formal agreement was drawn up, and the Caribbean Free Trade Association (CARIFTA) was formed.

On 1 July 1968, Dominica, Grenada, St Kitts and Nevis, Anguilla, St Lucia and St Vincent and the Grenadines joined CARIFTA. A few years later in 1971, Belize (then called British Honduras) joined as well. By this time, several of the states had achieved independence.

Did you know...?

The members of CARIFTA were:

- Antigua and Barbuda
- Barbados
- Belize
- Dominica
- Grenada
- Guyana
- Jamaica
- Montserrat
- St Kitts and Nevis
- Anguilla
- St Lucia
- St Vincent and the Grenadines
- Trinidad and Tobago

Exercise

1. What do the initials CARIFTA stand for?
2. Which countries first discussed the idea of a new trade association?
3. Name the countries that became members of CARIFTA.
4. What role did Trinidad and Tobago have in the formation of CARIFTA?

Objectives of CARIFTA

The main objective of CARIFTA was to unite the economies of the member countries, improve relationships between the states and, as a result of this, give them a powerful joint international presence.

The best way of doing this was to increase trade between members of the organisation. It was thought that this would also encourage development in the region.

The agreement encouraged member states to:

- buy and sell more goods between themselves
- diversify and expand the variety of goods and services available in the region
- make sure there was fair competition, especially for smaller businesses
- make sure that the benefits of free trade were equitably distributed among member states.

Trade between member states was **liberalised**. There was to be free trade between the member states. This meant that states did not charge each other tariffs (taxes or customs duties) on goods imported from other member states.

There were also no quotas on goods traded between member states, so states could trade as much as they liked.

Over and above this, CARIFTA also promoted industrial development of less developed states, the development of the coconut industry and an improved way to market agricultural goods.

Bananas being packed in Dominica for sale in the UK, as part of a special agreement between Caribbean islands and the UK.

Discussion

Do some research and then discuss whether CARIFTA was successful. Why/why not?

Exercise

5 What were the main objectives of CARIFTA?

6 Explain in your own words what free trade means.

7 What are the advantages of free trade?

8 Why do you think it was so important for newly independent states in the Caribbean to form strong ties?

9 Which countries played leading roles in the development of CARIFTA? Why?

10 Compare the West Indian Federation and CARIFTA. What were the similarities and differences between them?

11 Compile a timeline of the key dates of the history of CARIFTA.

Key vocabulary

CARIFTA

free trade

liberalised

CARICOM and CSME

We are learning to:

- define relevant terms and concepts: globalisation
- describe the Caribbean integration process from the 1950s to the present: CARICOM, CSME
- outline the objectives and membership of institutions/bodies which form part of the integration process: CARICOM, CSME.

CARICOM and CSME

The success of CARIFTA encouraged member states to broaden cooperation in the Caribbean. The CARIFTA agreements did not allow for the free movement of workers or of capital between the member countries, nor did it allow for the coordination of agricultural, industrial and foreign policies.

The result was an improved association called the Caribbean Community or **CARICOM**. This came into being with the signing of the Treaty of Chaguaramas, which was signed on 4 July, 1973 in Chaguaramas, Trinidad and Tobago. CARICOM replaced CARIFTA, although the CARIFTA Games and sporting events continued.

A meeting of CARICOM leaders.

Membership of CARICOM

CARICOM is an organisation of Caribbean states that promotes cooperation and integration between member states, especially in areas like trade and transportation. It also coordinates foreign policy. This has resulted in many benefits for the citizens of Caribbean states. People can move around freely to study and to look for work, and goods and services can be traded easily between these countries.

CARICOM was formed with the signing of an agreement between Trinidad and Tobago, Barbados, Jamaica and Guyana. The organisation grew quickly and now includes 15 member states:

- Antigua and Barbuda
- the Bahamas
- Barbados
- Belize
- Dominica
- Grenada
- Guyana
- Haiti
- Jamaica
- Montserrat
- St Lucia
- St Kitts and Nevis
- St Vincent and the Grenadines
- Suriname
- Trinidad and Tobago

The CARICOM flag.

Did you know...?

The CC on the CARICOM flag is like the links on a chain. A linked chain represents unity. The fact that the links are not complete represents a break with the colonial past. What do you think the colours of the flag represent?

Objectives

In 1989, the CARICOM heads of government agreed to advance the process of economic integration and to increase their ability to respond as a group to the challenges and opportunities of globalisation. This led to the creation of the CARICOM Single Market and Economy (**CSME**).

Globalisation is a process of making the world more connected, with goods, services and people moving and communicating easily and quickly all around the world.

The CSME allows for the free movement of money and skilled labour between member states, the right to set up a business in another member state, free movement of goods and a common trade policy.

Several other states have associate member status, including the British Virgin Islands, Turks and Caicos, Anguilla, the Cayman Islands and Bermuda.

Activity

Work in pairs and look online and in newspapers for interesting reports about CARICOM activities. Select a report, then describe what you have discovered to the class.

The objectives of CARICOM are, among other things, to improve standards of living and work, increase people in employed labour, expanding trade, greater productivity and improved trading relationships with other countries outside the region. The major activities of the group are to coordinate economic policies and development planning; designing special projects for the less-developed countries in the CARICOM membership, operating as a regional single market for many of its members and handling regional trade disputes.

Source: Jamaica Information Service website

What is the CARICOM Single Market and Economy (CSME)?

In 1989, it was decided to continue the good work of CARICOM, but to add to this by establishing the CSME to expand and deepen the integration in response to globalisation (the increasing interconnectedness in the world). This involved a review and updating The Treaty of Chaguaramas, which included the CARICOM Single Market and Economy, signed in 2001. The CSME made it much easier to trade and deepen relationships with other parts of the world.

Source: adapted from Caribbean Elections website

Exercise

1. What are the main objectives of CARICOM?
2. Why was the CSME agreement signed?
3. If they want to set up a new business, what advantages do business people from CARICOM member states have?
4. Compile a timeline of the key dates in both CARICOM and the CSME's history.

Key vocabulary

CARICOM

CSME

Organisation of Eastern Caribbean States

We are learning to:

- describe the Caribbean integration process from the 1950s to the present: OECS
- outline the objectives and membership of institutions/bodies which form part of the integration process: OECS.

OECS

The Organisation of Eastern Caribbean States (OECS) is an **inter-governmental** organisation formed in 1981 to promote unity and solidarity amongst its members.

OECS logo.

The origins of the OECS lie in the West Indian Federation, which was disbanded in 1962. When Trinidad and Tobago and Jamaica became independent of Britain in 1962, the remaining countries – Barbados, Dominica, Grenada, St Lucia and St Vincent and the Grenadines, Antigua and Barbuda, St Kitts and Nevis, Anguilla and Montserrat – formed a new organisation to continue dealings with Britain.

This eventually led to the 1981 Treaty of Basseterre, in which Antigua and Barbuda, Dominica, Grenada, Montserrat, St Kitts and Nevis, St Lucia and St Vincent and the Grenadines signed a formal agreement.

Membership of OECS

The OECS has 11 group members including the full Member States of Antigua and Barbuda, Commonwealth of Dominica, Grenada, Montserrat, St Kitts and Nevis, St Lucia and St Vincent and the Grenadines. These members are part of the Economic Union and received the full benefits of Economic Union like free movement of people and goods, with the British Virgin Islands, Anguilla, Martinique and Guadeloupe as associate members of the OECS.

Exercise

1. When was the idea of an OECS-type organisation first considered?
2. When was the OECS finally formed?
3. Which countries were in the OECS originally?
4. Name the countries that are in the OECS today.

Objectives of the OECS

The broad aim of the OECS is to promote economic growth, social inclusion and protection of the environment amongst its members.

Today, the main objectives of the OECS are to promote:

- regional integration
- the free movement, growth and development of people, goods, services and capital
- the security and well-being of citizens
- key economic priorities – including climate change, jobs, transportation, trade, energy, food security and production
- a high-performing organisation capable of delivering the strategic priorities.

The OECS also works to end poverty, build economic growth and address a range of social issues, such as education, health and social protection.

The headquarters of OECS.

Activity

Create a short video with 10 facts about the OECS, including facts about when it started, the work it does and some of its recent successes. Present your video to the class.

Research

Using the internet, go the OECS website look under 'Our Work' and select three of the areas the OECS works in to help regional integration. Write a short report of about 200 words, using illustrations. Try to choose three topics that are similar – for example, economic development, business development and trade.

Exercise

5 What are the two main broad aims of the OECS?

6 Outline the objectives of the OECS.

7 Explain in your own words what you think is meant by the objective 'Consolidating the architecture of regional integration'.

Key vocabulary

inter-governmental

Association of Caribbean States

We are learning to:

- describe the Caribbean integration process from the 1950s to the present: Association of Caribbean States
- outline the objectives and membership of institutions/bodies which form part of the integration process: Association of Caribbean States.

Association of Caribbean States

In 1994, the Association of Caribbean States (ACS) was set up to build on existing links in the Caribbean and to integrate the area further. This organisation does not include only Caribbean island states but also territories in South, and Central America. The organisation was formed with the aim of promoting the interests of the Caribbean region within its member states.

The 7th Summit of Heads of State for the Association of Caribbean States (ACS) at the Convention Palace in Havana, Cuba, 4 June, 2016.

The ACS was formed when US President Clinton put forward an idea for an organisation for Free Trade Area of the Americas (FTAA). The FTAA would encourage the movement of goods without any involvement by customs for North and South American and Caribbean countries.

Countries could not agree on the terms of the FTAA, so it was never formed. The ACS was formed in response to the proposed FTAA.

The agreement to form the Association of Caribbean States (ACS) was signed in Colombia in 1994. The **Secretariat** of the ACS is in Port of Spain.

Membership

In addition to the main member states, there are also **associate members** such as Aruba and Guadeloupe. Countries like Norway and the UK also have **observer status**, which means they can attend certain meetings. Currently there are 25 member states and 12 associate member states:

Antigua and Barbuda, the Bahamas, Barbados, Belize, Colombia, Costa Rica, Cuba, Dominica, Dominican Republic, El Salvador, Grenada, Guatemala, Guyana, Haiti, Honduras, Jamaica, Mexico, Nicaragua, Panama, St Kitts and Nevis, St Lucia, St Vincent and the Grenadines, Suriname, Trinidad and Tobago and Venezuela.

Did you know...?

The associate members of the ACS are as follows:

Aruba, Bonaire, British Virgin Islands, Curaçao, French Guiana, Guadeloupe, Martinique, Saba, St Barthélemy, St Martin, St Eustatius, and St Maarten.

Objectives

The ACS membership has identified five objectives for their organisation:

- the preservation and conservation of the Caribbean Sea – to ensure that the Caribbean region as a natural resource is protected for future generations
- **sustainable tourism** – protecting the environment, while developing long-term economic opportunities, which in turn creates job opportunities for the local community
- to develop greater trade between the nations
- natural disasters – to develop and put measures in place that will help protect countries and their economies in the event of a natural disaster (such as a hurricane), and to coordinate responses to natural disasters in the Caribbean
- transport – better air and sea routes between the member states and a focus on the safety of travellers in the region.

The ACS has Special Committees, each of which meet twice a year to discuss the organisation's objectives in relation to current regional issues. The Special Committees include:

- Trade Development and External Economic Relations
- Sustainable Tourism
- Transport
- Disaster Risk Reduction
- Budget and Administration.

Exercise

1. What is the main aim of the ACS?
2. Name two countries that are part of the ACS but not part of CARICOM.
3. Why do you think the preservation of the Caribbean Sea is a focus?
4. Discuss how transport within the region can strengthen economic development and cooperation.
5. What is sustainable tourism, and why is it important?
6. Write an essay with the title 'The role of regional agencies in facilitating regional integration'. Write 250–300 words.

Opening meeting of the 22nd meeting of the Association of Caribbean States in Havana, Cuba, 2017.

Project

Compile a report summarising what you have learned about the different organisations helping to foster integration in the Caribbean. Using the internet and what you have learned so far, name the member states involved in each organisation and list two main objectives for each organisation. Create a poster showing your findings, and present them to the class.

Key vocabulary

associate member

observer status

secretariat

sustainable tourism

Sport

We are learning to:

- identify non-political areas of cooperation within the Caribbean region: sports
- assess the role of regional agencies in facilitating the integration process.

Economic affairs were not the only concern of Caribbean leaders. In order to promote **unity** amongst people in the Caribbean, **integrated** sporting events were also set up. These have proved to be most successful.

CARIFTA Games

The CARIFTA Games were held for the first time in 1972. They consist of athletic field and track events, including sprints, middle-distance running races, hurdles, jumping events, throwing events and relay races between teams.

The Games are held annually. There are two categories: one for athletes under 17 years old, and the other for athletes under 20. Athletes are only allowed to compete if they are from countries that are members or associate members of CARICOM.

Sport can bring communities together.

Purpose of the CARIFTA Games

The CARIFTA Games were founded to improve relations between people of the English-speaking countries of the Caribbean. Since then, athletes from French- and Dutch-speaking countries have also been encouraged to take part.

Did you know...?

Cricket West Indies (CWI) is one of the oldest examples of regional cooperation. It was founded in the early 1920s, when it was called the West Indies Cricket Board.

Location of the Games

The CARIFTA Games have been held in many different countries, including Trinidad and Tobago, Jamaica, Barbados, the Bahamas, Martinique, Guadeloupe, Bermuda, Grenada, Turks and Caicos, St Kitts and Nevis and St Lucia. New sports facilities have been built in many places in order to host the Games.

Exercise

1. When were the CARIFTA Games first held?
2. Which sporting events feature in the CARIFTA Games?
3. What was the purpose of founding the CARIFTA Games?
4. In which countries have the Games been held?

Research

Work in pairs. Visit the Cricket West Indies website and research the mission, values and vision of this organisation. What do they aim to achieve?

Successful athletes

The CARIFTA Games have been a starting point for many athletes who have gone on to become world record holders, and world and Olympic champions. These include:

Usain Bolt (sprinter from Jamaica), Darrel Brown (sprinter from Trinidad and Tobago), Veronica Campbell-Brown (track and field athlete from Jamaica), Kim Collins (track and field athlete from St Kitts and Nevis), Pauline Davis-Thompson (sprinter from the Bahamas), Alleyne Francique (track athlete from Grenada) and Obadele Thompson (sprinter from Barbados).

The West Indies cricket team is made up of players from CARICOM countries.

West Indies cricket team

The West Indian cricket team, commonly known as the Windies, is one of the most successful cricket teams in the world.

The team is made up of players from CARICOM countries. It competes successfully in international tournaments and is an example of the benefits of regional cooperation between CARICOM countries. Cricket West Indies encourages regional development as part of the International Cricket Council's development programme.

Some of the best cricketers in the world come from the West Indies. Over the years, players like Sir Garfield Sobers, Gordon Greenidge, Brian Lara, Clive Lloyd, Malcolm Marshall, Sir Andy Roberts, Sir Frank Worrell, Sir Clyde Walcott, Sir Everton Weekes, Sir Curtly Ambrose, Michael Holding, Courtney Walsh, Joel Garner and Sir Viv Richards have made the Windies a force to be reckoned with.

Many players have been rewarded for their great contributions to the game of cricket.

The Windies have won the ICC Cricket World Cup, the ICC World Twenty20 and the ICC Champions Trophy. The Under-19 teams have also been successful.

Discussion

Your teacher will help you to arrange a class debate. You will discuss whether or not West Indies cricket benefits the Caribbean. Some of the class should argue that it does have benefits for the region, while others should suggest that is does not. Prepare your case and think of good reasons to back up your arguments.

Exercise

5 Which countries form the West Indies cricket team?

6 Work in pairs. Find out about the medals (gold, silver and bronze) that have been won by athletes from your country in the CARIFTA Games. Find pictures of the athletes and report back to the class.

Key vocabulary

integrated

unity

Education and medicine

We are learning to:

- identify non-political areas of cooperation within the Caribbean region: education, medicine
- assess the role of regional agencies in facilitating the integration process.

Education

In 1972, in order to increase integration, The Caribbean Examination Council (CXC®) was established. It is an institution that provides regional and internationally recognised secondary school leaving examinations which reflect the needs of the region, such as CSEC® and CAPE®. CXC® also helps to produce teaching materials and train teachers and to advise regional governments on education.

Students and their lecturer at the university campus in Kingston, Jamaica.

This University of the West Indies (UWI) developed from the University College of the West Indies, which had been established in 1948 as an independent external college of the University of London. The UWI became completely independent in 1962, at a time when many countries in the Caribbean achieved independence. This helped in efforts to make the region more autonomous and less dependent on former colonial rulers. The UWI aids in regional development by providing tertiary education and research facilities.

UWI is internationally recognised for its excellence. Graduates of the university have helped to provide leadership in Caribbean states and to promote economic and cultural growth. Graduates of the university include many current and former prime ministers as well as Nobel laureates and Rhodes Scholars.

> **Did you know...?**
>
> Sir Derek Walcott, the Caribbean poet and playwright who won the Nobel Prize for Literature in 1992, was a graduate of the University College of the West Indies. He studied in Jamaica.

The university has three main campuses:

- Mona – in Jamaica
- St Augustine – in Trinidad and Tobago
- Cave Hill – in Barbados.

There are several smaller campuses in other states, as well. The Open Campus of the university provides for online learning.

The university offers diplomas and degrees in engineering, humanities, education, law, medicine, science, agriculture and social sciences.

Exercise

1. How long has UWI been a fully independent Caribbean university?
2. What courses can you study at this university?
3. Analyse the role that UWI plays in the development of the Caribbean.

Medicine

Promoting good health is essential to the development of the Caribbean. There is widespread cooperation between healthcare providers across the Caribbean.

One example is the Caribbean Environmental Health Institute (CEHI). This was set up in 1989 by CARICOM to respond to the environmental health concerns of its members.

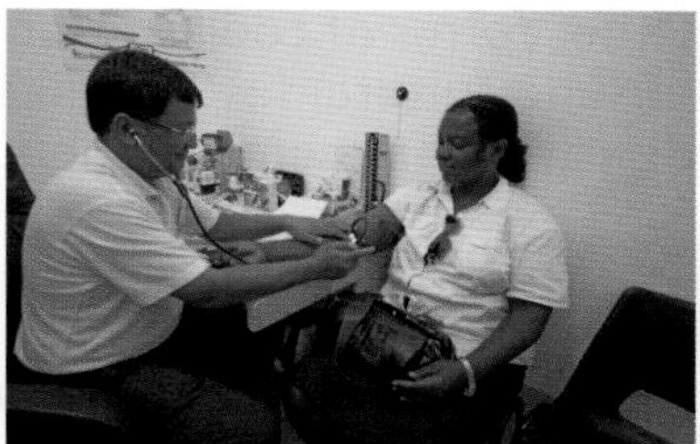

Promoting good health is essential to the development of the Caribbean.

The CEHI provides advice to members in all areas of environmental management, including:

- water supplies, liquid waste and excrement disposal
- solid waste management – for example, from shelters and health facilities
- water resources management – for example, collecting and distributing treated rainwater
- coastal management, including beach pollution
- air pollution, occupational health
- disaster prevention and preparedness, such as planning for floods
- natural resources conservation
- environmental institution development
- social and economic aspects of environmental management.

Currently, members of the CEHI include Anguilla, Antigua and Barbuda, the Bahamas, Barbados, Belize, British Virgin Islands, Dominica, Grenada, Guyana, Jamaica, Montserrat, St Kitts and Nevis, St Lucia, St Vincent and the Grenadines, Trinidad and Tobago, Turks and Caicos Islands.

Exercise

4. How and why is medical expertise shared across the Caribbean?
5. Why do you think it is important to share such expertise?
6. In your own words, explain the services that CEHI provides and why it is important to the well-being of the people of the Caribbean.
7. How is awareness about diseases created? Give an example of something you have seen or heard in your community.

Culture and disaster preparedness

We are learning to:

- identify non-political areas of cooperation within the Caribbean region: culture, disaster preparedness
- assess the role of regional agencies in facilitating the integration process.

Other forms of cooperation between Caribbean states include cultural festivals like CARIFESTA and a combined disaster management agency called CDEMA.

Culture (CARIFESTA)

Since this first festival in 1972 in Guyana, CARIFESTA has been strengthening the **cultural bonds** between the people of the Caribbean. The aims of CARIFESTA are as follows:

- to depict the life of the people of the region – their heroes, morale, myths, traditions, beliefs, creativeness and ways of expression
- to show the similarities and the differences between the people of the Caribbean and Latin America
- to create a climate in which art can flourish so that artists are encouraged to return to their homeland
- to awaken a regional identity in literature
- to stimulate and unite the cultural movement throughout the region.

The festival has achieved its aims and created numerous benefits for the people of the Caribbean. It has become a major tourist attraction that unifies Caribbean nations and expresses their diversity at the same time.

The festival has helped to create a unique **identity** for people from the Caribbean. The festival has also promoted cultural activities as a form of entertainment as well as creating opportunities for many artists to forge good careers.

Research

Work in pairs and find newspaper articles about CARIFESTA. Find out how the celebrations help to bring people of the region together. Report back to the class with a summary of what you have discovered.

Discussion

Work as a class and express your opinions about the benefits of CARIFESTA and its contribution to regional unity.

Exercise

1. What would you expect to see and do at CARIFESTA? Make a list of 10 items or activities.
2. What is a regional identity and how does CARIFESTA promote this?
3. How do you think the people of the Caribbean region have benefited the most from CARIFESTA?

Disaster preparedness (CDEMA)

CDEMA (the Caribbean Disaster Emergency Management Agency) was set up to coordinate responses to **natural disasters** such as hurricanes, volcanoes, earthquakes and tsunamis in CARICOM member states and associate member states. The responsibilities of CDEMA include:

- managing and coordinating disaster relief
- getting reliable information on disasters
- reducing or eliminating the impact of disasters
- setting up and maintaining adequate disaster response.

Case study

Read this press release issued by CARICOM after the 2010 earthquake in Haiti and answer the questions.

'More than 300 persons from 11 Caribbean Community (CARICOM) Member States and Associate Members have so far been involved in the response to the devastating earthquake which struck Haiti on 12 January. The Region's initial response was spearheaded by Jamaica, the sub-regional focal point with responsibility for the northern geographic zone of CDEMA which includes Haiti.

Personnel from Antigua and Barbuda, Barbados, Belize, the Bahamas, Dominica, Guyana, Grenada, St Lucia, St Vincent and the Grenadines and the British Virgin Islands provided support after the initial search and rescue, medical, security and engineering teams had been supplied by Jamaica within 48 hours of the earthquake.

CARICOM's continuing interventions in Haiti include: Emergency Response Coordination; Medical Assistance; Logistics, inclusive of the distribution of relief supplies and engineers assessments; Security; CARICOM Civilian Evacuation and Resource Mobilisation.'

Questions

1. How did CARICOM respond to the 2010 earthquake in Haiti?
2. Which members of CARICOM were involved in the response?
3. Which country led the response team? Why do you think they led it?

Activity

Write a report about the benefits of belonging to regional integration organisations. Outline the advantages and any disadvantages.

Did you know...?

Members of CDEMA include:

- Anguilla
- Antigua and Barbuda
- the Bahamas
- Barbados
- Belize
- British Virgin Islands
- Dominica
- Grenada
- Guyana
- Haiti
- Jamaica
- Montserrat
- St Kitts and Nevis
- St Lucia
- St Vincent and the Grenadines
- Suriname
- Trinidad and Tobago
- Turks and Caicos.

Discussion

Work as a class and express your opinions about the benefits of CDEMA to Caribbean unity. Has CDEMA really been effective? What more could be done to improve regional cooperation in this regard?

Key vocabulary

CDEMA
cultural bonds
identity
natural disaster

The Caribbean Court of Justice

We are learning to:

- identify non-political areas of cooperation within the Caribbean region: justice and law enforcement
- assess the role of regional agencies in facilitating the integration process.

The Caribbean Court of Justice

The **Caribbean Court of Justice (CCJ)** is the Caribbean regional **judicial** tribunal established on 14 February 2001. The CCJ is intended to be a hybrid institution, which means a mixture of two systems to produce something new. It includes a municipal court of last resort and an international court vested with original, compulsory and exclusive **jurisdiction** which was developed in response to the changes made in the Revised Treaty of Chaguaramas. The CCJ was set up to settle disputes related to the Revised Treaty of Chaguaramas. The Caribbean Court of Justice (CCJ) was officially opened in 2005. It is located in Port-of-Spain, Trinidad.

CCJ logo.

The CCJ is currently presided over by seven **judges**, including the President of the Court. These judges are qualified legal practitioners from the Caribbean Region and the Commonwealth.

Our Mission

Providing accessible, fair and efficient justice for the people and states of the Caribbean Community

Our Vision

To be a model of judicial excellence

Our Values

Integrity – Be honest, do right, stand firm

Courtesy and Consideration – Demonstrate care and respect for all

Excellence – Demonstrate the highest quality of service and performance

Industry – Be diligent, go above and beyond

Source: ccj.org/about-the-ccj/who-we-are/

Did you know...?

The Seal of the Caribbean Court of Justice (its symbol) is the winning design of two young men, Mr. Brent Matthew and Mr. Shawn Chong Ashing of Trinidad and Tobago following a CARICOM-wide competition in 2004.

The CARICOM states of Antigua and Barbuda, Barbados, Belize, Grenada, Guyana, Jamaica, St Kitts and Nevis, St Lucia, Suriname, Trinidad and Tobago, Dominica and St Vincent are the members of the CCJ.

The aim of the CCJ is to provide high quality justice to the people of the Caribbean by 'guaranteeing accessibility, fairness, efficiency and transparency' and 'delivering clear and just decisions in a timely manner'. The CCJ helps to reinforce regional integration by settling commercial disputes. It also brings a single vision to the development of law in the Caribbean region, which has lots of different cultures and historical backgrounds.

Case study

How the Caribbean Court of Justice benefits the Caribbean

In the long debate over the development of the Caribbean Court of Justice (CCJ) as the final court of appeal for the English speaking countries of the region, one of the main arguments in favour of the court has been the potential positive role it could play in the development of our local law-keeping. By this it is meant that having a court made up of individuals who have a greater connection to life in the region will lead to law-making that is more sensitive to local culture.

Those who have studied the CCJ's case law have concluded that these expectations have been met. A recent review of the decisions made by the CCJ stated that it acted very well, preserving the fine tradition of sound judicial reasoning from Commonwealth Caribbean courts.

An example of this is the October 2015 judgment of the CCJ in a case brought by several Maya peoples of Belize for damages that had occurred due to the government's failure to prevent private individuals from destroying their customary land ownership. The court ruled that the state was in breach (or had broken the law) for its failure to ensure that the Maya's constitutional right to property was protected. The court therefore confirmed that in some circumstances the state must actively protect the constitutional rights of its citizens.

Source: adapted from Caribbean Journal website

The CCJ brings a single vision in the development of law in the Caribbean region.

Exercise

1. Which countries are members of the CCJ?
2. Explain the role of the Caribbean Court of Justice.
3. Who can bring a dispute to the CCJ?
4. Explain why the CCJ is important in the Caribbean region.

Key vocabulary

Caribbean Court of Justice

judge

judicial

jurisdiction

Regional integration and cooperation

We are learning to:

- analyse ways in which the individual, businesses and countries benefit from regional integration.

The benefits and achievements of regional integration and cooperation

Integration in the Caribbean has brought many benefits to the region.

Free movement of goods, labour and capital

Regional integration has improved the ability to move goods, **labour** and **capital** freely across the region, increasing opportunities to grow regional economies and to improve levels of employment.

Unemployment is a big problem within the Caribbean region, but access to greater resources can lead to better job opportunities, a larger population can offer more skills and a larger regional economy is more attractive for investment.

Regional integration has given businesses and industries in the Caribbean access to a larger market.

Expansion of trade

Regional integration has given businesses and industries in the Caribbean access to a larger market. Trade expansion means a diversification of products available to larger markets, which leads to greater economic growth. Regional integration assists trade expansion because:

- the entire region becomes a market of goods and services starting from within the region
- the region can trade more effectively on the world market.

Various **trade agreements** between member countries of organisations such as CARIFTA, the removal of trade barriers and a larger market to trade in have resulted in more goods being traded between Caribbean countries. There is also a greater awareness in the world about goods and services provided by the Caribbean.

Discussion

Have a class discussion about the ways young people and adults can help promote Caribbean integration and the development of a Caribbean identity.

Exercise

1. In your own words, explain the benefits of regional integration for trade. Write 100 words.
2. How can unemployment be reduced by greater regional integration?

Improvement in the quality of life

Regional integration, along with steady economic growth and prosperity, means that there is more money available for social programmes (better housing, health care, **sanitation**). It also creates jobs, which means people have more money. There is better access to education, as well – for example, the University of the West Indies. Member states also help each other to combat crime through the Regional Security Service.

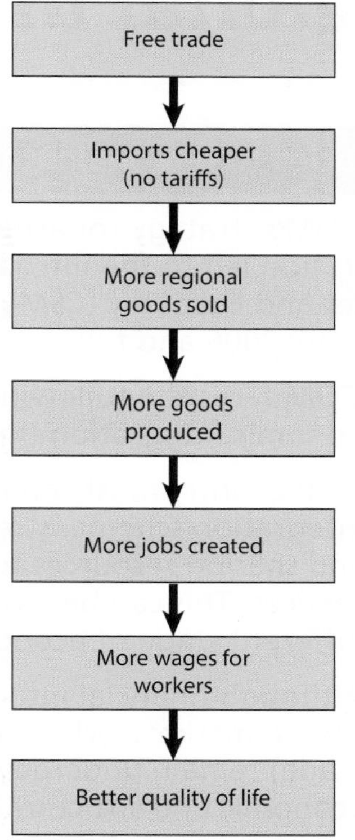

The benefits of regional integration.

Increased cooperation among member states

Regional integration has increased cooperation among the member states. Participation in organisations such as CARIFTA (trade), CARICOM/CSME (economy), OECS (unity), ACS (heritage and sustainable tourism), CARIFESTA (culture) and CDEMA (disaster preparedness) contributes to increased cooperation between member states.

Closer cooperation between member states also helps to reduce the cost of government (CARICOM, for example, provides many services that individual countries could only provide for themselves at a much higher cost), reduces duplication of effort and increases bargaining power with markets outside the region. Member states that work closely together create a stronger community sense and a closer-knit region that already has a long shared history.

Better response to global environment

Regional integration offers greater opportunities for the region to compete on a global scale and to take part in globalisation. Working cooperatively to produce certain goods reduces the costs of production and offers economies of scale. This helps to make the Caribbean region more competitive on a global scale. However, retaining a strong regional market also means that the region does not need to rely on global markets in times of global economic difficulty.

Project

Work in groups to create a jingle or advertisement that informs individuals and businesses about ways they can support regional integration.

Exercise

3. In your own words, explain how regional integration can improve the quality of life in the region. Write 100 words.
4. Name the organisations that help to improve regional integration and explain what they do.
5. What are the obstacles to regional integration?

Key vocabulary

capital

labour

sanitation

trade agreement

Obstacles to regional integration

We are learning to:

- discuss some of the obstacles and barriers to regional integration.

Obstacles to regional integration

CARICOM's strategy for achieving complete economic integration led to the introduction of the Caribbean Single Market and Economy (CSME). It was formally established on 1 January 2006 and fully established by 2015.

CARICOM faces the following main challenges in its quest for economic integration through the CSME.

1. Each country must complete the intraregional integration scheme, strengthening trading relationships and sharing resources to improve the delivery of public services. This can be a challenge if each country is at a different stage of economic development.
2. Although financial integration has moved quickly, capital markets (where savings and investments are made) remain underdeveloped. Developing shared economic and structural policies is still work in progress.
3. The lack of a regional body that has the power to help transform community decisions into legally binding policies has been a challenge for integration.
4. Where the decision-making process is based on the idea that each member state retains its sovereign authority, progress can be slow. Decision-making often takes a long time.
5. Due to the fact there are no regional rules about cooperation, each decision must rely on shared national interests and shared goals. Not all countries will have the same priorities.

Project

The European Single Market is a long-established single market. Work in a group to look at Europe's Covid-19 response. During the pandemic, what benefits did European people experience from being in a single market? What downsides were experienced? For both pros and cons, you should look into vaccines and border control measures.

Activity

Work in groups to design a game based on promoting regional integration and the removal of the obstacles.

Your board game might have these components:

1. Game board: map of the Caribbean with pathways between countries.
2. Player tokens: representing different Caribbean nations.
3. Obstacle cards: highlighting challenges to regional integration.
4. Collaboration cards: Providing solutions and strategies for overcoming obstacles.
5. Resource cards: representing shared resources like trade agreements, cultural exchanges, and joint projects.

Give your game a name and come up with a set of rules. You could use AI or free online game makers to help you.

6. Differing export and production structures and income levels mean it can be challenging to integrate economic and structural policies.

Is integration worth the challenges?

The Caribbean authorities generally agree that integration should remain a top priority and greater collaboration is crucial to tackle common challenges. Research finds that further integration of trade and greater labour mobility within the region can generate significant benefits. These benefits include increased GDP and increased employment levels.

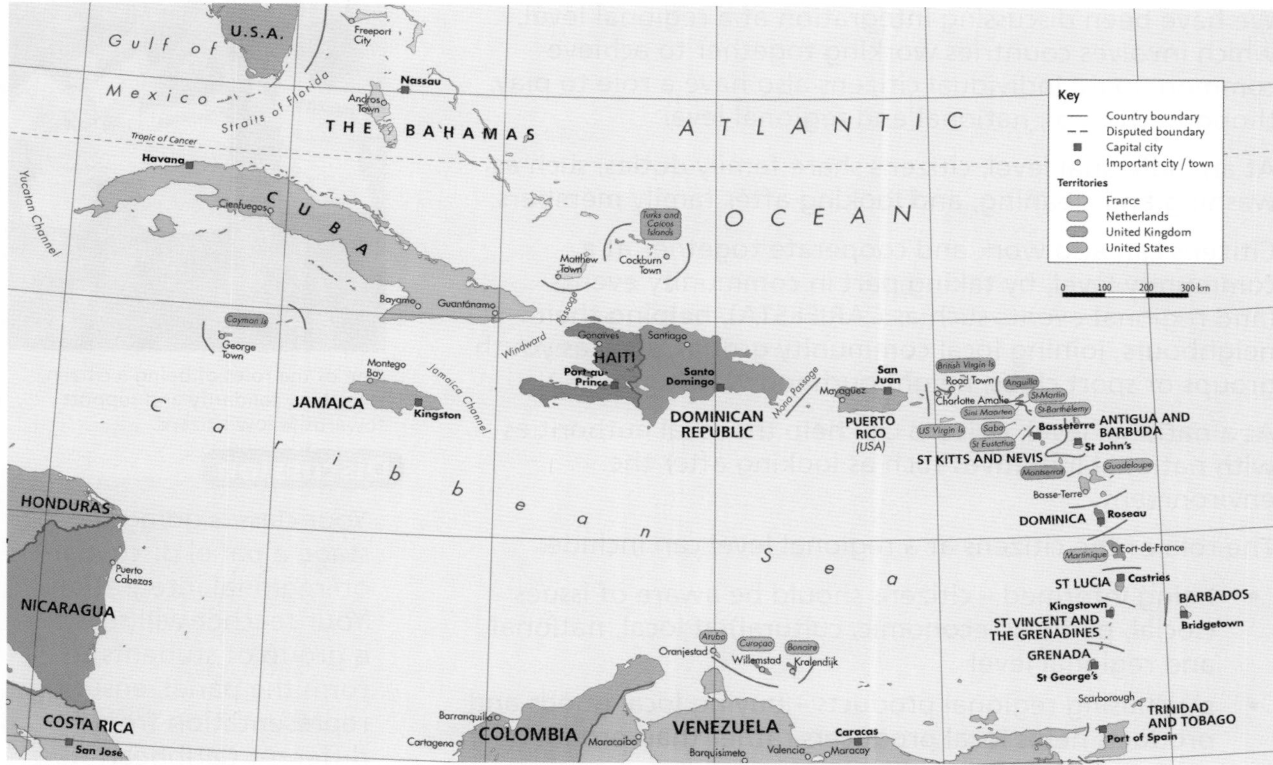

The Caribbean: Political map.

Exercise

1. Explain economic integration in your own words, giving examples.
2. Why might countries within the Caribbean region find it hard to make decisions together?
3. Write a paragraph explaining what challenges Jamaica might experience in particular in relation to regional integration, giving examples.

Regional integration: the role of individuals, businesses and states

We are learning to:

- discuss ways the individual, businesses and countries can deepen regional integration
- role of individual citizens and business organisations in the integration process.

Role of the individual

We have been discussing integration at a regional level, which involves countries working together to achieve common goals. Individual citizens also have a role to play, though – at local, national and regional level.

At an individual level, citizens share family duties, such as washing and cleaning, and looking after family members.

Citizens can also work and cooperate together at a community level, by taking part in community events (and regional events such as CARIFESTA), helping their neighbours, joining local community groups, such as youth groups or sport clubs, neighbourhood watch groups.

At a national level, citizens can help the local authorities with national initiatives such as looking after the environment.

The role of the citizens at a regional level can include:

- being informed – citizens should be aware of issues (social, political, economic, cultural) at local, national and regional level
- purchasing regional products – buying local goods and products helps local producers rather than producers in other parts of the world
- showing solidarity and mutual support towards regional fellow citizens – the Caribbean is a multicultural region and on each island there are people from different cultural backgrounds; it is important to respect people who come from different backgrounds.

One of the roles of being a citizen, is to show solidarity and support towards fellow citizens.

Discussion

Your class is going to stage a panel discussion on regional integration. Your teacher will select a group of students to form the panel, ensuring representation from different Caribbean nations. Panel members should prepare brief presentations on how regional integration impacts individuals. The panel discussion should include opening statements, individual presentations, and a concluding discussion. The rest of the class is the audience and should interact with questions and comments.

Exercise

1. Name three ways an individual can help with regional integration at an individual level and a regional level.
2. Give examples of things that citizens should stay informed about.

Role of business organisations

The role of businesses in regional integration include:

- increasing range of goods and services – businesses have an important role to play in creating a wide range of goods and services for the region. Increased goods and services means more jobs;
- providing opportunities for investment and employment – companies often need **investment** to expand or bring in new equipment, and this attracts investors, which in turn can create employment. In return, the investors are looking to make more money themselves;
- competition – increased competition can help to raise employment and boost sales outside the region, which in turn increases earnings and improves living standards;
- **multinational companies** – large companies that are based in different countries in the region and that often produce a number of different products. They produce goods which are used in the region, are exported outside the region and employ large numbers of people within the region. Examples in the Caribbean include:
  - Massy Group – machinery, engineering, retail, real estate, insurance, finance, energy and gas
  - ANSA McAL – retail, car industry, manufacturing, media, finance
  - TCL Group – cement and ready-mixed cement products.

Massy Group is a multinational company which works in engineering, machinery, finance, retail, real estate, insurance, energy and gas.

Research

Research a multinational company that is present in the Caribbean. Identify the different types of industry they are involved in, and where. Write a short report of around 100 words and use photos if you can find them.

The role of countries

The role of government includes making sure that:

- legislation works across the region
- policies across the region work for all members of the region in a similar, or same, way
- government agreements are followed, such as environmental protection agreements
- citizens are aware of the objectives and benefits of integration.

Project

Create a brochure that outlines the benefits of integration to individuals, businesses and countries. To illustrate your brochure, use images from magazines, the internet or newspapers.

Exercise

3. Explain the role of businesses in regional integration.
4. How can multinational companies help regional integration? Give an example of a multinational company.
5. Explain how governments can help regional integration.

Key vocabulary

investment

multinational company

Regional integration: non-traditional areas of cooperation

As well as regional integration through things like political alliances and trade agreements, there are other factors that bring Caribbean nations together. These include:

- relationships between people through marriage, family and friendship
- humanitarian initiatives, such as programmes for asylum seekers and the prevention of human trafficking.

Relationships

Personal relationships can help to foster regional integration in a number of ways, including:

- Promoting cultural understanding and trust
- Enabling communication channels between people from different countries
- Creating networking opportunities, both personally and professionally
- Helping to resolve conflicts
- Encouraging different communities to come together.

Kyle and Marica recently got married.

Exercise

1. Look at the picture of Kyle and Marica who recently got married and are living in Portland. Kyle is from Jamaica and Marcia is from Trinidad and Tobago. List some of the ways their marriage could help to foster regional cooperation, as well as some of the ways their relationship may already have done.
2. Can you think of any obstacles that Kyle and Marcia might face because they are from different Caribbean countries? Draw a table to list the obstacles in the left-hand column, and possible solutions in the right-hand column.

Project

Carry out three interviews with friends and family to ask them about examples of non-traditional regional cooperation, such as relationships between people in different parts of the Caribbean. What do they think the benefits are? Use what you find out to create a short presentation to share with the rest of the class.

Humanitarian organisations

Humanitarian organisations are groups which work to help improve the lives and opportunities of people. For example, UNICEF is an international charity dedicated to helping children in need with offices in Barbados, Guyana and Jamaica.

Exercise

1 Why do you think UNICEF has offices in three different Caribbean countries?

2 List three ways that a humanitarian organisation such as UNICEF can contribute to regional integration.

Activity

You are going to take part in a team building activity called 'All Aboard'.

1. Your teacher will divide you into equal groups and provide you with a piece of cardboard, newspaper or tarpaulin, (representing the Caribbean region). Each group will consist of students representing Caribbean citizens, Caribbean governments, NGOs, and businesses that operate in the Caribbean.
2. Your teacher will fold the cardboard, newspaper or tarpaulin over and over again and all members of the group must try to remain on it.
3. Your teacher will take pictures of each group as they try to achieve this feat.

Discussion

As a class, talk through these questions:

- what did you notice about the groups that were able to keep everyone on board?
- what did that suggest about what the countries in the region need to do to achieve the level of integration desired?
- Can non-traditional areas of cooperation be successful without the economic and political areas of cooperation?

Questions

See how well you have understood the topics in this unit.

1. Match the key vocabulary word **(i–vii)** with its definition **(a–g)**.

i) *regional integration*
ii) *integrate*
iii) *social integration*
iv) *racial integration*
v) *economic integration*
vi) *interdependence*
vii) *region*

a) when people of all cultural groups, sexes and ages live and work together in an area
b) an area of the world – for example, the Caribbean
c) the joining or working together of countries that are near to each other, in order to make them economically and politically more powerful
d) when two or more things or people rely on each other or help each other
e) bring together ideas and people so that they work together or become part of the same group
f) when people from different cultural groups live and work together on an equal basis
g) cooperation in business, such as trading and finance

2. Which organisation was the first attempt at integration by Caribbean states?

3. Match the dates **(i–vi)** to the events **(a–f)**:

i) *1958*
ii) *1962*
iii) *1965*
iv) *1973*
v) *1981*
vi) *1989*

a) CARIFTA formed
b) CSME formed
c) West Indian Federation formed
d) Treaty of Basseterre/OECS formed
e) West Indian Federation disbanded
f) CARICOM formed

4. Complete this table with ticks (✓) to show which groups the Caribbean countries have belonged/belong to.

	West Indian Federation	CARIFTA	CARICOM	ACS	OECS	CDEMA	CEHI
Anguilla							
Antigua and Barbuda							
the Bahamas							
Barbados							
Belize							
British Virgin Islands							
Colombia							
Costa Rica							
Cuba							
Dominica							
Dominican Republic							
El Salvador							
Grenada							
Guatemala							
Guyana							
Haiti							
Honduras							
Jamaica							
Mexico							
Montserrat							
Nicaragua							
Panama							
St Kitts and Nevis							
St Lucia							
St Vincent and the Grenadines							
Suriname							
Trinidad and Tobago							
Turks and Caicos							
Venezeula							

Grade 9 Unit 2 Summary

Regional Integration

In this chapter, you have learned about:

- Regional integration as a priority of Caribbean countries since the 1950s
- How social, racial, economic and political integration can strengthen a group
- How Caribbean countries established bilateral agreements and lessened their dependence on European colonists
- The West Indies Federation being the first attempt at regional integration in 1958
- The objectives for the countries that participated in the West Indies Federation
- The reasons for the dissolution of the West IndiesFederation in 1962
- The Caribbean Free Trade Association (CARIFTA) as the second attempt at regional integration in the Caribbean.

Non-political areas of cooperation within the Caribbean region

In this chapter, you have learned about:

- The Caribbean countries that participated in CARIFTA and their main objective
- The organisation, membership and objectives of the OECS
- The mission, membership and aims of the ACS
- The main purpose of the CARIFTA Games and the countries that have hosted the Games
- The West Indies cricket team as an example of strength through cooperation
- Regional cooperation in education through organisations such as CXC and UWI
- CARICOM's investment in medicine as an area of regional cooperation
- How CARIFESTA shows regional cooperation in culture
- The establishment of CDEMA to respond to disasters
- The establishment of the CCJ as the regional judicial tribunal in 2001

Regional integration

In this chapter, you have learned about:

- The benefits and achievements of regional integration and participation
- The obstacles to Caribbean regional integration
- The role of individuals, businesses and states in achieving regional integration.

Checking your progress

To make good progress in understanding different aspects of Caribbean integration and global links, check to make sure you understand these ideas.

- ☐ Understand the term *regional integration* and the history of the integration process in the Caribbean.
- ☐ Understand objectives and membership of institutions/bodies which form part of the integration.
- ☐ Write an essay about the role of regional agencies in facilitating regional integration.

- ☐ Identify non-political areas of cooperation within the Caribbean region.
- ☐ Analyse ways in which the individual, businesses and countries benefit from regional integration.
- ☐ Discuss the ways young people and adults can help promote Caribbean integration and the development of a Caribbean identity.

- ☐ Discuss ways the individual, businesses and countries can deepen regional integration.
- ☐ Explain the role of businesses in regional integration.
- ☐ Explain how governments can help regional integration.

- ☐ Discuss the role of the individual in regional integration.
- ☐ Explain the benefits of integration.
- ☐ Explain how integration and cooperation help economically and in other ways.

SOCIAL STUDIES

Unit 3: Social Issues in Jamaica

Objectives: You will be able to: 

Social problems

- define a social problem.

Juvenile delinquency and crime

- examine issues that affect Jamaica and the world and develop action plans to solve these issues.

Sexual Health

- define sexually transmitted infections
- gather and interpret data on sexual health and use data to draw conclusions.

Teenage pregnancy

- gather and interpret data on teenage pregnancy and use data to draw conclusions
- analyse the consequences of teenage pregnancy on Jamaican society.

Child abuse and domestic violence

- gather and interpret data on social issues and use data to draw conclusions
- analyse the consequences of social problems on the Jamaican society.

Human trafficking

- gather and interpret data on human trafficking and use data to draw conclusions
- analyse the consequences of human trafficking on Jamaican society.

Poverty

- examine poverty as an issue that affects Jamaica and the world and develop action plans to solve it.

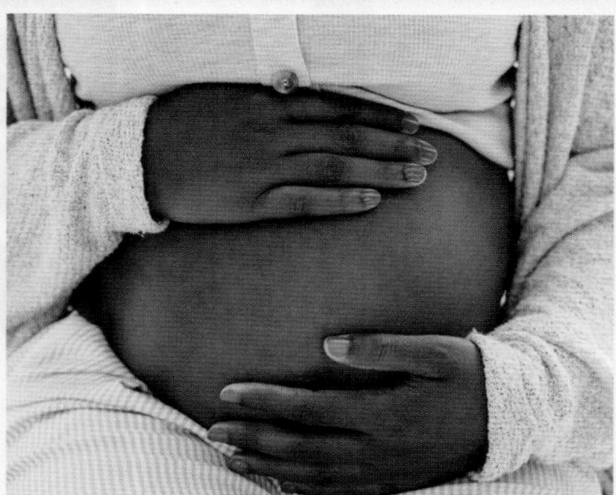

Social problems

We are learning to:

- define and describe social problems.

A social problem is an issue within a community which affects a number of people, and is seen by the community as needing to be resolved. A social problem is usually characterised by:

- harm to those directly affected
- harm to others indirectly
- involving a criminal activity
- involving behaviour considered to be deviant or wrong without being illegal
- relating to the physical or mental health of the community
- involving cost to the community or government
- negatively affecting the development of Jamaica.

Juvenile crime is an example of a social problem.

Discussion

In small groups, make a list of the social problems that affect the area where you live. Discuss the causes of these social problems.

Activity

Describe each of the following images, explaining how they are examples of social problems:

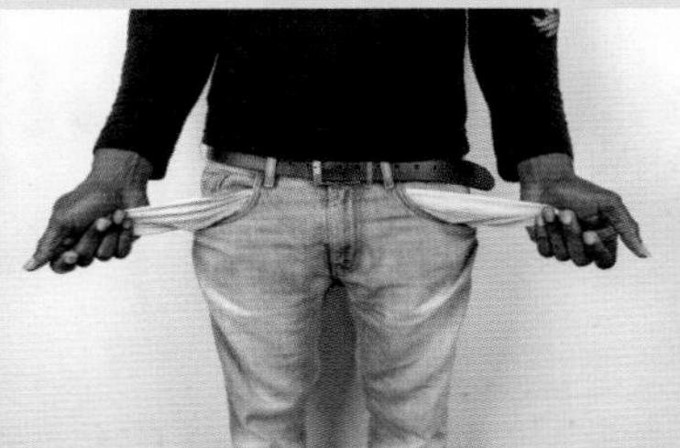

Imagine you are the Prime Minister of Jamaica. What steps would you take to reduce these social problems?

Gang Crime

Gangs, organised crime and violence are Jamaica's biggest social problems. With the second highest murder rate in the Latin American and Caribbean region in 2019, Jamaica's problems with violence are often related to gangs. Between 2008 and 2018, gang-related violence was responsible for 56% of murders in Jamaica, with a high of 78% in 2013. Jamaica also has high rates of domestic violence. These social problems are difficult to resolve as the causes are often complex and deep rooted.

Activity

Work in groups and consider the following questions.

1. What is meant by 'organised crime'?
2. Look up data on murders in Jamaica. Find the percentage of murders linked to gang-related activity for the most recent year that data is available.
3. Why is it difficult to understand the causes of gang crime?

Discussion

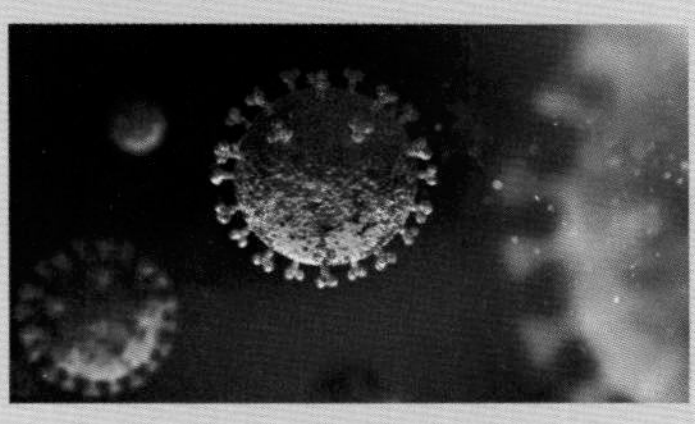

The global pandemic has had a huge impact on all our lives.

How might the global pandemic caused by the spread of Covid-19 lead to more social problems?

Exercise

1. Explain in your own words what is meant by a social problem.
2. What does 'deviance' mean? Give an example.
3. Give three examples of criminal behaviour.
4. Write a paragraph explaining why some social problems occur.

Juvenile delinquency and crime

We are learning to:

- examine issues that affect Jamaica and the world and develop action plans to solve these issues.

Crime

In most communities, **crime** is a serious problem. It can take on many forms, ranging from minor offences like vandalism and stealing, to major offences such as murder, gang violence, armed robbery and rape. Gangs are often associated with drugs and crime in Jamaica.

The factors influencing crime in Jamaica can be classified as social and economic in nature. Some of these factors include:

Gangs are often associated with drugs and crime in Jamaica.

Unemployment and poverty

Being out of work can cause a number of problems, including poverty which causes many to feel deprived and desperate. In 2020, the unemployment rate in Jamaica was at approximately 7.95%, which is a slight decrease from previous years. In general, unemployment is on a downward trend after reaching its highest point at over 15% in 2013. However, Jamaica's unemployment rate is still quite high. Those who are not in work may turn to crime as a way to survive and buy goods. The Covid-19 pandemic will likely cause an increase in unemployment rates.

Greed and the desire for power and status

For some individuals, wanting expensive consumer goods such as designer clothes, cars or other items may be seen as very important. This may lead to frustration if a person feels that they are unable to gain these goods through hard work or education. These items are seen as giving status and power, as other people may look up to those who are seen as rich. Some people may turn to crime to achieve this power and status through material items.

Violent and dysfunctional family backgrounds

Being brought up in a violent or dysfunctional home may cause people to turn to crime as they may be unable to seek family for support or financial help. People who experience violence in their childhood may also be likely to be more violent themselves, leading to more crime in society.

Association with delinquent peers

As children grow up, they may end up being friends with those who commit crime and act in deviant ways. This can lead to people being encouraged or forced into criminal behaviour as a result of peer pressure.

The presence of gangs in communities

One major cause of crimes in Jamaica is the presence of gangs in local communities. These gangs regularly commit crimes and recruit young people into their groups to help them. It is very difficult for members to leave the gang once they join and they may be intimidated or pressured into committing crimes and deviant acts against their will.

Children in Conflict with the Law

According to the Office of the Children's Advocate, approximately 400 children are in conflict with the law at any given time in Jamaica. Both male (71%) and female youths (29%) may come into conflict with the law. The average age of those involved in conflict is 15–16 and the most common reason is uncontrollable behaviours, followed by the carrying of weapons.

Source: Office of the Children's Advocate (2011). A Study of the Profile of Children in Conflict with the Law in Jamaica.

Action plan

Some of the strategies to prevent crime and juvenile delinquency include:

- educating people about the causes and effects of juvenile delinquency and crime
- offering guidance for parents to help their children avoid juvenile delinquency and crime
- counselling services for those directly or indirectly involved with juvenile delinquency or crime
- social intervention programmes
- improving relations between citizens and law enforcement.

Some of the strategies to combat crime can include:

- making sure that crimes are punished fairly
- crime prevention programmes, such as community policing, presentations at schools, anti-crime campaigns
- awareness campaigns showing the effect that crime has on individuals and society.

Activity

In groups, research examples of social intervention programmes. Examine how they help to address the issue of crime.

Key vocabulary

crime

Exercise

1. In your own words, outline why juvenile delinquency and crime are an issue in Jamaica.
2. What are some of the strategies used to combat juvenile delinquency crime issues?
3. Create a poster highlighting crime as a social problem, along with ways to solve it.
4. Explain what is meant by social and economic factors.
5. Give two examples of crimes that a person may commit if they experience poverty.
6. Write a paragraph explaining the reasons why young people may join gangs and the issues this creates for society.

Sexual health

We are learning to:

- define sexually transmitted infections
- gather and interpret data on social issues and use data to draw conclusions about social issues.

One social problem in Jamaica relates to people's sexual health. Understanding the need for protecting yourself against sexually transmitted infections is an important issue that affects the whole of the population, but especially young people who need to be informed about the risks and precautions needed to remain healthy.

Sexually Transmitted Infections

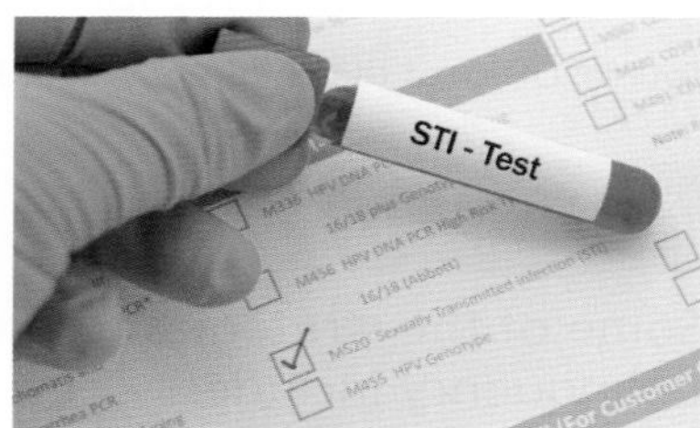

STI tests are very important.

A **sexually transmitted infection (STI)** refers to an infection or virus that is passed from one person to another during sex or by exchanging bodily fluids with another person. There are many types of STI that are common in Jamaica including **HIV**.

Chlamydia

Chlamydia is one of the most common bacterial sexually transmitted infections. The majority of people with this infection have no symptoms. Persons can be tested for this infection with a swab or a urine sample.

Gonorrhoea

This is another common sexually transmitted bacterial infection which can also be tested for. Symptoms include discharge, burning with urination, or burning or itching in the genital area.

Both chlamydia and gonorrhoea can be easily treated with oral antibiotics. However, women who are not treated may develop pelvic inflammatory disease, which can lead to infertility, chronic pelvic pain and other problems.

Hepatitis B

Hepatitis B is a virus that is carried in the blood. Persons can get infected through sexual contact or through injection with a contaminated needle which can occur in illegal drug use. Hepatitis B infection can cause severe liver disease, but it is preventable by a vaccine.

Syphilis

Syphilis spreads very easily. It can be a devastating disease which, in the late stages, may affect many organs of the body. Fortunately, because of screening and treatment, it is less common than it has been in the past.

All these sexually transmitted infections can be transmitted to a baby during childbirth and some can cause serious illness and sometimes death of a baby. It is recommended that pregnant women be tested for all these infections to avoid these consequences.

Key vocabulary

AIDS

HIV

sexually transmitted infection (STI)

HIV/AIDS

The HIV rate in the general population of Jamaica is 1.3%. The rate is much higher in vulnerable populations. Additionally, women and girls are increasingly infected by HIV, and girls in the 15–19 age group are three times more likely to be infected with the virus than young men in the same age group. Stigma (negative labelling) and discrimination, particularly in relation to the most-vulnerable populations, prevents people from accessing relevant health information and services.

HIV is a virus that causes the disease **AIDS**. There is no cure for HIV/AIDS at present, although the effects of the disease can be treated. HIV/AIDS can be transmitted through unprotected sex; untested blood transfusions; by sharing razors and syringes; through contact with infected blood or other bodily fluids; and mothers with HIV or AIDS can sometimes pass the infection onto their babies in childbirth.

The spread of HIV/AIDS is associated with different factors. Some of these include unprotected sex, and having multiple partners. Some groups are more vulnerable than others due to factors such as poverty, gender and inequality. HIV/AIDS can seriously affect the lives of persons who are infected, especially if they are unable to access or afford necessary treatment. Along with breakdown in health, infected persons sometimes are affected mentally and emotionally as they try to cope. It is therefore important to have the support of family and friends. If the spread of HIV/AIDS increases and becomes uncontrolled we may see further impact on families, communities and the country as a whole.

Action plan

Some of the strategies to help prevent STIs include:

- using condoms during sexual activity, which reduces the risk of infection
- government campaigns on prevention by providing information and advice
- campaigns in schools
- distribution of free condoms
- avoiding touching other people's blood and dirty syringes
- taking regular tests, if you're sexually active, to check for infection

Activity

Write a story about someone who becomes infected with HIV. Describe how other people react to this person and what he or she does in order to live with the disease.

AIDS is no longer considered a death sentence should anyone become infected. Governments should work to ensure easy access to medication and treatment for infected persons. Where possible, these should be made available at reduced costs. There should also be systems through which infected persons and their families can receive counselling and support. To ensure the spread of HIV/AIDS is further contained, the government should also develop systems and programmes to reduce the factors influencing the spread among vulnerable groups and educate the wider population about the disease and how to assist persons who may be affected.

Exercise

1. How successful have HIV/AIDS awareness campaigns been in Jamaica?
2. To what extent are people more open about their HIV/AIDS status today? Explain.

Teenage pregnancy

We are learning to:

- gather and interpret data on social issues and use data to draw conclusions about social issues
- analyse the consequences of social problems on Jamaican society.

Although teenage pregnancy rates have declined slightly in recent years, they are still fairly high. The fact that 18% of all births in Jamaica occur to teenagers means it continues to be a social problem. One major challenge is the fact that teenage mothers often drop out of the school system, and have little support from the 'baby-fathers' in bringing up their children. This has a double negative effect – on the young mother, whose opportunities for development are reduced; and on the child, who may not receive the benefits that a better-equipped mother could provide in terms of parenting.

Eighteen per cent of all births in Jamaica are to teenage mothers.

There are a number of causes of teenage pregnancy including:

- ignorance and myths regarding contraception
- failure to access free contraception (often due to embarrassment or unawareness of their availability)
- behaviour (high-risk sexual activity at a young age; poor contraceptive use; involvement in crime; alcohol and substance misuse)
- education-related factors (low educational attainment; disengagement from school and education; leaving school at 16 or before with no qualifications)
- family/home background factors, such as wanting to be a parent; poverty; being a child of teenage parents; in care; sexual abuse/exploitation
- environmental (the area a young person lives in, unemployment rate).

Activity

Research some of the programmes and strategies that have been introduced to address teenage pregnancy. Discuss their effectiveness, and make a list of the strengths and weaknesses of each one.

Action plan

- Offering confidential, non-judgemental, empathic advice to young people about sex and relationships
- Ensuring young people understand their information will be kept confidential
- Providing contraceptive services and advice about teen pregnancy and abortion
- Encouraging use of condoms and other forms of contraception
- Making sure that schools and other education settings provide contraceptive services
- Offering a return to education for teenage mothers.

Case study

The Women's Centre Foundation of Jamaica (WCJF) was set up in 1978 in response to the high level of teenage pregnancy. The organisation operates as a company and is supported by the government through the Ministry of Culture, Gender, Entertainment and Sport. At the beginning, there was one centre located at 42 Trafalgar Road, Kingston 10. The Foundation has grown since then and now includes 7 main centres and 11 outreach stations, island wide.

The Foundation offers the following services:

1. continuing education for adolescent mothers 17 years and under
2. counselling for 'baby-fathers', their parents and parents of adolescent mothers
3. day care facilities for (i) babies of adolescent mothers and (ii) babies of working mothers
4. walk-in counselling service for women and men of all ages
5. peer counselling training for in-school youths
6. counselling for clients in the Child Diversion Programme.

Since it began, the WCJF has assisted 46 989 adolescent mothers.

Women's Centre of Jamaica Foundation
1978 Celebrating 40 years 2018

The Women's Centre Foundation of Jamaica.

Research

Go to YouTube and search for 'reintegrating school-age mothers'.

In this video, Dasmine Kennedy, 2017 Echidna Global Scholar, describes her work with school-age mothers in Jamaica. Make notes on the causes and consequences of teenage pregnancy. Create a presentation for your class on this social problem, including graphs and other statistical facts.

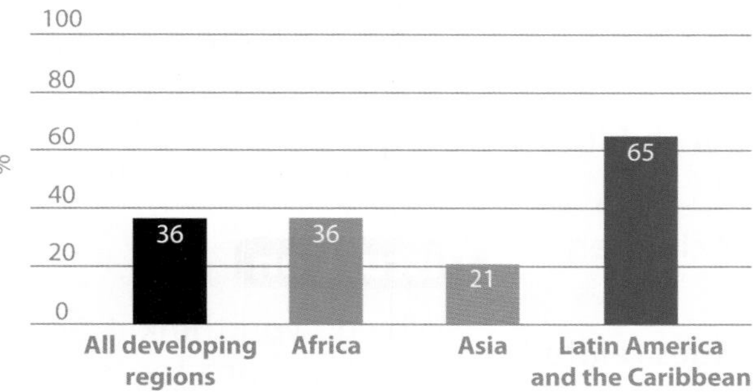

Unplanned births to adolescents younger than 15 are more common in Latin America and the Caribbean than in other developing regions.
Source: The Sexual and Reproductive Health Needs of Very Young Adolescents Aged 10-14 in Developing Countries: What Does the Evidence Show? (2017)

Project

Create a poster which gives information about five effects of teenage pregnancy.

Exercise

Look at the graph above.

1. What is meant by 'unplanned births'?
2. Why do you think that teenage pregnancies are more common in Latin America and the Caribbean than in other developing regions?
3. Write a report suggesting strategies that could reduce teenage pregnancies in Jamaica.

Child abuse

We are learning to:

- gather and interpret data on social issues and use data to draw conclusions about social issues
- analyse the consequences of social problems on Jamaican society.

Child abuse is when a child is intentionally harmed by an adult or another child – it can be over a period of time but can also be a one-off action. It can be physical, sexual or emotional and it can happen in person or online. It can also be a lack of love, care and attention – this is neglect.

According to the **Office of the Children's Registry** (OCR), in Jamaica:

- Almost 70 000 cases of child abuse were reported in Jamaica over eight years, from 2007, with a significant increase in the number of cases reported in 2015.
- Neglect continues to be the most common issue reported, making up 51% of all reports.
- According to the **Child Protection and Family Services Agency** (CPFSA), some 1 644 reports of neglect were received by the National Children's Registry between April and September in 2019.

Neglect is the most common issue in child abuse.

Did you know...?

The CPFSA, or the Child Protection Family Services Agency and the OCR, the Office of Children's Registry's role is to receive reports of children who have been, are being or are likely to be abandoned, neglected, physically or sexually abused, or are otherwise in need of care and protection.

Action plan

The government developed the National Plan of Action for an Integrated Response to Children and Violence (NPACV) 2018–2023, funded partly by the **United Nations Children's Fund** (UNICEF). This includes the following strategies:

1. Strengthened policy to ensure the protection of children from all forms of violence and exploitation.
2. Improved quality of, and access to, services for children affected by violence.
3. Family and community capacities to address issues related to children and violence.
4. Enhanced public education about violence prevention, the care of child victims of violence, and children's rights.
5. Monitoring and evaluation of the NPACV.

Discussion

Why do you think it might be hard for children to report child abuse? Discuss ways that children can be encouraged to speak up about abuse.

How do you report child abuse?

Persons wishing to make a report to the OCR can call 1-888-PROTECT

(1-888-776-8328) or 908-2132, 822-7031, 878-2882, 618-5888, 631-8933 and 631-8908.

Persons can also complete a reporting form and submit it to the OCR's head office at 12 Carlton Crescent, Kingston 10, or fax to 908-2579 or email it to: reports@ocr.gov.jm.

Exercise

1. Explain what is meant by child abuse in your own words.
2. What type of child abuse is the most common in Jamaica?
3. Write a paragraph explaining the key strategies to tackle child abuse by the government of Jamaica.

Activity

Plan an awareness day in your school on Children's Day about child abuse. Design and produce a display board including current statistics, facts and policies, as well as information on how to report child abuse.

Children make historic appeal in Parliament to #ENDviolence

On 19 November 2019, on the eve of World Children's Day, a group of children became the first in Jamaican history to address Parliament in a Special Session on Violence against Children. They were 7-year-old twins Ngozi and Tafari Wright, 10-year-old Keino King and 18-year-old Shaneille Hall.

Ngozi, who opened the presentation, made a powerful statement on behalf of fellow Jamaican children. "We LOVE our country. But we hate the violence that is hurting the bodies, minds and spirits of Jamaican children. We hate the violence that is making children so afraid. We hate the violence that is taking their lives." She shared their experiences of violence and the action they want the Jamaican government to take to address it.

The Special Session marked the end of a series of activities led by UNICEF Jamaica to commemorate the 30th anniversary of the Convention on the Rights of the Child.

UNICEF provides funding to many charities and organisations which protect children.

Exercise

4. Why do you think that girls are more likely to experience sexual abuse than boys?
5. Explain in your own words why this leads to increased rates of AIDS/HIV among young girls.
6. What strategies could be introduced to help prevent sexual abuse of children?

Discussion

Do you agree that it is more powerful or influential when children make their appeal in parliament against child abuse?

Key vocabulary

child abuse

Child Protection Family Services Agency

Office of Children's Registry

United Nations Children's Fund

Domestic violence

We are learning to:

- gather and interpret data on social issues and use data to draw conclusions about social issues
- analyse the consequences of social problems on Jamaican society.

Domestic abuse is a pattern of behaviour on the part of the abuser designed to control his or her partner. It can happen at any point in a relationship, including after a couple has split up. There are various forms of abuse, including:

- physical (when someone hurts or harms a person on purpose)
- emotional (when someone acts in a way which causes distress to a person)
- sexual (when a person is sexually abused, they're forced or tricked into sexual activities. They might not understand that what's happening is abuse or that it's wrong)
- financial (when someone is taken advantage of for economic reasons).

The majority of domestic abusers are male, and victims female.

Femicide is defined as a homicide in which the victim is a woman or a girl. Jamaica has the second highest rate of femicides in the world, according to United Nations data in 2019. Explanations include:

- financial problems in couples
- some people with very traditional beliefs may think they have the right to control their partner, and that women are not equal to men. These are known as **patriarchal** views, in which some men see themselves in a position of dominance over 'their woman'
- according to the 2016 Jamaica Women's Health Survey, 70% of Jamaicans believe that the man is the head of a household, and that the place of a woman is to do the domestic work and raise children
- low self-esteem, extreme jealousy, difficulties in regulating anger and other strong emotions, or when they feel inferior to their partner
- children who were brought up seeing violence in their parents are more likely to carry out abuse against their own partners.

However, things are changing. More and more women are working and becoming less **dependent** on their partners financially, which means that they can leave an abusive partner more easily.

Key vocabulary

dependent

domestic abuse

femicide

patriarchal

Action plan

The National Strategic Action Plan to Eliminate Gender-Based Violence in Jamaica (2016–2026) recommended:

- continue trying prevention programs, develop the most promising ones, and study how well they work. Encourage reporting of domestic abuse
- make penalties for domestic violence consistent and firm
- increase funding for support services
- change the way family courts handle cases involving domestic violence to make sure they are fair
- help women to become economically independent.

In **France**, reports of domestic violence have increased by **30%** since the lockdown on 17 March, 2020.

In **Cyprus** and **Singapore** helplines have registered an increase in calls of **30%** and **33%**, respectively.

In **Argentina** emergency calls for domestic violence cases have increased by **25%** since the lockdown in 2020.

Increased cases of domestic violence and demand for emergency shelter have also been reported in **Canada, Germany, Spain, the United Kingdom** and **the United States.**

The Covid-19 pandemic has led to an increase in domestic violence around the world.

Did you know...?

According to the WHO (World Health Organization), almost 30% of all women who have been in a relationship have experienced physical and/or sexual violence by their intimate partner.

Public campaigns are important in preventing domestic violence.

Exercise

1. Name the different types of domestic violence.
2. Men are less likely to report domestic violence than women. Why do you think this is?
3. Produce a PowerPoint highlighting the key causes and effects of domestic violence, as well as strategies to reduce it.

Human trafficking

We are learning to:

- gather and interpret data on social issues and use data to draw conclusions about social issues
- analyse the consequences of social problems on Jamaican society.

Human trafficking is the action or practice of illegally transporting people from one country or area to another, typically for the purposes of forced labour or sexual exploitation.

Most victims are people living in poverty, women and children enticed from rural parts of the country to urban areas by family members or newspaper classified job postings. After they are recruited, victims are forced into prostitution. **Sex tourism** in resort areas has been identified as a problem. This is where people visit a place to pay for sex.

In Jamaica, women have been trafficked from the Dominican Republic, Russia, Eastern Europe and Cuba, to work in the sex trade. Some Jamaican women and girls have been trafficked to Canada, the United States, the Bahamas, and other Caribbean destinations for sexual exploitation.

Campaign against human trafficking.

Action plan

According to the National Taskforce Against Trafficking in Persons (NATFATIP) this crime is known to be the most under reported in the world. This makes it a challenging area to tackle. Here are some current strategies:

- The Trafficking in Persons, Prevention, Suppression and Punishment Act became law in Jamaica in 2007, with the mission of identifying, punishing and preventing human trafficking, and to help protect vulnerable potential victims as well as those rescued from captivity.
- In 2014, an operation named 'Operation ID-Fix' was introduced, leading to the arrest of 41 individuals involved in people trafficking. The campaign involved 31 investigations and identified and rescued 12 victims.
- In 2015, the Jamaican police force implemented its Counter-Terrorism and Organised Crime (C-TOC) Investigation Branch with a unit dedicated to combating trafficking in persons.
- Other actions include educating people, especially young people about the dangers of people trafficking, and to encourage awareness about false job adverts, and how to report people they are concerned about.

Exercise

1. Explain what is meant by human trafficking in your own words.
2. What makes someone more likely to be trafficked?
3. Why is human trafficking a difficult problem to tackle?

According to the Jamaican Information Service, in order to identify potential victims of people trafficking, be aware that victims may:

- appear fearful or anxious when in the presence of his or her 'employer'
- be a minor or an adult who has been forced into prostitution or other 'jobs'. He or she might also try to mask this activity
- live with his or her 'employer'
- hesitate to speak to others freely
- respond to questions with answers that are seemingly scripted
- not be in possession of his or her identification documents (if he or she is an adult)
- not be attending school (if he or she is a child)
- show signs of physical abuse
- receive little or no payment for 'work' done.

Exercise

4. Describe the signs that indicate that someone might be experiencing human trafficking.
5. What role does National Taskforce Against Trafficking in Persons (NATFATIP) play in trying to prevent human trafficking?
6. Select one of the strategies being used by the National Taskforce Against Trafficking in Persons (NATFATIP) and explain how effective you think this strategy might be.

Did you know...?

It is estimated that hundreds of Jamaicans are or have been victims of human trafficking. However, between 2010 and 2016, only 62 victims were rescued.

Human trafficking is a serious social problem in Jamaica.

Activity

Imagine you are working for the Jamaican government and you are in charge of reducing human trafficking. Develop a strategy for reducing human trafficking and raising awareness. What actions would you take and why?

Key vocabulary

human trafficking

sex tourism

Poverty

We are learning to:

- examine issues that affect Jamaica and the world and develop action plans to solve these issues: poverty.

Poverty

Poverty is the state of being poor and not having enough money to live a comfortable life. The poverty rate in Jamaica fluctuates but is still considered high. This issue is part of the national development plan to reduce poverty levels to below 10% by 2030. A larger proportion of the population now falls below the poverty line and inequality has risen, in many instances increasing vulnerabilities of the most-at-risk populations, including women and young people. Poverty in Jamaica is caused by:

- unemployment and low levels of income
- regional inequality of income and wealth
- global inequality of income and access to resources
- lack of access to education
- volatile economies (that is, prone to change)
- the absence of government-funded social care programmes for poorer families
- an income ceiling, as a result of the level of education or skills training received
- gender inequality and exclusion from parts of society.

Poverty is also often closely linked to crime and violence, although of course some families living in poverty are also strong, happy and stay away from crime. Some researchers have suggested that there are three main types of poverty in Jamaica:

- families who have been poor for many generations
- families who are poor because people in the family have lost their jobs due to economic conditions
- families who are poor for part of the year, because the work they do is seasonal – as is the case with some jobs in the hotel industry.

Activity

Work in groups and conduct a survey on poverty in Jamaica. Your teacher will help you. Different groups can focus on different issues. For example:

- How many people live in poverty in Jamaica?
- How many people are homeless in Jamaica?
- Are there more men or more women who are living in poverty?
- What help is available from the government to help people in poverty?
- What help is available for people in poverty from the government, charities or NGOs?

Would you say that this family in Jamaica lives in poverty? Do people have different ideas about what poverty means?

Action plan

Some strategies to combat poverty include:

- increasing economic growth, which leads to higher employment and income
- higher levels of investment, improvements in productivity
- better education and training
- improving social services, to support families that are less well off
- improving opportunities for poorer countries to trade with the more well-off countries
- greater foreign investment.

Poverty is an issue all around the world.

Case study

The National Policy on Poverty and National Poverty Reduction Programme (NPP/NPRP) was launched in March 2018. The NPRP supports the National Policy on Poverty and is expected to contribute directly to the policy goals of eradicating extreme (food) poverty by 2022 and reducing national poverty to less than 10% by 2030. Its actions include:

- setting up the National Poverty Reduction Programme Committee (NPRPC) to oversee the implementation, monitoring and evaluation of the NPRP
- addressing extreme poverty and basic needs
- encouraging economic empowerment, helping people to develop their human capital
- helping people to become more able to avoid poverty by offering support and education
- improving basic community support in relation to food poverty.

Source: National Poverty Reduction Programme from Planning Institute of Jamaica website.

Activity

Work in pairs. Find out what living below the poverty line means in Jamaica. Make notes and do research. Then make a short presentation to the class about what it means to live in poverty.

Discussion

Work in groups. Brainstorm ideas that you think could be used to help reduce poverty in Jamaica. Write down all your ideas, then focus on two that you think are practical and workable. Present your ideas to the rest of the class.

Exercise

1. In your own words, outline the main types of poverty in Jamaica, and their causes.
2. What strategies are there to combat poverty?

Key vocabulary

poverty

Questions

See how well you have understood the topics in this unit.

1. A social problem is:

- **a)** any issue or behaviour that has negative consequences for large numbers of people and that is generally recognised as an issue or behaviour that needs to be addressed
- **b)** a beneficial behaviour in society
- **c)** an issue that only affects young people
- **d)** a set of issues that relates only to the environment.

2. STI stands for:

- **a)** socially transmitted ideas
- **b)** sexually transfused issues
- **c)** sexually transmitted infections
- **d)** sexually transmitted ideas.

3. Give three examples of STIs.

4. ____________ refers to a young person who commits deviant or illegal behaviour.

- **a)** Juvenile
- **b)** Ancestor
- **c)** Criminal
- **d)** Juvenile delinquent

5. True or False? Domestic violence only affects women and children.

6. Correct this statement: 'Teenage pregnancy in Jamaica is below international averages'.

7. Explain three characteristics of a person who is experiencing human trafficking.

8. Write a short definition of the following terms:

- **a)** sex tourism
- **b)** neglect
- **c)** exploitation.

9. Make a list of strategies to reduce crime in Jamaica.
10. Give two examples of ways that human trafficking is being tackled in Jamaica.
11. Explain how patriarchal attitudes in Jamaica may lead to domestic violence against women.
12. Give two examples of social problems people are more likely to experience if they live in poverty.
13. Find and read a blog or newspaper article about a social issue in Jamaica. Summarise the causes and effects of the social issue in two paragraphs.
14. Imagine that you work for an organisation that supports people who have been trafficked. Write an essay of about 200 words describing your role.
15. Carry out a day of action in your school, raising awareness of one of the social problems that you have been learning about.

Grade 9 Unit 3 Summary

Social problems

In this chapter, you have learned about:

- The characteristics of social problems
- Juvenile delinquency and crime
- The link between crime, unemployment and poverty
- The link between crime, dysfunctional families and delinquent peers
- Gangs in communities and their impact on crime
- Action plans to address the associated issues.

Sexual health and teenage pregnancy

In this chapter, you have learned about:

- Sexually transmitted infections (STIs)
- HIV and AIDS
- Strategies to prevent STIs
- Analysing the consequences of teenage pregnancy on Jamaican society
- Action plans to address teenage pregnancy.

Child abuse and domestic violence

In this chapter, you have learned about:

- The frequency and effects of child abuse in Jamaican society
- The strategies in the National Plan of Action for an Integrated Response to Children and Violence
- What is meant by domestic violence
- The issue of domestic violence and its effects on the victims and the wider society
- The components of the National Strategic Action Plan to Eliminate Gender-Based Violence in Jamaica.

Human trafficking and poverty

In this chapter, you have learned about:

- Human trafficking and the ways it is evident in Jamaican society
- Strategies to combat the occurrence of human trafficking
- The causes and types of poverty in Jamaica, and the efforts to alleviate it.

Checking your progress

To make good progress in understanding social problems in Jamaica, check that you understand these ideas.

- ☐ Explain and use correctly the term *social problem.*
- ☐ Describe three social problems in Jamaica.
- ☐ Explain the difference between juvenile delinquency and crime.

- ☐ Explain and use correctly the term *poverty.*
- ☐ Name the causes of poverty.
- ☐ Explain the possible solutions to poverty.

- ☐ Explain and use correctly the term *sexually transmitted infections.*
- ☐ Name three types of sexually transmitted infections.
- ☐ Explain three strategies to reduce sexually transmitted infections.

- ☐ Explain and use correctly the term *human trafficking.*
- ☐ Describe the causes and effects of human trafficking.
- ☐ Explain why teenage pregnancy rates are high in Jamaica.

End-of-term questions

Questions 1–6

See how well you have understood ideas in Unit 1.

1. Explain what is meant by globalisation, giving examples.
2. Explain what is meant by diaspora, giving examples.
3. Match these definitions to the correct terms:
   - **a)** heritage
   - **b)** cultural diffusion
   - **c)** socialisation
   - **d)** culture

   - **i)** The way of life of a group of people
   - **ii)** The internalisation of norms and values
   - **iii)** The spread of cultural beliefs and social activities from one group of people to another
   - **iv)** the legacy of physical artefacts and intangible characteristics of a group or society that is inherited from past generations
4. Briefly describe how Jamaican culture has spread around the world.
5. How have global cultures affected life in Jamaica?
6. Explain how technology and globalisation are helping to preserve Jamaican culture.

Questions 7–11

See how well you have understood ideas in Unit 2.

7. Outline the functions of CARICOM, CSME, OECS, CCJ.
8. Provide two examples of the positive effects of regional integration.
9. Give two examples of the economic benefits of multilateral agreements.
10. Make a list of examples of sporting and education based cooperation in the Caribbean.
11. Give two examples of what it means to be a citizen of the Caribbean.

Questions 12–16

See how well you have understood ideas in Unit 3.

12. Explain what is meant by a social problem.

13. What are the main social problems experienced by young people in Jamaica? Write a short paragraph to explain.

14. Write a short essay of six paragraphs in which you explain the problems linked to poverty in Jamaica. You should give examples of the consequences of poverty.

15. Explain what strategies the government have in place to tackle child abuse.

16. Create a spidergram showing:

a) the causes of human trafficking

b) the signs that someone is being trafficked

c) Jamaica's government responses to tackle human trafficking.

SOCIAL STUDIES

Unit 4: Development and Use of Resources: Impact on National Growth and Development

Objectives: You will be able to:

Demographic patterns in Jamaica

- outline the factors that contribute to national development
- assess the ways in which Jamaica develops its natural and human resources.

National development and contributing factors

- distinguish between gross national product and gross domestic product
- outline the factors that contribute to national development.

What are human resources?

- define and use correctly the terms resource, human resource, human capital, physical resources, skills, talent, knowledge, ability
- assess the importance of human resources to a country's economic development
- examine the importance of education in developing our human resources.

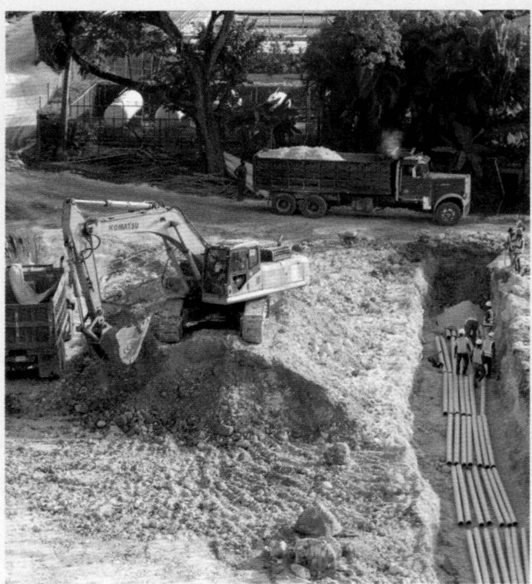

Our physical resources

- explain how our natural resources are used
- assess the ways in which Jamaica develops its natural and human resources.

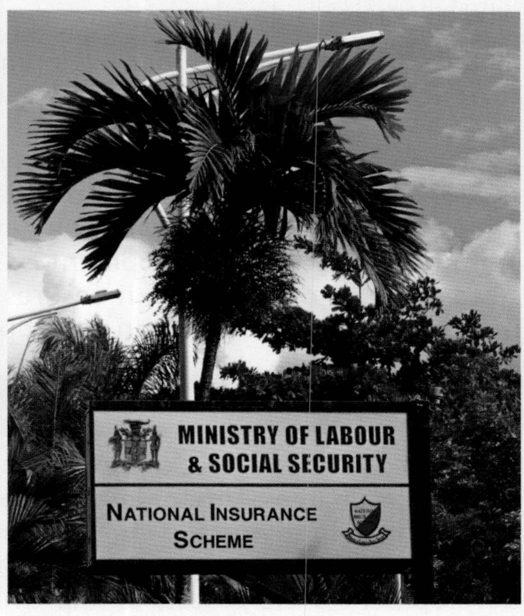

Oil and gas production; Agriculture; Using our natural resources

- explain how we use oil and gas
- evaluate the importance of the development of a country's human and natural resources, and the effects of using them.

Jamaica's National Development Plan (Vision 2030)

- explain Jamaica's National Development Plan (Vision 2030)
- evaluate the proposed performance indicators and targets which are used to measure progress (Vision 2030).

Key concepts

We are learning to:

- distinguish between economic growth and development; sustainable development, urban and rural development
- outline factors that contribute to national development.

In Grades 7 and 8 you learned about **development**, which is a process that leads to growth, progress, positive social and economic changes in a country. In this section we explore different types of development and consider the ways in which Jamaica is developing.

Finite resources in Jamaica are those which are non-renewable, such as bauxite.

Sustainable development is development that meets current needs without compromising the ability of future generations to meet their own needs. This means that improvements and advances in society can continue in the long-term without relying on and depleting our **finite natural resources** or damaging the natural environment. This means that such development is environmentally sustainable, in other words, it ensures that the natural world is preserved alongside human development.

Sustainable urban and rural development

There are different types of development for different geographical areas. **Urban development** refers to growth and progress in towns and cities, whereas **rural development** refers to growth and progress in countryside areas. Rural development is the process of improving the quality of life and economic well-being of people living in often relatively isolated and sparsely populated areas.

Urban development in Jamaica.

Research

Carry out some research on the population globally. Find out how many people live in rural areas compared with urban areas. Give three reasons why this is.

Urban and rural life.

Urban and rural population in Jamaica, 2018

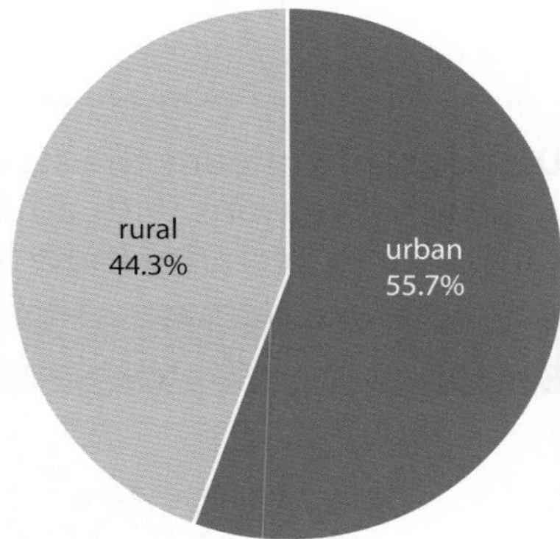

Where there is development, population growth tends to occur more rapidly.

Did you know...?

Over the past 15 years, Jamaica's population growth has slowed dramatically and was down to 0.26% as of 2019.

Discussion

Discuss the advantages and disadvantages of living in rural and urban areas. Make a list of each.

Exercise

1. What is the difference between urban and rural development?
2. Look up the word demography. What does it mean?
3. Suggest reasons why Jamaica's urban population is larger than its rural population.

Key vocabulary

development

finite natural resources

rural development

sustainable development

urban development

Demographic patterns in Jamaica

We are learning to:

- outline the factors that contribute to national development
- assess the ways in which Jamaica develops its natural and human resources.

Demography means the study of population. Demographic patterns change all the time, for a range of reasons with a range of effects. Demographic changes include birth and death rates, life expectancy (how long people are expected to live), as well as migration rates.

The distribution of population in Jamaica

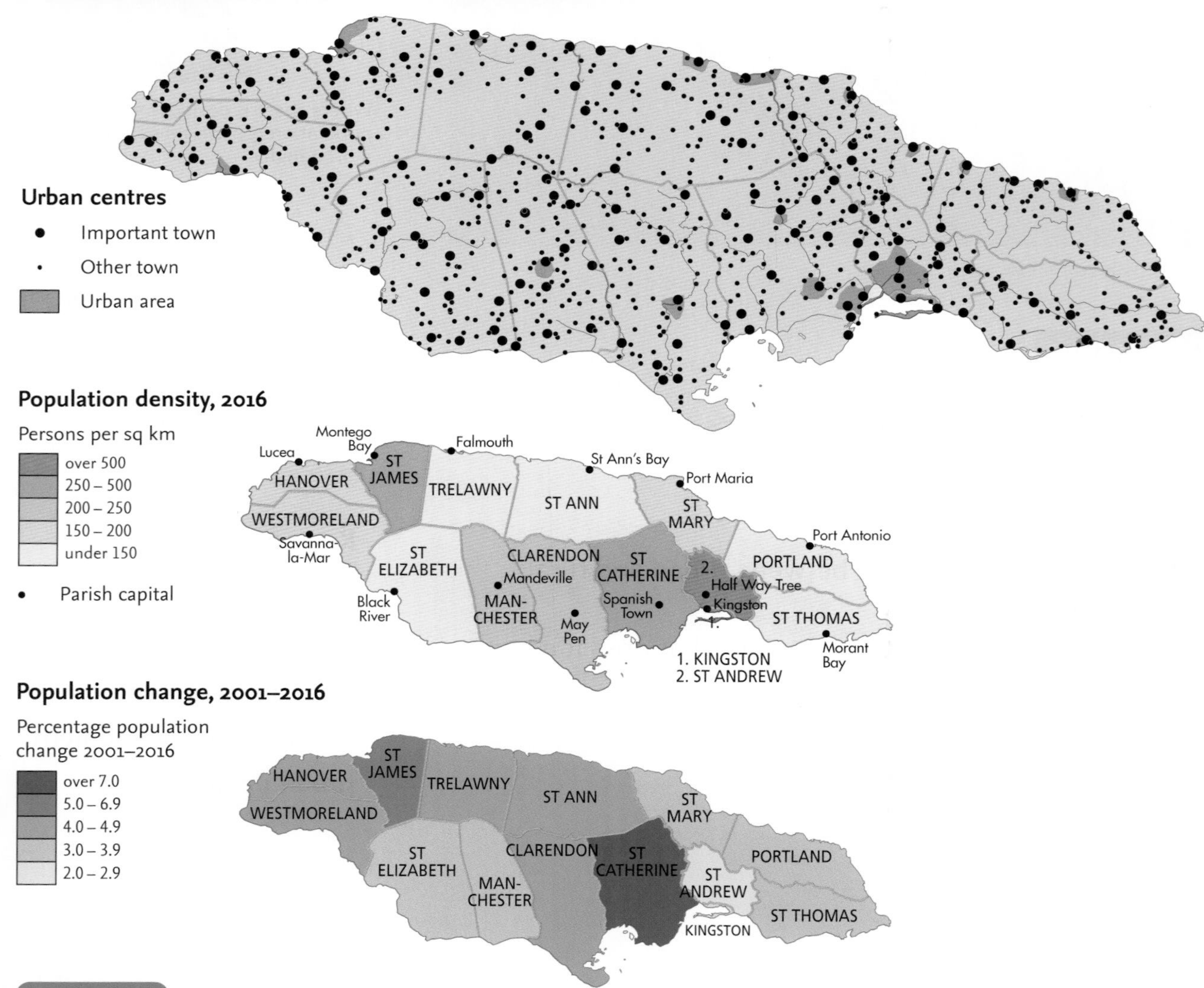

Exercise

1. Name three of the main urban centres in Jamaica.
2. In which parishes is the population most and least dense in Jamaica?
3. Where has been the greatest population change in Jamaica? Why do you think this is?

Population structure

In order to understand development in a country, it is important to understand the age of the population. This is because it is important to know how many people are of working age and able to contribute to the economic development of the country and also the number of people who are too young or too old to work (**dependants**). In Jamaica this is changing dramatically.

A **population pyramid** is a graph that shows the age–sex distribution of a given population. It a visual profile of the population's residents. Sex is shown on the left/right sides, age on the *y*-axis, and the percentage of population on the *x*-axis. Each grouping (e.g. males aged 5–9) is called a **cohort**.

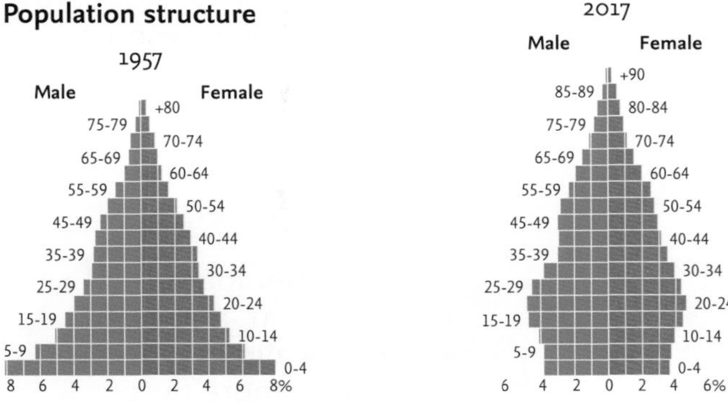

Each full square represents 1% of the total population.

Did you know...?

In Jamaica, the elderly now constitute 11.3% of the population today, up from 5% in 1850, and this is projected to rise to 25% by 2050.

Exercise

4. Describe the main changes in age distribution in Jamaica from 1957 to 2017.
5. Why do you think we are seeing a growth in the ageing population?
6. If old people are less able to work, what effect might this have on Jamaica's economy?

Key vocabulary

cohort
demography
dependant
population pyramid

National development

We are learning to:

- distinguish between economic growth and development; gross national product and gross domestic product.

What are economic growth and development?

Economic growth refers to an increase in the amount of goods and services produced per head of the population over a period of time:

- an increase in the production of goods and services in an economy
- increases in capital goods, labour force, technology, and human capital can all contribute to economic growth.

Development as we saw, is the process that leads to growth, progress, positive social and economic changes in a society. These changes include improvements in the standards of living for the people and an increase in the country's wealth or economic resources.

How does economic growth occur?

How does economic growth occur?

1. Increase in the amount of physical **capital goods** in the economy. Newer, better, and more tools, for example, mean that workers can produce more goods. For example, a fisherman with a net will catch more fish per hour than a fisherman with a sharp stick. This however requires money to be put aside to buy the capital goods (tools, for example).

2. Technological improvement. Improved technology allows workers to produce more output. This requires savings and investments. For example, using a machine to help you to produce part or all of your goods, saves a lot of time and energy.

3. A strong **labour force**. Having a healthy population and lots of people of working age is really important to economic growth.

4. Developing **human capital**. You explored the idea of human capital in Grade 8 – it refers to the skills, knowledge, and experience possessed by an individual or population. For economic growth it is important to develop the skills necessary to create goods and services in your work force.

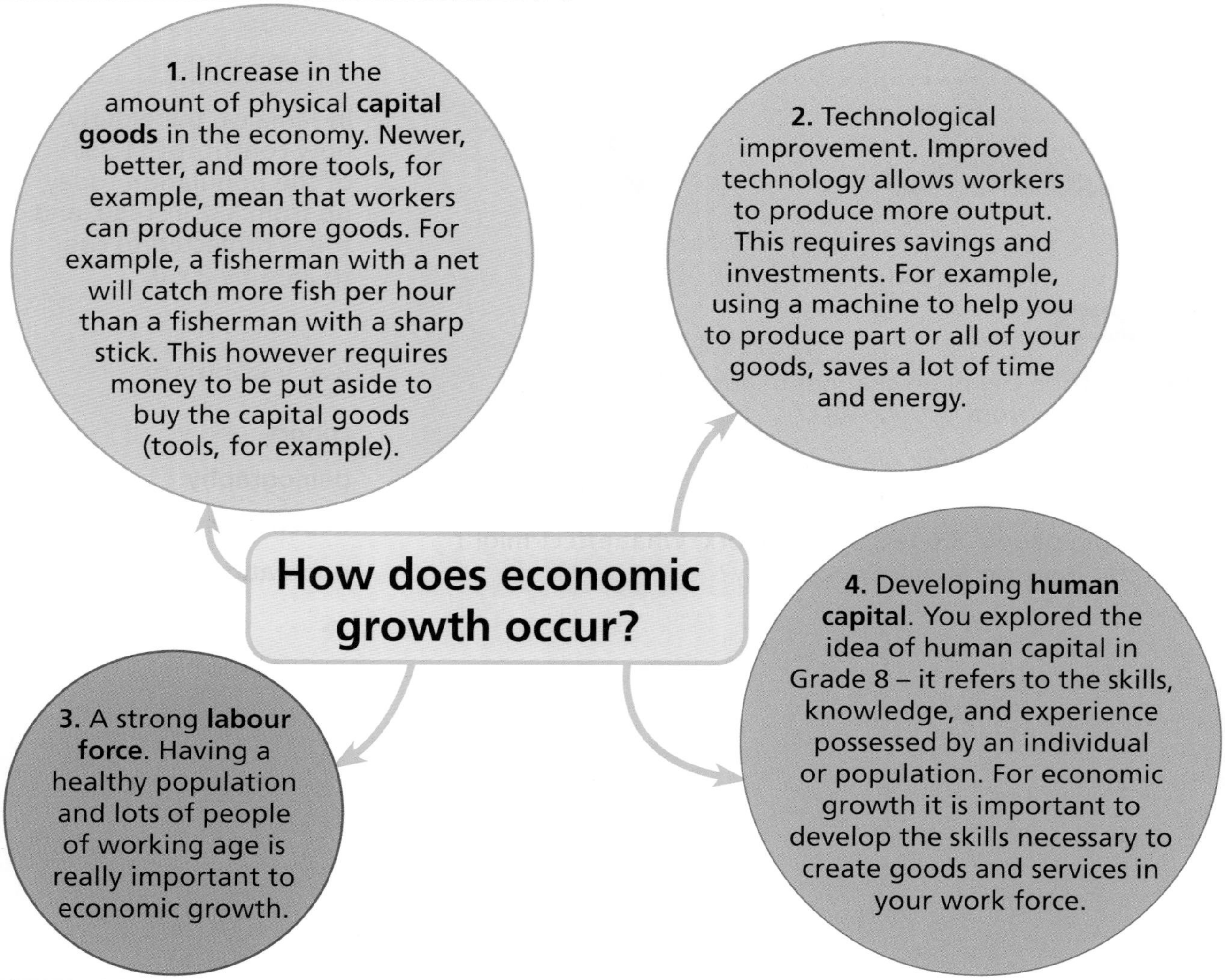

Rural farming.

Urban farming.

Small-scale farming.

Building.

The development of roads.

The introduction of technology.

What is gross national product and gross domestic product?

Gross domestic product (GDP) is the value of a nation's finished goods and services during a specific time period. It takes into account all that a country earns within a year. A related but different measurement, the **gross national product (GNP)**, is the value of all finished goods and services owned by a country's residents over a period of time, including the earnings of those who reside outside of the country.

Both GDP and GNP are two of the most commonly used measures of a country's economy, both of which represent the total value of all goods and services produced over a defined period.

- GDP is based on only the economy of Jamaica.
- GNP includes the overseas economic activities performed for example, by Jamaican people and businesses in other countries.

Exercise

1. Explain what is meant by economic growth.
2. Explain in your own words why economic growth occurs.
3. Explain the difference between the gross national product and gross domestic product.

Project

Pretend that you are the minister of Economic Growth and Job Creation. Make a 3 minute video of you presenting ideas to the nation that will create economic growth.

Did you know...?

The gross domestic product (GDP) in Jamaica was worth 15.72 billion US dollars in 2018.

Key vocabulary

capital goods
economic growth
human capital
Gross Domestic Product (GDP)
Gross National Product (GNP)
labour force

What factors contribute to national development?

We are learning to:

- outline the factors that contribute to national development
- evaluate the importance of the development of a country's human and natural resources.

Sustained economic growth within a country will have a positive effect on the national income and level of employment, and this, in turn will lead to higher living standards for the people. A growing economy is also good because it means people are able to pay more tax, which means more money or revenue for the government, which can be used for further development of an economy.

Important factors that affect the economic growth of a country are:

- *Human resources*: The quality and quantity of available human resource can directly affect the growth of an economy. The quality of human resource is dependent on its skills, creative abilities, training, and education. If the human resource of a country is well skilled and trained then the output would also be of high quality.
- *Natural resources*: Involve resources that are produced by nature either on the land or beneath the land. The resources on land include plants, water resources and landscape. The resources beneath the land or underground resources include oil, natural gas, metals, non-metals, and minerals, provide an opportunity for economic growth.
- *Capital*: Involves land, building, machinery, power, transportation, and medium of communication. Being able to acquire capital means economic growth is more possible.
- *Technological development*: Technology involves application of scientific methods and production techniques. Countries that have invested in technological development grow rapidly as compared to countries that have less focus on technological development.
- *Social and political factors*: These play a crucial role in economic growth of a country. Social factors involve customs, traditions, values and beliefs, which contribute to the growth of an economy. Social factors also include policies and programmes related to the health and education of the population. Political factors include policies and programmes a government may implement to promote growth in the economy.

Bauxite is an important natural resource for Jamaica.

Human Development Index

The **Human Development Index (HDI)** is a statistical measurement of **life expectancy**, education, and per capita (per person) income indicators, which are used to rank countries into different levels of human development.

The HDI was developed and collected by the **United Nations** to measure the level of social and economic development within countries around the globe. This index is a tool used to follow changes in development levels over time and to compare the development levels of different countries.

Specifically, HDI is measured by three components:

- the mean (average) years of schooling
- life expectancy at birth. This means how long a person is expected to live on average
- gross national income (GNI) per capita, or by person. This means the value of a country's final income in a year, divided by its population.

The HDI was established to place emphasis on individuals, and in particular, their opportunities to be able to do satisfying work and have a good quality of life. This was thought to be a better measure than simply looking at the income of a country, or economic growth alone.

This index can also be used to examine the various policy choices of nations; if, for example, two countries have approximately the same GNI per capita, then it can help to explain why they produce different human development outcomes.

The HDI is not perfect, for example, it does not measure important factors such as job satisfaction or people's feeling of job security. It also does not measure the level of freedom in a country.

Exercise

1. Explain what 'HDI' means, using your own words.
2. How is HDI measured?
3. State one problem with using the HDI to measure development?

HDI is measured by the mean average of years of schooling, life expectancy and the GNI per capita.

Did you know...?

Jamaica's HDI value for 2017 was 0.732 positioning it at 97 out of 189 countries and territories.

Research

Carry out research into the countries with the highest and lowest HDI globally. Suggest reasons why these countries occupy the top or bottom ranking. What can we learn from this activity about changes needed in Jamaica?

Key vocabulary

Human Development Index

life expectancy

United Nations

What are human resources?

We are learning to:

- define and use correctly the terms resource, human resource, human capital, physical resources, skills, talent, knowledge, ability
- look at the characteristics of human resources
- explain the difference between human and physical resources.

Developing human resources

An **economy** is made up of businesses that provide **goods** and **services** to meet people's needs. In order to provide goods and services, we use capital.

Traditionally, there were three kinds of capital: **resources**, land (or natural resources) and labour.

- A resource is defined as anything natural or physical that can be used to create wealth or improve the standard of living of people. For example, people use land to grow crops or to mine metals and minerals.
- Natural resources come from the natural environment, for example wood, water and soil. **Physical resources** are other tangible resources made by man, such as buildings and equipment.
- **Human resources** are people and their various **skills**, **talents** and **abilities**. People such as teachers, doctors, farmers, office workers, engineers, scientists and shop keepers all have skills that they use to provide goods or services.

The ball is a physical resource. The player, his talent and his skill are all human resources.

Characteristics of human resources

Human resources (HR) has several meanings:

- workers or employees who work for an employer;
- talents, skills, **knowledge** and experience that can only be found in people.

Training and education are aspects of human resource development.

Activity

For each of the following, brainstorm the physical and human resources that it requires:

a) a school

b) a restaurant.

HUMAN RESOURCES

Similarities and differences

Today, economists talk about two kinds of capital – **physical capital** (including land, which is a physical resource) and human capital.

- Physical capital, including land, is a physical resource that cannot make or provide anything by itself. Physical capital refers to assets that have been made or found that we use to produce goods and services.
- Human capital refers to people, skills, training, experience, education and knowledge. It can only be found in people.

An economy needs human capital and physical capital to run smoothly. Skills are special abilities people have that have been learned or developed.

Who makes up a country's human resources?

Think about the population of our country. The young and old people in the country are not able to work. Children and teenagers are still at school.

The working-age population is made up of people between the ages of around 17 or 18 up to about 65.

However, younger people are part of the next generation's human resources. For this reason, education is also considered an important part of human resources.

Exercise

1. Choose the correct term to complete each sentence.

resource	human	physical	skill

   a) A ___________ is something that we use.
   b) Wood is an example of a ___________ resource that we use to make different products.
   c) Someone who has a special ___________ for music or dance may go on to become an artist.
   d) The ___________ resources of a country lie in its people.

2. List two main differences between human and physical resources.
3. Look at the picture of the people making up the word 'human resources' on the opposite page. What does this picture tell you about human resources?

Project

Create a concept map to show how skills, talent, knowledge and ability relate to human resources.

Choose a working person you know. Collect and present information about the person's skills, talents, knowledge and ability.

Key vocabulary

ability
economy
goods
human resources
knowledge
physical capital
physical resources
resources
services
skill
talent

Factors influencing human resources

We are learning to:

- explain factors that influence the development of human resources.

There are several factors that influence the development of human resources:

- quality
- quantity
- composition
- skills development/enhancement
- creativity.

Learning is at the core of skills development in any country.

Quality

Quality is a measure of excellence. The quality of a country's human resources is directly linked to its skills development and education. Education includes schools, colleges, universities, training centres and programmes that help adults increase their skills.

Quantity

In a very small country, with a very small population, there is likely to be a smaller **quantity** of people making up its human resources. A bigger country is likely to have a bigger pool of human resources.

Composition

Population **composition** refers to the make-up or characteristics of people in a population, such as **gender**, age, ethnicity, occupation or religion.

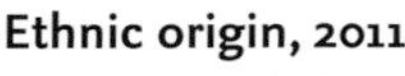

Ethnic origin, 2011

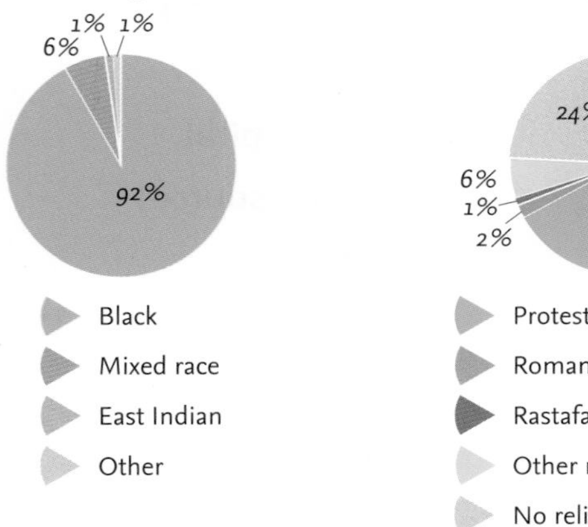

Religion, 2011

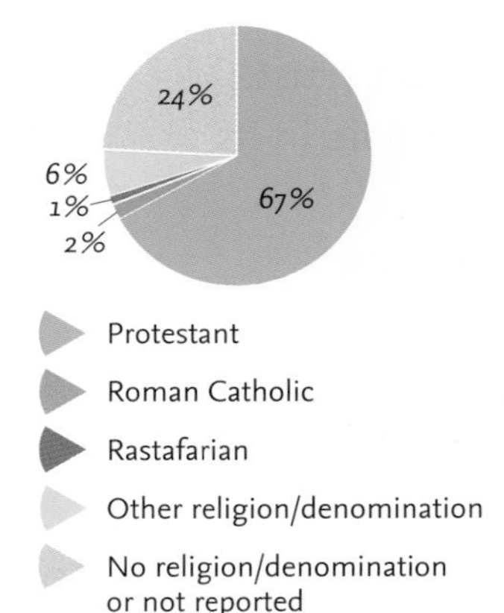

Ethnic origin and religion, 2011, Jamaica.

Skills development/enhancement

A skill is an area of expertise or ability to carry out activities or job functions involving ideas, things and/or people.

Skills development is where a country, economy or firm provides education and training for its workers so they can improve their existing skills and develop new ones. We also talk about skills enhancement, which is the improvement of existing skills.

- **Unskilled** workers are people who want work, but they do not have any special skills. Their job options are limited to work such as cleaning or labourer jobs.
- Semi-skilled workers have some training in using tools or machinery. For example, a labourer who has learned to drive a tractor is a semi-skilled worker.
- A **skilled** worker has some training in a particular field and can work independently.
- Highly skilled workers have very specialised skills and knowledge, and can also usually supervise others.

If the people in a country are constantly developing their skills, the human resources of the country get stronger and more able to provide goods and services for its population.

Creativity

Creativity is a person's capacity to use their imagination to come up with original or new ideas and solutions. We often associate creativity with artistic work such as drawing, painting, music or dance. However, people may be creative in the ways they solve problems, from real-life problems to maths and science.

Exercise

1. What are the factors that influence human resources?
2. Explain each, using your own words.
3. For each of the following jobs, say whether it is unskilled, semi-skilled, skilled or highly skilled. Give reasons for your answers.

   a) doctor
   b) secretary
   c) pilot
   d) farm labourer
   e) machinist
   f) painter

Research

Choose one of the factors from these pages and research a product, or industry, in Jamaica and find out how that factor influences the development of human resources in that product/industry.

Activity

Create a mind map showing the factors that influence the development of a country's human resources. Add to the mind map using the information on these pages.

Key vocabulary

composition
creativity
gender
quality
quantity
skilled
unskilled

Human resources and economic development

We are learning to:

- assess the importance of human resources to a country's economic development.

Human resources and economic development

Economic development is the activity of improving a country's **standard of living** by creating jobs, supporting **innovation** and new ideas, creating **wealth** or making improvements to people's **quality of life**.

Car assembly plants help to provide economic employment and economic development to the country.

When a country has a high standard of education and training, with investment in human resources, there are many benefits to the economy. Skilled, educated people can offer:

- a variety of skills, which in turn offer a range of goods and services
- creative innovations
- expertise that can lead to better planning and use of resources
- new manufacturing and agricultural practices, which can provide for the country's needs more efficiently
- an increase in the wealth generated for the country
- improved creativity allowing people to solve problems facing the country
- increased levels of **production** so that more goods and services become available
- improved standard of living
- more jobs and opportunities
- drops in poverty and crime levels.

Exercise

1. In your own words, explain how economic development depends on human resources.
2. Research the types of economic development that you can find in Jamaica.
3. Outline five benefits to a country's economy that skilled people can offer.

Activity

Write two paragraphs of approximately 250 words on what skilled and educated people can give to a country's economy.

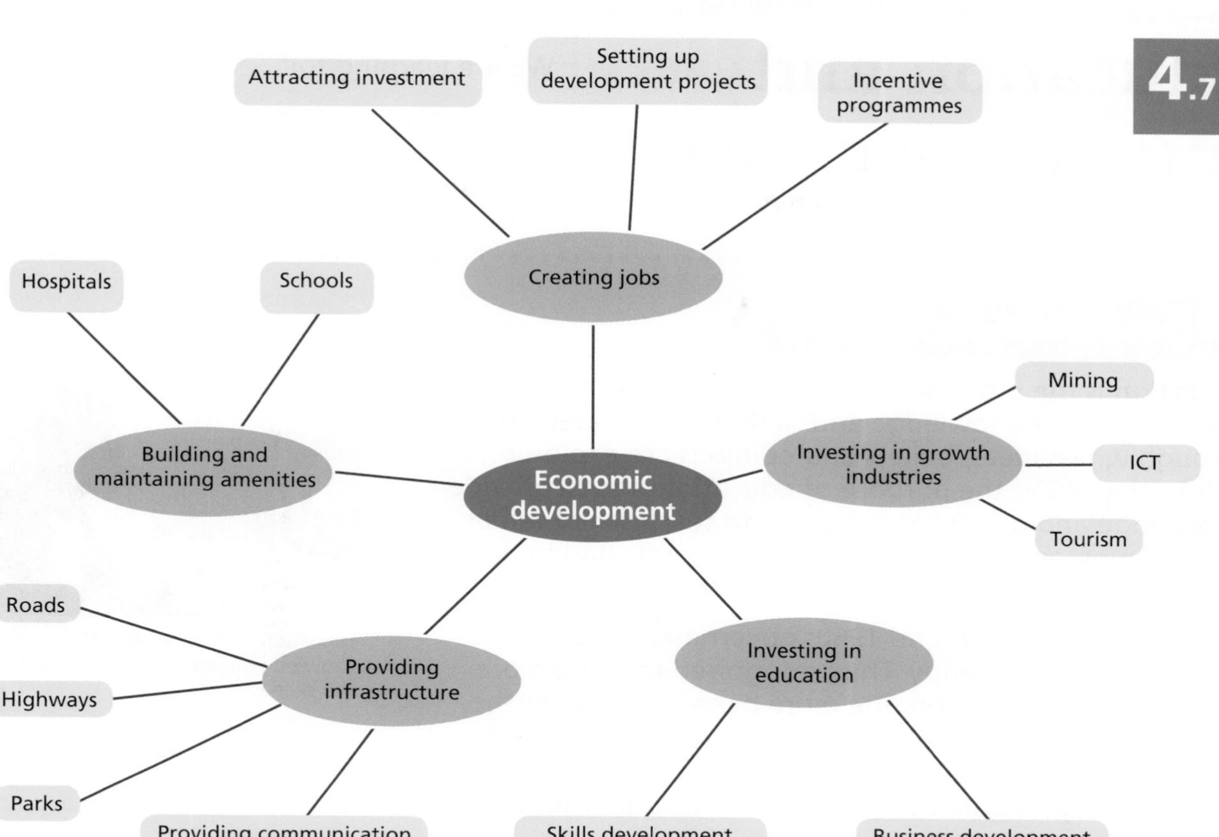

Activities that form part of economic development in Jamaica.

Exercise

4 Look at the mind map on this page. For each of the following aspects of economic development, list at least five skilled jobs it involves:

   a) building a hospital
   b) establishing a school
   c) providing communication infrastructure.

5 How do you think each of the following could help economic development?

   a) The government offers a free computer training course for 500 school-leavers.
   b) A business offers internships to 20 students.
   c) A bank offers training bursaries for students studying economics and finance, on condition that the students work at the bank for at least one year after qualifying.

Key vocabulary

economic development
innovation
production
quality of life
standard of living
wealth

Education and human resources

We are learning to:

- define and use correctly the term education
- examine the importance of education in developing our human resources.

Education and the labour force

Education is the process through which the teaching and development of knowledge and skills are facilitated, and through which ideas, beliefs and opinions are explored. Before the 1950s, the purpose of education was to provide knowledge and understanding, and to teach social values and customs, as well as religion. Governments had budgets for education, but it was seen as a burden on the state.

However, in the 1950s and 1960s governments began to see education differently. They recognised that the more educated the population, the more beneficial it is for the economy (as well as for themselves). Education became part of economic development. For Jamaica, this was an important change. Today, education is seen as an investment to:

- improve skills in the labour force
- produce knowledge and expertise to create new products
- create new markets and opportunities
- pass on cultural values and traditions
- transform the political landscape.

In the past, Jamaica's workforce had a shortage of highly skilled workers. This slowed down economic development. Companies who needed more highly skilled workers had to employ people from other countries. In the budget for 2019/20, the Ministry of Education, Youth and Information received the second largest amount with $109.4 billion. Some of this money goes towards school feeding programmes, free transport for students, book rental programmes and scholarships, as well as towards building schools and training centres, and training teachers.

Education is the teaching of knowledge, ideas, opinions, beliefs and skills.

Discussion

In groups, define the term education and discuss the importance of education in developing our human resources. Brainstorm your ideas and write them up in a large mind map.

Exercise

1. How has the view of education changed since the 1950s?
2. Define the term 'education'.
3. Give three reasons why education is seen as an important investment in Jamaica.

Activity

Take the ideas from your discussion. Use them to create a poem, song or poster showing how education benefits the nation.

Training

The term **human resource development** (HRD) is used when we talk about **employees** developing their personal and professional skills, knowledge and abilities. It focuses on developing the best labour force possible, so that the company and its employees can achieve their work goals and deliver excellent service to customers or clients.

Training can start earlier. Once a student has graduated from secondary school, they can do further training in institutions such as:

- colleges and technical colleges
- universities
- online colleges or training websites.

People who go on to do further training after school may have a wider choice of careers open to them. They can also earn more money.

Once a person is employed, it is still important that they continue to develop their skills and abilities. Some companies and **employers** may offer:

- **on-the-job training** – training whilst working, to help develop skills within a job
- **mentorship** (or coaching) – another more experienced employee gives advice and support to someone less experienced
- **succession training** – where the employee's skills and abilities are developed to prepare them for promotion
- **tuition assistance** – an employee can go on additional training courses to help build up their knowledge and skills.

After secondary school, students can do further training in online colleges or training websites.

Did you know...?

The Human Employment and Resource Training Trust/National Service Training Agency Trust (HEART/NSTA) is known to most Jamaicans as 'HEART'. It is the leading human development agency in Jamaica.

Exercise

4 Why do you think people choose to spend the time and money on further study? Give at least two reasons.

5 Why would employers choose to offer training to their employees?

6 Write a sentence about the role of education in HRD for:

a) companies

b) employees

c) the country.

(Hint: What does education do for the human resources in each of these categories?)

Key vocabulary

education

employee

employer

human resource development

mentorship

on-the-job training

succession training

tuition assistance

Our physical resources

We are learning to:

- define and use correctly the terms physical environment, physical resources and natural resources
- describe the physical resources found in Jamaica and the Caribbean
- explain how our natural resources are used.

Our physical environment and resources

Resources are things that humans use to meet their needs. For example, in early times we used clay to make pots and bowls and then iron to make tools and weapons. Today we use many different resources for many different needs.

Our resources come from our **physical environment**. This is the part of the environment made up of physical factors we can see and use, such as water, soil and mountains. **Natural resources** are things that occur naturally, including:

- air, water and soil
- biological resources such as plants and animals
- raw minerals
- space and land
- wind, geothermal, tidal and solar energy.

Most natural resources are physical resources. **Physical resources** are things we can physically see and touch. In the Caribbean, our main physical resources are oil (petroleum), natural gas, asphalt, bauxite, rivers and forests (for timber).

We can classify resources into two types:

- renewable resources that we can replace or grow back, such as rivers and forests
- non-renewable resources that are difficult or impossible to grow back or replace, such as petroleum and natural gas.

Exercise

1. Define the following terms:
   a) physical environment **b)** physical resources
   c) natural resources.
2. List six physical resources found in the Caribbean.

Did you know...?

Some of the physical resources of the other Caribbean countries include:

- **Anguilla** salt, fish
- **Antigua and Barbuda** the islands' location, pleasant climate
- **Barbados** petroleum, fish
- **Dominica** timber, hydropower
- **Grand Cayman** fish, climate
- **Grenada** timber, tropical fruit
- **Guyana** bauxite, gold, diamonds
- **Montserrat** the island's location
- **Saint Kitts and Nevis** arable land
- **Saint Lucia** forests, sandy beaches, minerals (pumice)
- **Saint Vincent and the Grenadines** hydropower, arable land
- **Trinidad and Tobago** petroleum, natural gas

How we use petroleum

Petroleum is a fossil fuel mined from deep under the Earth's surface. We rely on petroleum for many uses, including:

- fuel for cars and for large transport, including bunker fuel (for ships), jet fuel and diesel fuel
- synthetic materials such as synthetic rubber (used for car tyres and shoe soles) and synthetic fibres (polyester, nylon and acrylic)
- plastics made from chemicals found in petroleum
- products made from petrochemicals such as paints, make-up, photographic film and some medicines
- pesticides and **fertilisers** used in agriculture.

How we use other natural resources

- Natural gas is also a fossil fuel. It is found in the Earth's crust, usually under the sea. It has many uses including heating, cooling and cooking.
- Asphalt is a type of black, sticky pitch. It is used in the construction of roads.
- Bauxite is a mineral and is principally used to make aluminium, which is used to make cans, cooking utensils, and window and door frames.
- Limestone is an important component of construction materials, including quicklime, slaked lime, cement and limestone slabs. It is also crushed and used to make roads.
- Sand and gravel are used to mix concrete, cement and other building materials.
- Rivers are an important source of fresh water and provide homes for aquatic life, as well as plants and animals that live on river banks.
- Forests are important living **ecosystems**. Trees help to **filter** the air in the atmosphere and provide homes for animals and plants. Mangrove forests help to protect the shoreline from damage during floods and storms and are important breeding areas for many types of fish and sea organisms.

Even though petroleum does not occur naturally in Jamaica, it is an important resource for us because of its many uses.

Research

In groups, choose one of the following resources to research: petroleum, bauxite, asphalt, gypsum, gravel.

Find out where it is found in the Caribbean, how it is collected and what it is used for.

Trinidad and Tobago has the world's largest deposits of asphalt at the La Brea Pitch lake, near San Fernando, Trinidad.

Key vocabulary

ecosystem

filter

physical environment

physical/natural resources

Exercise

3. Name two fossil fuels found in the Caribbean.
4. Describe one use for each of the following resources:

   a) bauxite **b)** asphalt **c)** natural gas.
5. Create a documentary or PowerPoint presentation on the main natural resources found in the Caribbean, and some of the important uses of these resources.

Locating our natural resources

We are learning to:

- assess the ways in which Jamaica develops its natural and human resources.

The natural resources in Jamaica

Geography and climate influence where we find natural resources. Jamaica is well known for its bauxite deposits.

Did you know...?

Jamaica's mineral resources include metallic ores such as bauxite and industrial minerals such as limestone, gypsum, silica sand, marble, sand and gravel.

Location of mineral resources

Minerals are substances found in the Earth's crust. Usually they occur in very small amounts. However, in some places minerals are **concentrated** enough to make it worthwhile to extract them. Minerals such as limestone, gypsum and gravel are obtained by **quarrying** – a way of cutting into rock or ground to obtain stone and other materials. We obtain fossil fuels such as petroleum and natural gas by drilling.

Mineral resources and mining in Jamaica

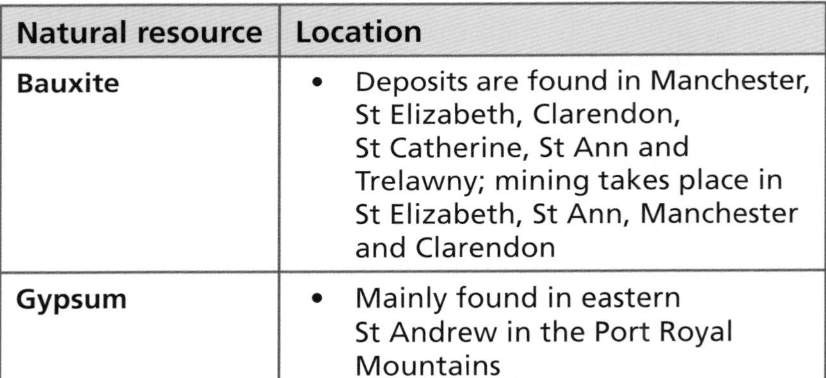

Natural resource	Location
Bauxite	• Deposits are found in Manchester, St Elizabeth, Clarendon, St Catherine, St Ann and Trelawny; mining takes place in St Elizabeth, St Ann, Manchester and Clarendon
Gypsum	• Mainly found in eastern St Andrew in the Port Royal Mountains

Bauxite mine in Saint Ann.

Jamaica has many natural resources spread all around the country. Many of the minerals are mined and the raw materials exported. The stone quarries produce aggregates for the local construction market including building sea defences. The map on the opposite page shows the location of areas where mining is done.

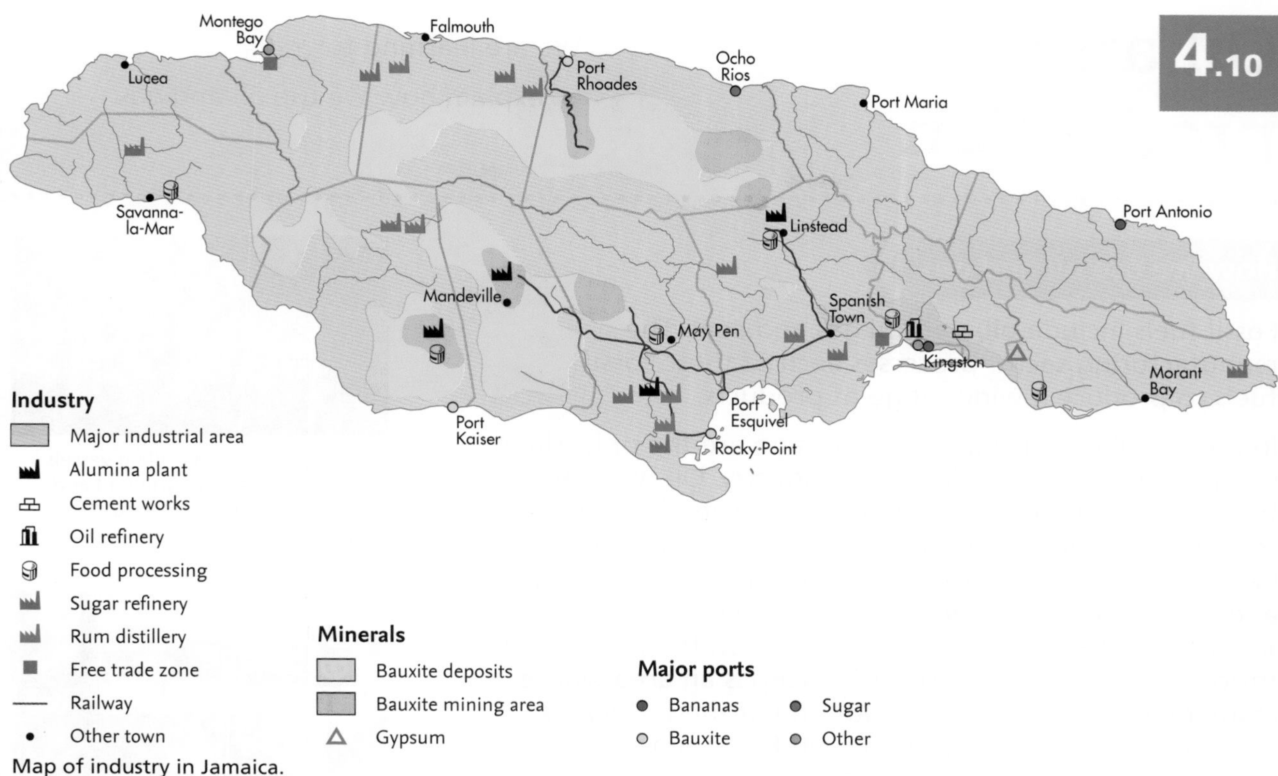

Map of industry in Jamaica.

Exercise

1. Trace a blank map of Jamaica. Draw the symbols to represent where the following resources are found:

   a) bauxite **b)** gypsum.

2. Using the map above, make a table showing the minerals found in Jamaica and their locations.

3. **a)** Which mineral is mostly mined in Jamaica?

   b) Which mineral is found mainly in the centre of Jamaica?

   c) Write a paragraph discussing the uses of Bauxite.

Key vocabulary

concentrated

quarrying

Oil and gas production

We are learning to:

- explain how we use oil and gas.

How we use oil and gas

Fossil fuels include **oil**, natural gas and **coal**. The manufacturing sector processes each of these fossil fuels to produce a wide range of products.

In the Caribbean, Trinidad and Tobago are the only islands where there is an established oil industry. Oil was discovered there in the 20th century and oil production is now one of the country's most important industries. Most of the other Caribbean countries, including Jamaica import oil, fuels and petroleum. Recently, the Petroleum Corporation of Jamaica (PCJ) discovered a live oil seep on the island — the third one to be discovered. An oil seep is an area where crude oil naturally seeps through the ground. However, what has been found is not enough for commercial production.

Offshore oil rig and drilling vessels in Chaguaramas Bay, Trinidad and Tobago working on oil industry project at sea.

The Petrojam plant in Kingston processes Jamaica's petroleum.

Energy and Minerals

Oilfield · Gasfield · Oil pipeline · Gas pipeline · Oil refinery · Transshipment terminal · Major container port · Bauxite · Gold/silver · Nickel

Oil production

Thousand barrels per day

Trinidad & Tobago · Cuba · Suriname · Belize · Barbados

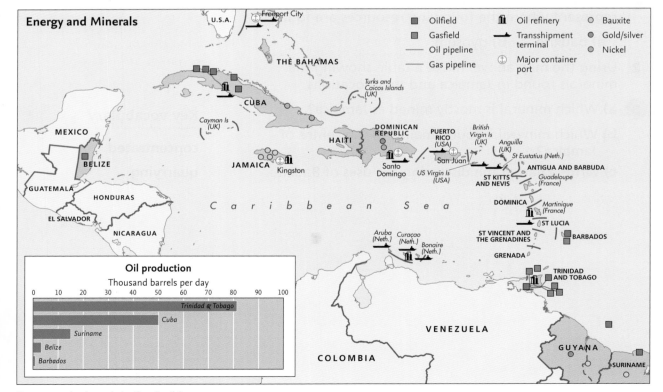

Energy and minerals in the Caribbean.

Oil companies drill deep into the Earth's crust to obtain the oil, which they suck up into **pipelines**. Large **tanker ships** carry the oil to **refineries**.

The **refining process** separates oil into different chemicals. Most of the oil is refined into fuel, but the refining process also leaves many residual **petrochemicals**, which are used to produce a huge range of products. Products of the refining process include:

- fuel and diesel oils for cars, buses and trucks, and fuels for ships and aeroplanes
- **gas** used as a fuel for heating and cooking
- **kerosene** used for lighting and heating
- chemical products, such as pesticides and fertilisers
- plastics used for toys and other products, synthetic rubber
- lubricating oils and greases used for transport and industrial uses
- bitumen used for road surfacing
- synthetic fibres, such as nylon, acrylic and polyester, used for clothing and other materials
- paints, detergents and cosmetics.

Coal is a type of soft carbon rock that burns easily. Miners dig for coal at coal mines. Most coal is burned at power plants to generate electricity.

Natural gas is used for heating and cooking, generating electricity and as a fuel for vehicles such as cars. It is also used to produce plastics and organic chemicals, including **fertilisers**.

Exercise

1. What is a fossil fuel?
2. What is meant by the refining process?
3. Write a paragraph explaining how oil is used in daily life.

Activity

You know that cars, planes and trains all use fossil fuels, and that their by-products are used in the production of plastics and fertilisers. Make a collage entitled 'Everyday products that involve the use of fossil fuels'.

Did you know...?

Many experts believe Jamaica has the potential to produce oil commercially based on deposits offshore. New estimates indicate there are some 229 million barrels of recoverable oil and gas offshore Jamaica.

Key vocabulary

coal
fertiliser
gas
kerosene
oil
petrochemicals
pipeline
refinery
refining process
tanker ship

Agriculture

We are learning to:

- evaluate the importance of the development of a country's human and natural resources.

Agriculture is another word for farming. Farming uses our natural resources to produce food for people to eat. The main resource it uses is land.

Farming makes changes to the environment

Land is a renewable resource. However, agriculture involves many processes that change the natural environment through:

- land clearing
- tilling the soil (turning over the soil to break it up and make it fine enough to grow new seedlings)
- irrigation.

Farmers do many things to **maximise** the yield of their crops. **Yield** is the amount of fruits or vegetables that the farmer harvests per square unit of area. Maximising yield means getting the highest amount of crops possible from the area of land available. In order to increase yield, farmers may:

- use **insecticides** and **pesticides**
- apply chemical fertilisers – these add nutrients to the soil, helping plants to grow faster and produce more fruits or vegetables
- plant a single crop over a large area of land – this is known as **monocropping**.

These techniques all form part of **conventional agriculture** – the type of agriculture used on large farms. However, each of these techniques introduces problems for the natural resources that the farmer uses.

A farmer watering his crop.

Research

Research one of the following problems caused by conventional farming:

- soil erosion
- agricultural run-off
- **deforestation**.

Draw a labelled picture to show how the problem is caused.

Exercise

1. What do you understand by 'monocropping'?
2. In your own words, explain how a farmer can increase the yield of his crops.
3. Carry out research into the problems of monocropping.

Project

Research the crops that are grown in your country. Find a photo of each crop, and add these to your portfolio.

Conventional agriculture – positives and negatives

4.12

Conventional agriculture has several benefits for the farmer.

- Large-scale farming is less work for the farmer; for example, driving a tractor is less work than using a hand plough, and a farmer can irrigate a much larger area with a sprinkler system than with a hand-watering system.
- Cheaper than labour – using technology and chemicals reduces the number of workers the farmer employs.
- Very high yields – chemical fertilisers, insecticides and pesticides allow the farmer to get more crops out of each square unit of land.

Conventional agriculture can also damage the main resource it relies on – the land.

- Clearing land for farming destroys habitats for many animals and plants.
- Monocropping destroys biodiversity and can wipe out many local crop varieties.
- Once crops are harvested, the land is bare. Bare soil easily becomes eroded by wind and rain.
- Insecticides and pesticides pollute the environment.
- Fertilisers run off into the water cycle and can cause unnatural amounts of algae to grow in seas and rivers. This uses up oxygen in the water, causing the death of many aquatic plants and animals.

Solutions – sustainable agriculture practices

There are many ways that farmers around the world are working towards making agriculture more **sustainable**.

- Crop rotation – planting different crops each season helps to **replenish** some of the nutrients in the soil.
- Natural forms of fertiliser instead of chemical fertilisers.
- Using local **varieties** of crops with greater resistance to local pests and diseases than imported varieties.
- Planting different varieties of the same species instead of monocropping, such as several varieties of rice in one paddy, make it more likely they will not be destroyed by a single pest attack.
- **Mulching** prevents water from evaporating so it reduces the need for irrigation.

Discussion

For each of the following resources, discuss why it is important for farming, and how it may be damaged by farming: soil, water, plants.

A farmer using a tractor to plough the field in St Elizabeth parish.

Activity

Visit a nearby farm or invite a farmer to speak to your class. Find out:

Which crops are farmed there? Does the farmer use any sustainable methods?

Complete a report in response to these questions (of about 250 words).

Key vocabulary

agriculture
conventional agriculture
deforestation
insecticide
maximise
monocropping
mulching
pesticide
replenish
sustainable
variety
yield

Using our natural resources

We are learning to:

- evaluate the positive and negative effects of using our resources
- explain the causes of global warming and climate change.

Positive effects of using physical resources

The two most important effects of using our natural resources are improvements in people's daily lives and job creation.

Fossil fuels provide electricity to light and heat our homes, fuel to power factories, cars, planes and trains, materials for many different products (e.g. plastic, nylon, acrylic and other synthetic materials), fertilisers and chemicals that help our crops, and jobs associated with the mining, refining, transport, manufacturing and processing industries.

A cruise-liner moored in Ochos Rios port town. The cruise-line industry is important in the Caribbean.

Materials such as asphalt, gypsum, limestone, gravel, sand and other materials allow us to construct roads and buildings. Handling these materials creates jobs in the construction and manufacturing industries.

We use land to grow crops for food, and to provide space for housing and other buildings. Land is an important resource to create jobs in the construction and agricultural industries.

Water

- All living things rely on water to live.
- Water is an important solvent. It is used for washing and cleaning, and as a base for many medicines.
- Water is a cooling agent. In industry, water is used to cool down machinery. We also freeze water in order to preserve food.
- Many boats, ships and other vessels travel by sea and by river. In the Caribbean, the cruise-liner industry is an important part of the tourist industry.
- Water provides food – many types of food come from the sea or from rivers. Examples include fish and shellfish. Seaweed is an important source of food as well as medicines.
- Water can also provide power through hydroelectric plants, which generate electric power.

Research

Brainstorm all the ways you use physical resources in one day in your life, from the moment you wake up to the moment you go to bed. Think of all the things you use that are made of or rely on physical resources. Draw a big mind map of all your ideas.

Negative effects of using physical resources

Using physical resources has negative effects too. The main negative effect is damage to the environment.

- Pollution is the introduction of impurities that can damage the land, air or water. At Riverton City Dump in Kingston, where land is used to dispose of waste materials, there are high levels of toxic chemicals in the soil and in the air.
- **Exploitation** means using too much of something and making the resource unavailable for future generations.
- Destruction of habitats – mining, quarrying, clearing land and farming all destroy the environment. This damages habitats for other species as well as humans.
- Damage to sustainable resources – industries such as agriculture involve processes that cause damage to the land so that it cannot grow crops in future.

Jamaica suffered its first major oil spill in 1981 when the tanker ERODONA spilled 600 tonnes of fuel oil after grounding at Port Kaiser.

Global warming and climate change

Burning fossil fuels increases the carbon levels in the atmosphere, which is gradually causing the atmosphere to retain more heat. This causes average temperatures to rise, a process known as **global warming**, which could cause disasters for life on Earth.

- The ice caps at the north and south poles are melting at a fast rate, causing a rise in sea levels.
- Higher sea levels could cause the flooding or disappearance of coastal cities and low-lying islands.
- Changing sea levels cause increases in storms, flooding and tidal waves.
- Increased drought and desertification occur in dry areas.

Discussion

Of all the physical resources you have looked at, which one offers the most positive effects for human life? Which one offers the most negative effects? Discuss your opinions.

Exercise

1. Name two important effects of how we use our physical resources, and give two examples of each.
2. Draw up a table listing two positive and two negative consequences of using our natural resources.
3. Give three reasons why global warming could be disastrous for life on Earth.
4. Why is water so important to us? Give three reasons.

Key vocabulary

exploitation

global warming

Which factors hinder economic growth and development?

We are learning to:

- outline the factors that prevent economic growth and development.

The economic growth of a country may be hindered due to a number of factors, such as limited production of manufactured goods and limited external trade, also large debts and changes in government spending. Generally, the economic growth of a country is negatively affected when there is a sudden rise in the prices of goods and services, or when there is recession in the global market. Along with economic and political factors, environmental factors can also hinder development, especially in cases where countries may have experienced a major natural disaster.

Economic recession

Recessions can be defined as a period of temporary economic decline during which trade and industrial activity are reduced, generally identified by a fall in GDP in two successive quarters. These result in higher unemployment, lower wages and incomes, and lost opportunities more generally. Education, private capital investments, and economic opportunity are all likely to suffer in the current downturn, and the effects will be long-lived. For example, The Statistical Institute of Jamaica, STATIN, recently released **data** showing the economy contracted or shrank by 18% for the second quarter of 2020, between April and June. This means Jamaica is officially in a recession. The decline was caused primarily by the continued spread of Covid-19 and the measures which were put in place to try to reduce it, such as lockdown, where many businesses were temporarily shut down. With hotels and tourism temporarily suspended, economic development are likely to be hit hard, and rates of poverty are likely to increase as a result.

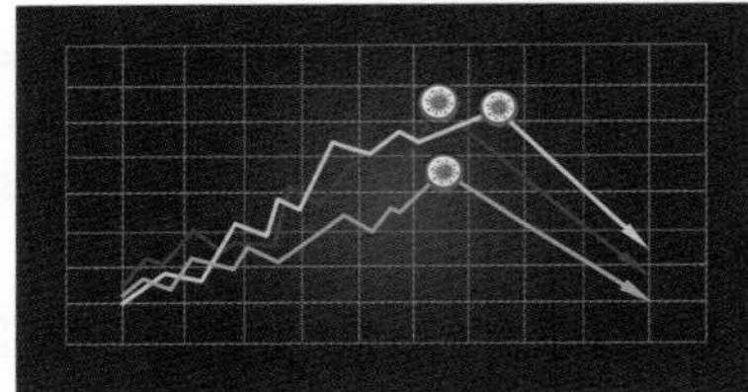

Recessions can be defined as a period of temporary economic decline.

Natural disasters

Major natural disasters have severe negative short and long-term effects on economic development. Natural Disasters tend also to have long-term consequences for development and poverty reduction. Natural disasters cause significant financial pressures on budgets, with short-term impacts and wider long-term development implications. Natural disasters generally mean that government spending

Clarence Bryan and Mazlyn Richard's home was destroyed by Hurricane Gilbert. They lived at Top Hill in the parish of St Thomas – the first place the storm hit.

has to prioritise the damage caused by the event, as well as ensuring basic needs are met by those who lose their homes. For example, the former Prime Minister Edward Seaga said that Hurricane Gilbert in 1988 caused $8 billion damage in Jamaica, with half of the nation's homes badly damaged and one out of every five dwellings destroyed, leaving over 500 000 people homeless. Natural disasters require significant rebuilding of infrastructure such as roads and energy supplies, as well as other costs.

Climate change

Climate change, is a long-term shift in global or regional **climate** patterns. Oftentimes climate change refers specifically to the rise in global temperatures from the mid-20th century to present, a phenomenon known as global warming.

Climate change and development are closely linked. Poor people will feel the impacts first and worst (and already are) because of living in places that are more likely to experience the effects of climate change and lesser ability to cope with damage from severe weather and rising sea levels.

Climate changes have meant that Jamaica is at increased risk of multiple natural hazards (hurricanes, floods, droughts) and human-induced hazards (bush fires). This has been a major challenge to sustainable development. Social issues such as poverty, people building settlements in high-risk areas, environmental degradation, and poorly constructed roads and housing have added to this vulnerability.

Discussion

Which factors do you think are most important in affecting economic growth? Place them in order of importance and be ready to explain why.

Exercise

1. Explain what is meant by an economic recession.
2. Explain how natural disasters affect economic growth.
3. Write a paragraph explaining the effects of the Covid-19 pandemic on economic growth in Jamaica.

Effect of hurricanes can be devastating.

Activity

See if you can remember the difference between human and natural disasters from Grade 8. Make a list of examples.

Discussion

As a class, discuss the main effects of climate change on Jamaica. Discuss why this is most likely to affect the poor and vulnerable, giving examples.

Key vocabulary

climate change
climate
data

Jamaica's National Development Plan (Vision 2030)

We are learning to:

- explain Jamaica's National Development Plan (Vision 2030)
- recite Jamaica's National Vision Statement
- analyse Jamaica's National Goals (Vision 2030)
- evaluate the proposed performance indicators and targets which are used to measure progress (Vision 2030).

What is Vision 2030?

As we saw in Grade 8, Vision 2030 Jamaica, launched in 2007, is Jamaica's first long-term National Development Plan which aims to put Jamaica in a position to achieve developed country status by 2030. It is based on a comprehensive vision:

"Jamaica, the place of choice to live, work, raise families, and do business."

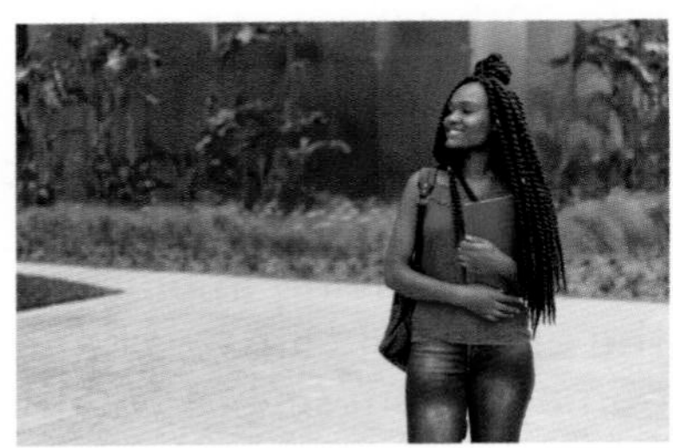

"Jamaica, the place of choice to live, work, raise families, and do business."

This vision means a major transformation from a middle income developing country to one which provides its citizens a high quality of life and world-class standards in areas including education, health care, nutrition, basic amenities, access to environmental goods and services, civility and social order.

These different areas are essential to ensure the country makes progress towards a more sustainable society which integrates and balances the economic, social, environmental, and governance areas of national development.

Source: Visit the United Nations website and search for 'Sustainable Development'.

What are the national issues that Vision 2030 seeks to improve?

According to the National Plan, Vision 2030 was developed in the midst of a global financial and economic crisis which at the time, was considered the most serious since the Great Depression of 1929. It is an attempt to try to resolve short and long term problems facing the country and to encourage growth and development.

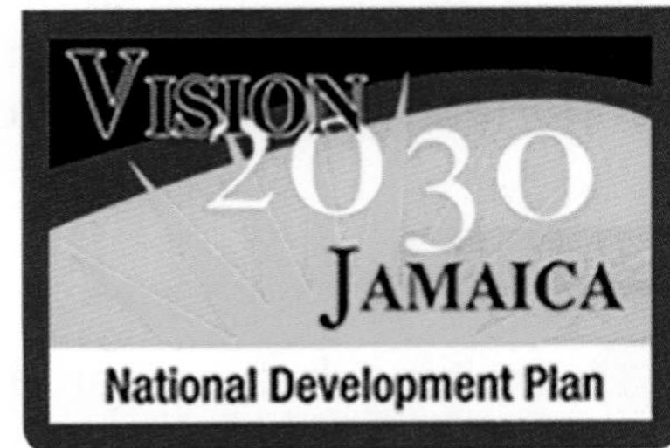

Vision 2030 comes with a National Development Plan.

Along with the financial problems affecting Jamaica at the time, other issues included:

- poor economic growth
- high levels of national debt
- unacceptable levels of unemployment and poverty

- high levels of crime and violence
- low levels of skills, weak business and industry
- very rapid urbanisation, migration and globalisation which have had a negative impact on the structure and stability of the Jamaican family.

Where other plans failed to be effective before Vision 2030, this plan involves both the public and the private sector as well as charities and other organisations, to make sure that the vision is shared.

Source: Visit the United Nations website and search for 'Sustainable Development'.

What are the four goals of Vision 2030?

Vision 2030 Jamaica is built on four goals for our country's development. These goals overlap and need to be pursued together in order to achieve the vision. They give greater detail on the vision statement. These goals are presented below.

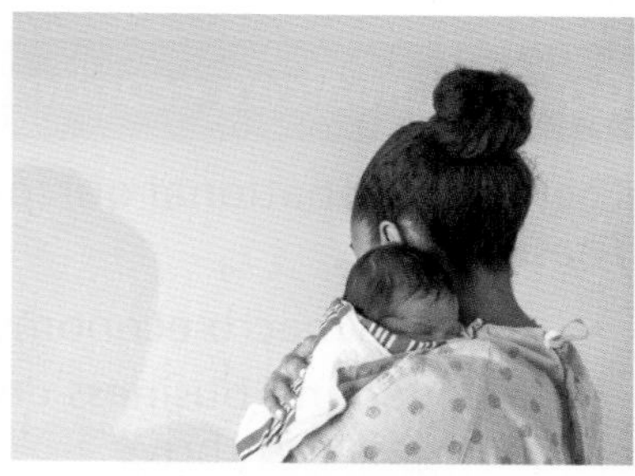

Child mortality rate is falling...

Goal 1: Jamaicans are empowered to achieve their fullest potential

- A healthy and stable population – making sure that everyone in society is in the best health and has free healthcare when they need it.
- World-class education and training – making sure that education is high quality and checked regularly.
- Effective social protection – making sure those who are vulnerable, or who have disabilities are protected and cared for.
- Authentic and transformational culture – making sure that important heritage sites are protected and valued.

Progress:

- ✓ Most progress has been made with Goal 1
- ✓ Improved life expectancy, child mortality rate, grade 4 literacy rates, grade 4 numeracy rates, a higher percentage of people in work, higher secondary level enrolment rates among others
- ✗ However, increasing levels of poverty, including rural poverty, as well as the effects of non-communicable diseases (e.g. diseases of the circulatory system, cancer, respiratory among others)
- ✗ In the area of education, attendance is falling.

... but education attendance is falling too.

Goal 2: The Jamaican society is secure, cohesive and just

- Security and safety – making sure that people feel safe and secure from crimes and bad behaviour.
- Effective governance – making sure that Jamaica is run properly and fairly by the government.

Progress:

- ✓ Some related indicators such as control of corruption, accountability, government effectiveness and some crimes are showing some movement towards the target
- ✓ In the area of governance, the majority of the indicators have shown improvements over the baseline year of 2007 and are moving toward target.
- ✗ Overall, however Goal 2 is making least progress, with no indicator meeting or exceeding the 2015 target.

Some indicators show that the corruption and some crimes are moving towards the Goal 2 target.

Goal 3: Jamaica's economy is prosperous

There are six national outcomes for this national goal. These are:

- a stable macro economy (large scale)
- an enabling business environment – a place where business can thrive
- strong economy – making sure that businesses are secure and not likely to fail
- energy security and efficiency – making sure that there is a good supply of gas and electricity at all times and that there is little waste
- a technology-enabled society – good access to the internet and forms of technology
- internationally competitive industry structures – making sure that businesses are able to compete with businesses in other countries.

Progress:

- ✓ Under Goal 3, 46% of the targets were either met for 2016/17 or moving towards meeting the target
- ✓ The greatest gains under Goal 3 were realised in terms of small-scale economic factors such as increased tourism and lower inflation rates

Large hotel complexes contribute to the economy.

✗ However, unemployment rate and labour market efficiency continue to be worse than the baseline year 2007.

Goal 4: Jamaica has a healthy natural environment

In a competitive global market, the natural environment plays an impactful role in the success of any country's economy.

The national outcomes for this goal are:

- sustainable management and use of environmental and natural resources – making sure that the natural resources of Jamaica are protected and conserved
- hazard risk reduction and adaptation to climate change – making sure that plans are in place to help protect people against things like natural disasters
- sustainable urban and rural development – making sure that building and planning is carefully planned and checked to ensure that the environment is also protected.

Hurricane preparedness comes under Goal 4.

Progress:

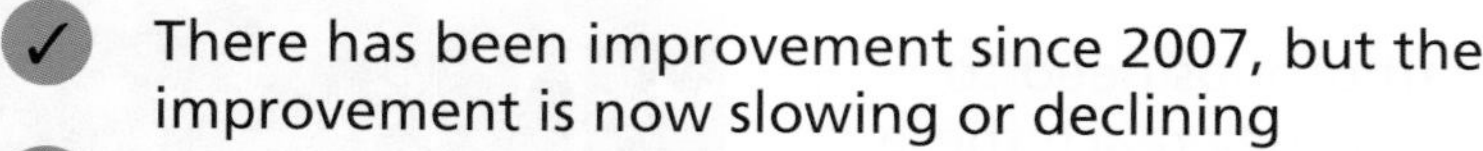

✓ There has been improvement since 2007, but the improvement is now slowing or declining

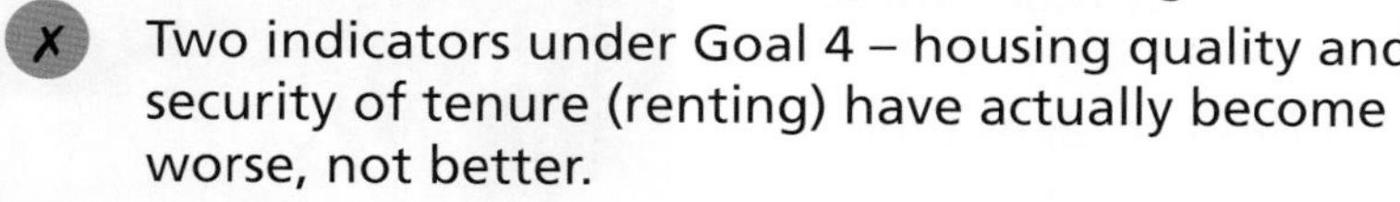

✗ Two indicators under Goal 4 – housing quality and security of tenure (renting) have actually become worse, not better.

Exercise

1. Place the goals in order of progress, explaining why you have put them in that order.
2. Why do you think it is challenging for all targets to be met?
3. Imagine you are writing a report for the Jamaican government recommending ways to improve progress. What would you recommend?

What is the overall progress of Vision 2030?

There are 12 working groups that meet regularly to monitor the progress being made in reaching the goals of Vision 2030. Progress in the achievement of the goals and outcomes of Vision 2030 Jamaica is measured through the use of what are called *national outcome indicators* aligned to the 4 goals and 15 national outcomes.

- 67.2% of these outcomes have shown improvement since the year 2007 based on results to 2016/17
- 31.3% showed no improvement or worsened since 2007.

What are the challenges of achieving the goals of Vision 2030?

The goals of Vision 2030 are ambitious and involve a lot of careful planning and hard work. There are several reasons why achieving the goals of Vision 2030 are difficult, or challenging:

- cost – the goals require a lot of investment from the government
- commitment – people from different groups need to be very dedicated to making sure that they reach these goals
- changing people's beliefs and attitudes – it takes time to encourage people to think differently and believe in the values of Vision 2030
- educational performance of boys – currently lower than girls, meaning they are less likely to make progress and meet their goals
- parenting skills – making sure that parents are raising their children with positive parenting and to believe in themselves
- positive values of honesty are not always present.

Discussion

Discuss areas of good progress. Why do you think it was possible to make progress in these areas? Why was it more challenging to make progress in other areas?

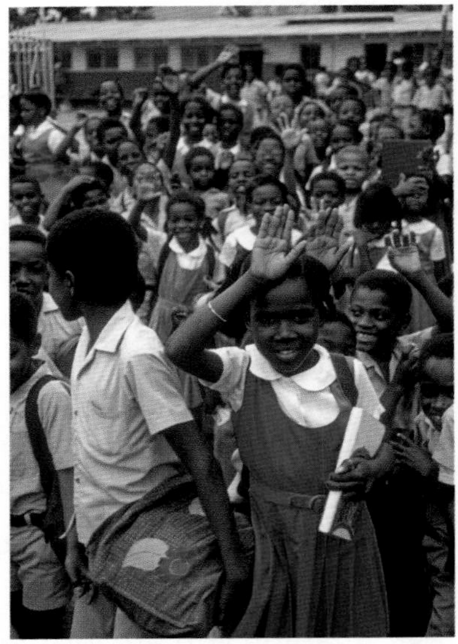

Teaching the younger generations about the 2030 values for Jamaica will be very important.

Dashboard of Performance 2009 – 2015/16		
Green	Yellow	Red
Life Expectancy at Birth	Human Development Index	Gross enrolment rate at tertiary level
Population Growth Rate	Percentage of labour force that is certified	Poverty headcount ratio
Grade 4 Literacy Rates (male, female)	Control of Corruption Index	Case Clearance Rate
Annual inflation rate	Fiscal balance as a percentage of GDP	Government Effectiveness Index
Debt to GDP ratio (fiscal year)	Nominal GDP per capita	Real GDP annual growth rate
Percentage change in foreign exchange earnings from tourism	Percentage of renewables in energy mix	Ease of Doing Business Ranking
Percentage of children in consumption quintile 1 receiving PATH benefits	Agriculture production index	Unemployment rate
Housing Quality Index	Category 1 Crime Rate	Proportion of households with access to secure tenure
Hazard damage as a percentage of GDP	Environmental Performance Index	Poverty in rural areas

Green – Met or exceeded target (2015).
Yellow – Improved over baseline but did not meet target (2015).
Red – Equal to or worse than baseline year of 2007.
Source: vision2030.gov.jm

Exercise

1 What is the largest percentage in terms of outcomes?

2 What percentage of outcomes worsened?

3 What does this pie chart suggest about the progress of Vision 2030 overall?

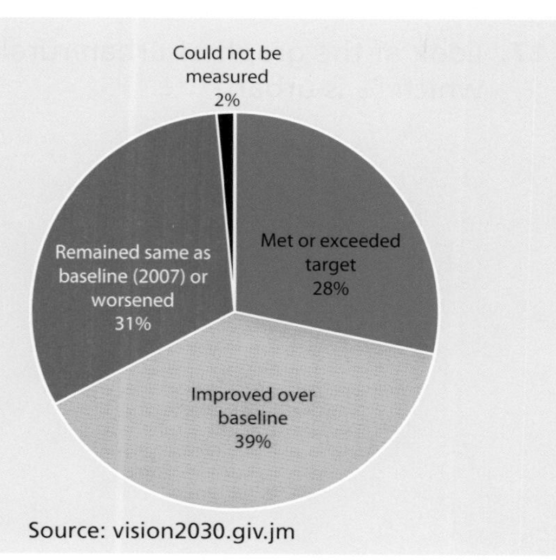

Source: vision2030.giv.jm

Questions

See how well you have understood the topics in this unit.

1. Explain what is meant by the following terms:
   a) urban
   b) rural
   c) climate change
   d) human resources.
2. True or false? HDI stands for Human Directory Index.
3. In your own words, explain what is meant by sustainable development.
4. What is the difference between human and natural resources?
5. Explain how economic development is measured.
6. Identify three natural resources of Jamaica.
7. What do population pyramids tell us?
8. How has the age distribution in Jamaica changed since the 1950s?
9. Identify three factors that shape human resources.
10. What is the difference between gross domestic product and gross national product.
11. Give some examples of sustainable development in Jamaica.
12. What is the vision statement for Vision 2030 in Jamaica?
13. Identify a goals in Vision 2030 that is already making good progress.
14. What is national development? Give some examples.
15. When was Vision 2030 launched in Jamaica?
16. Write a paragraph explaining why there is a lack of progress in meeting some of the goals in Vision 2030.
17. Look at the graph of urban/rural population in Jamaica. Which % is rural and which % is urban?

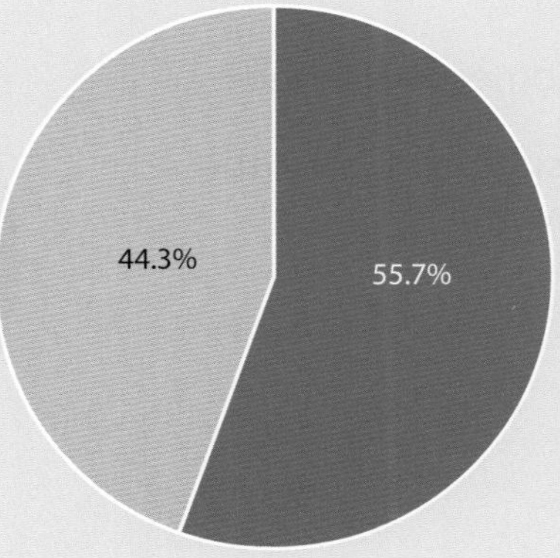

18. Look at the map and answer the questions.

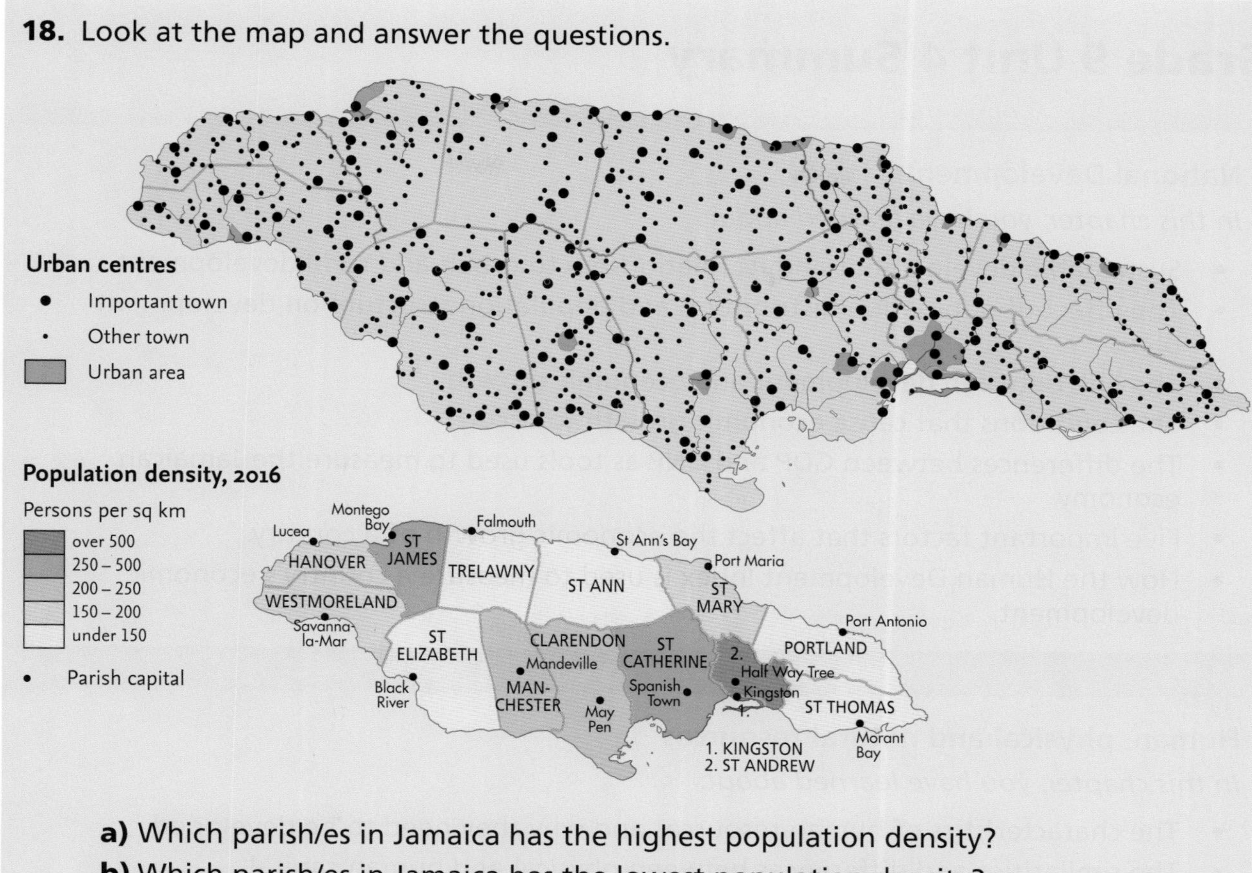

a) Which parish/es in Jamaica has the highest population density?
b) Which parish/es in Jamaica has the lowest population density?
c) Which parish has the largest urban centre?
d) What industry accounts for the high density of population in Clarendon parish?
e) Which parish has the fewest urban centres? Why do you think this is?
f) How do you account for the parish with the largest population density?

Grade 9 Unit 4 Summary

National Development

In this chapter, you have learned about:

- Sustainable development and its relationship to urban and rural development
- The effect of population distribution and population structure on development plans
- The link between development and economic growth
- The conditions that cause economic growth to occur
- The differences between GDP and GNP as tools used to measure the Jamaican economy
- Five important factors that affect the economic growth of a country.
- How the Human Development Index is used to measure a country's economic development.

Human, physical and natural resources

In this chapter, you have learned about:

- The characteristics of human resources and why they need to be developed
- The similarities and differences between physical and human capital
- The factors that influence the development of human resources
- How developed human resources benefit a country's economy
- The roles of education and training in human resource development
- The physical environment and resources that human resources use for economic development
- How oil and gas is used to manufacture products in the Caribbean
- The changes that farming makes to the environment and sustainable agriculture
- The positive and negative effects of using our physical resources
- The factors which limit economic growth and development.

Jamaica's National Development Plan (Vision 2030)

In this chapter, you have learned about:

- The national issues that Vision 2030 seeks to address
- The four goals of Vision 2030
- The progress made towards achieving the goals of Vision 2030, and the obstacles to achieving these goals.

Checking your progress

To make good progress in understanding development and the use of resources, check that you understand these ideas.

- [ ] Explain and use correctly the term *sustainable urban development.*
- [ ] Describe how development may be influenced by climate change.
- [ ] Explain how sustainable development is possible.

- [ ] Explain and use correctly the term *Human Development Index.*
- [ ] State the goals of Vision 2030.
- [ ] Explain the difference between natural and human resources.

- [ ] Explain and use correctly the term *economic growth.*
- [ ] Name ways in which economic growth are measured.
- [ ] Explain the difference between gross domestic product and gross national product.

- [ ] Explain and use correctly the term *population pyramid.*
- [ ] Describe the ways in which the progress of Vision 2030 is measured.
- [ ] Outline the progress made with achieving the goals of Vision 2030.

Unit 5: The Structure of the Jamaican Government

Objectives: You will be able to:

Functions of government

- define the relevant terms: government, constitution, democracy, referendum, secession and anarchy
- list the functions of a government.

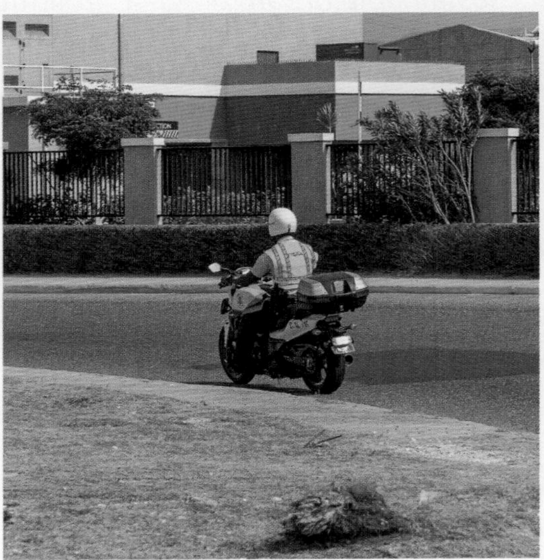

How democracies work

- outline the main characteristics of a democracy
- explain non-confrontational ways to bring changes in government.

The reasons for government

- examine the reasons for having a government
- examine the consequences for citizens and a country if there is no government.

Structure of central government

- explain the composition of each branch of government
- evaluate the role of each branch of government
- analyse the systems of checks and balances in the Jamaican government.

Structure of local government

- explain the composition of each branch of government
- evaluate the role of each branch of government.

Functions of central and local government

- evaluate the role of each branch of government
- describe the extent to which the Members of Parliament are carrying out their functions.

Functions of government

We are learning to:

- define the relevant terms: government, constitution, democracy, referendum, secession and anarchy
- list the functions of a government.

Government

A **government** is a group of people who manage the affairs or goals of a country, as well as regulating the activities of its society. In most countries today, governments are elected by the **citizens** of a country. The main functions of government include:

- making and enforcing laws to help maintain order
- providing economic policies that that will allow businesses to create jobs and provide services
- providing public services like education, health care, road building, and utilities such as electricity and water
- protecting its citizens with police and armed forces
- working with other countries to promote trade and international cooperation.

Democracies are countries in which all eligible citizens have an equal say or participation in the decisions that affect their lives.

Democracy

Democracy is a form of government in which all **eligible** citizens have an equal say or participation in the decisions that affect their lives. Most Caribbean countries are democracies.

- Democracy is based on the **principles** of fairness, justice, respect and honour.
- Everyone should be treated equally and fairly, and with respect.
- There should be respect for the law, for human rights and for civil liberties.
- There should be free and fair elections to choose people who will govern.
- The people who are elected to serve should do so with honour and be held accountable for what they do.

Research

Work in pairs and do some research on a recent referendum held in a different country. What question did the voters have to consider? What was the outcome of the referendum?

Exercise

1. Research and write your own definition of government and democracy. Add them to your portfolio.
2. What are the main functions of government? Think of an example from your country for each one.
3. Does Jamaica have the characteristics of a democracy?

Key vocabulary

anarchy
citizen
constitution
democracy
eligible
government
law and order
principle
secession

Constitution

The **constitution** is a written document that sets out the laws by which a country is governed. It outlines:

- how government is structured
- the powers of government
- the rights and responsibilities of its citizens
- how governments are chosen
- the role of the civil service.

Referendum

A referendum is an opportunity for eligible people to vote on a particular issue. Referendums play an important role in modern democracies, because they allow people to have a say in how they are ruled. A referendum on continued membership of the Federation of the West Indies was held in Jamaica on 19 September 1961. Voters were asked 'Should Jamaica remain in the Federation of the West Indies?' The result was 54.1% voting 'no', resulting in the country leaving the federation and its dissolution in 1962. Voter turnout was 61.5%

Secession and anarchy

When a country or group separates from a larger group to which it belongs, this is known as **secession**. An example includes the withdrawal of Southern states from the federal union in 1860/61 at the start of the American Civil War.

Anarchy is when **law and order** break down in a country and is often characterised by an absence of government, political disorder, and confusion and lawlessness.

Discussion

Discuss what you already know about the constitution of Jamaica and make notes on what it covers and how it has been updated.

Discussion

The countries of the Caribbean have formed many groups to promote regional integration. Discuss what advantages or disadvantages integration could have for the region. Is your country part of the OECS or CARICOM? Discuss whether you think your country should secede from these groups.

Exercise

4 On which principles is democracy based?

5 Research and write your own definitions of constitution, referendum, secession and anarchy. Add them to your portfolio.

6 Complete this quiz by matching each term to the statement that fits best.

i) government	**a)** the principles and laws by which a country is governed
ii) democracy	**b)** when a country or group separates from a larger group or country
iii) constitution	**c)** a system of government
iv) referendum	**d)** the power and authority to rule a country
v) secession	**e)** when law and order break down
vi) anarchy	**f)** when people vote on an issue

How democracies work

We are learning to:

- outline the main characteristics of a democracy
- explain non-confrontational ways to bring changes in government.

Characteristics of a democracy

The characteristics of a democracy include:

- that elections are fair and are open to all citizens of voting age
- the establishment of basic human rights and the protection of those human rights
- tolerance, cooperation and compromise; for example, citizens have the right to free speech and can form political parties unopposed
- the right to challenge a government's decisions.

Voters lining up in Jamaica to elect their government representatives.

An important characteristic of a democracy is **majority rule** and **minority right**. When decisions are made based on the majority of the population's wishes, this could easily lead to the oppression of those who did not agree or vote along with the majority. Minority rights keep this from happening by taking an individual's rights and needs into account along with the majority rule.

Direct and representative democracy

Democratic governments exist around the world and fall into the categories of **direct** and **representative democracies**.

- Direct democratic governments allow citizens of legal voting age to establish rules and laws, and permit citizens to directly participate in making public policy.
- Representative democracies use elected officials for rule-making, so it is more feasible for smaller communities.

Exercise

1. Explain in your own words the characteristics of a democracy.
2. Explain in your own words the two categories of democracy.

Discussion

In groups, use the internet to research either the conflicts in Syria or those in Venezuela. What type of democracy do they have in those countries? Why do you think it is the citizens who are suffering?

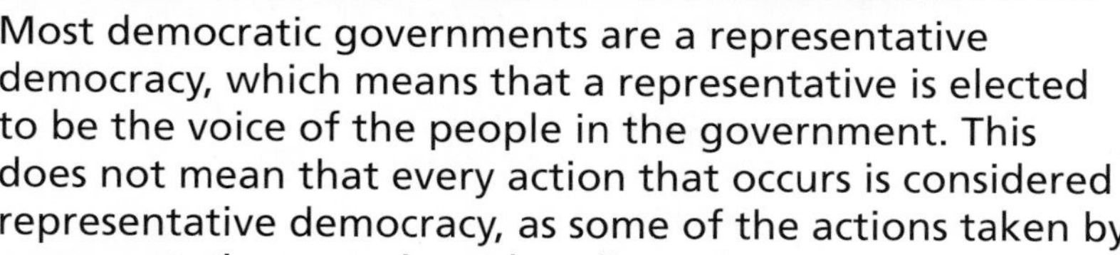

Characteristics of a representative democracy

Most democratic governments are a representative democracy, which means that a representative is elected to be the voice of the people in the government. This does not mean that every action that occurs is considered representative democracy, as some of the actions taken by representatives are viewed as direct democracy.

The representative or governing body may put forward a mandate or referendum on a law, which can stem from meetings held by representatives in the area they represent or groups from the area requesting the changes. This can also apply to a nominee calling for votes to be re-counted in an election. These are all direct actions that do not proceed to be voted on by the people, although they can be requests or suggestions from them.

A representative democracy allows freedom of speech, the press and religion, allows personal liberties, and is a peaceful, non-violent way of running the country.

Non-confrontational ways to bring changes in government

Non-confrontational means dealing with situations in a calm, **diplomatic** manner that is not aggressive or threatening. In a political sense, this means bringing about changes by peaceful means, through:

- peaceful protests, marches or strikes
- writing protest letters
- forming pressure groups against the government
- having free and fair elections
- non-violent civil rights movements.

Exercise

3. Does Jamaica have a direct or representative democracy?
4. In what ways can changes in government be made by using non-confrontational means?
5. Working in groups, brainstorm examples of the characteristics of a representative democracy in a Caribbean country of your choice.

Key vocabulary

diplomatic
direct democracy
majority rule
minority right
non-confrontational
representative democracy

The reasons for government

We are learning to:

- examine the reasons for having a government
- examine the consequences for citizens and a country if there is no government.

Why do we need a government?

All **modern states** have governments, although they are not always the same. The governments cost a lot of money to run, so we need to ask ourselves, why do we need a government?

We need a government for the following reasons:

- Convenience – humans are gregarious (social) beings. As such, it is more convenient and practical for a group of people to make rules and laws than for each member of the entire country to become involved.
- Qualification of leaders – all the people in a country cannot spend all their time making rules; instead, this authority is given to their leaders who are most qualified to do so.
- A group accomplishes more than an individual – as most governments comprise a group of persons, they are more able to get things done, because a group can accomplish jobs that are too big for one individual to do.
- Law and order – in order for a country or society to move forward, and for the citizens to have freedom to live without fear for their lives and property, there must be law and order. Selecting a government and giving it powers to make and maintain laws helps to ensure order in a country. Without a government, there would be chaos, confusion and anarchy in society.

Police officers help to protect the community.

Did you know...?

Governments help to make laws, enforce order, create economic policies; provide services like health, education, police, fire services, armed forces, transport infrastructure, water, electricity, rubbish and sewage collection, national security, leadership at home and abroad; and work towards the goals that the country would like to achieve.

Exercise

1. What helps to ensure law and order in a country?
2. Why do you think it is easier to run a country as a group than as individuals?
3. Write a paragraph of 300 words outlining why a country needs a government.

Case study

What would happen with no government?

Imagine what it would be like if the government in your country was unable to provide these services.

- Laws – who would protect you? It would be difficult to resolve conflicts in a peaceful way and people would be able to do as they pleased. Imagine if people were allowed to set up private armies and take any land that they wanted for themselves.
- Law enforcement – what would happen if there were no police? Who would look after the citizens?
- Economic policies – what would happen if there were no policies encouraging trade? How would the economy work? How would overseas deals be negotiated? Would there be any banks? Where would we keep our money?
- Basic services – where would you get water? How you would you cook if you had no gas or electricity? How would you be able to watch television and surf the internet?
- Education – where would you get your teaching from? What would happen if there were no rules at your school? What would happen if there were no school governors or local authority?
- Health care – what would happen if there were no hospitals, community care, doctors, maternity wards, chemists?
- Road regulations – what would happen if there were no traffic rules to ensure that people use roads in a sensible way? The roads would be chaotic. What would happen if there was an accident?
- Refuse collection – imagine if people were allowed to throw their rubbish anywhere and no one collected and disposed of it.
- National security – what would happen if we no longer had the army and coastguards? Who would protect the country?

Questions

1. Work in groups and brainstorm this question: If there was no government, what would be the consequences for your country?
2. Create a mind map to record your ideas.
3. Choose the five most important reasons for having a government and present these to the rest of the class.

Discuss your ideas as a class and draw up an agreed list of reasons for having a government.

Research

Work in groups and find out what basic services the government provides in your area. Make a list of these services.

Bin bags waiting for collection and disposal – who would take care of these if no one collected them?

Key vocabulary

modern states

Structure of central government

We are learning to:

- explain the composition of each branch of government
- evaluate the role of each branch of government
- analyse the systems of checks and balances in the Jamaican government.

The Government of Jamaica

Jamaica is a constitutional monarchy with King Charles III as head of state. He is represented by a Governor-General appointed on the recommendation of the Prime Minister. The country is a parliamentary democracy with a bicameral legislature and party system, based on universal adult suffrage (being able to vote).

A constitutional monarchy refers to a system of government in which a monarch (the head of a royal family) shares power with a constitutionally organised government.

A parliamentary democracy is a **system** of **democratic** governance of a state where the executive, or those leading the country gain their **power** from their ability to command the confidence of **parliament**, and are also held accountable to that parliament.

A bicameral legislature or parliament is one that contains two separate assemblies who must both agree when new laws are made. For example, the UK Parliament is **bicameral** because both the House of Commons and the House of Lords are involved in making legislation.

The 21 senators are appointed by the Governor-General, 13 of them on the advice of the Prime Minister, and eight on the advice of the Leader of the Opposition. The House of Representatives has 63 directly elected members. The Governor-General appoints the Prime Minister (the MP best able to lead the majority of the House) and Leader of the Opposition. The Cabinet (Prime Minister and at least 11 ministers) has executive responsibility. Elections are held at intervals not exceeding five years.

The Jamaican government is divided into three branches – the **Legislature**, the **Executive** and the **Judiciary**. These three branches cooperate and interact but they also help to ensure fairness in the government. The three branches of the government operate according to the constitution of the country.

The Head of State

In some countries the head of state is the **Governor-General**. In these countries the role is ceremonial as the Prime Minister usually has full authority. The Governor-General is the representative of the King. In other countries the **President** is the head of state, who does not sit in Parliament, but who has the power to call Parliament to a sitting, to extend the sitting of Parliament and to dissolve or end Parliament. The President exercises power in consultation with the Prime Minister and the leader of the Opposition.

Prime minister, Andrew Holness and Governor-General, Patrick Allen, in 2016.

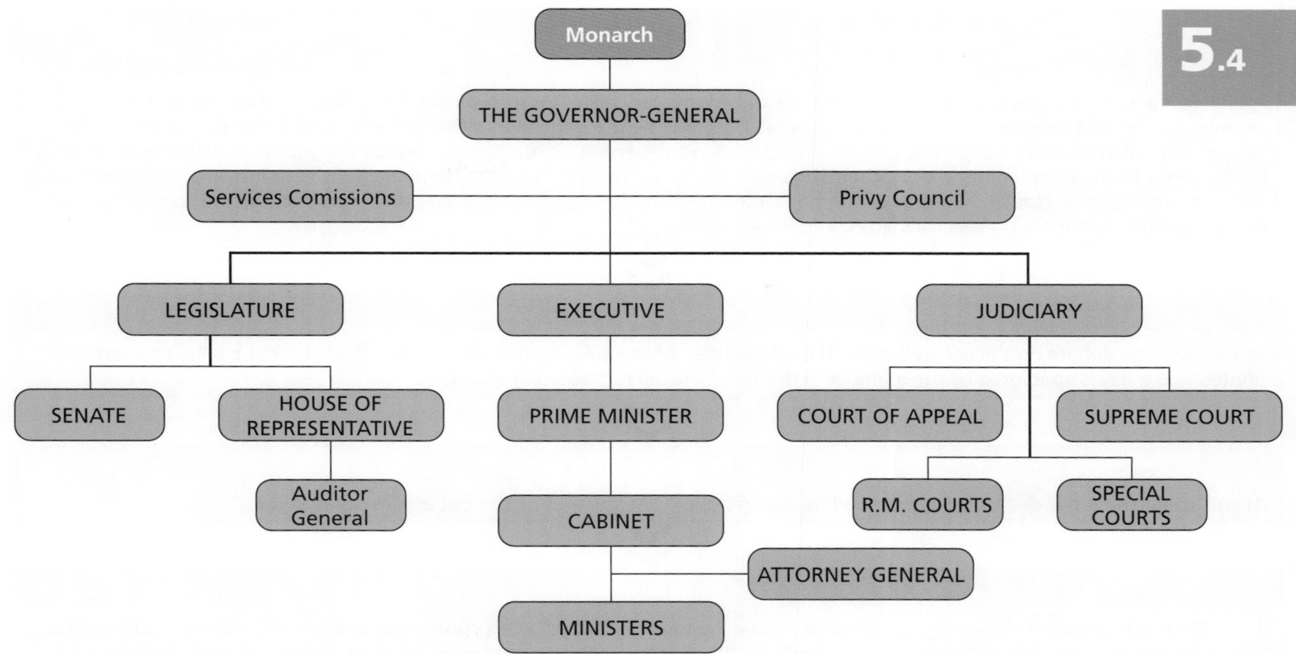

Once a year, at the official opening of Parliament, the Governor-General of Jamaica delivers the "Throne Speech". As well as this, his/her role is to grant assent to Bills passed by the two Houses of Parliament.

The maximum life of a Parliament is five years, at the end of which Parliament must be dissolved and a general election held.

The Legislature

The Legislature is also known as the **Parliament**. The Legislature makes laws, approves national budgets, amends the constitution and monitors the executive actions of government. In some countries it is made up of two houses: the Upper House (**Senate**) and the Lower House (**House of Representatives**). This is called a **bicameral system**.

The Senate is made up of appointed members usually selected by the Prime Minister and the Leader of the Opposition and then appointed by the Governor General. **Senators** are usually independent, which means they are not part of a particular party. However, they have knowledge and expertise that can be useful nationally. The **representatives** or Members of Parliament are elected by the people and are part of particular political parties. Members of Parliament have responsibility to represent their constituency. Jamaica has a bicameral system.

In some countries such as Dominica and St Vincent and the Grenadines there is only one house in the Legislature. This is called a **unicameral system**.

How a Bill Becomes Law

A Bill is an act of Parliament in draft, and no Bill can become law until it is approved by the Houses of Parliament and receives the formal assent of the Governor-General. Bills may be introduced in either the House of Representatives or the Senate (no Bill involving finance can be first introduced in the Senate). "Public Bills", which are set up to affect Government policy, are introduced by Ministers or other officers of the Government. "Private Members' Bills" are introduced by any other member of the House, whether of the governing party or the Opposition. After a Bill has been introduced in the House, it must pass through several stages, known as "readings".

First Reading:

At this stage no debate on the Bill is allowed. The "short title" of the Bill is read by the Clerk of the House, the Bill is ordered to be printed and a day is appointed by the member in charge of the Bill for "second reading".

Second Reading:

At this stage the Bill is debated fully at the "second reading". At the end of the debate a vote is taken.

Committee Stage:

If the Bill passes its second reading, it moves on to the "committee stage". This committee involves the whole House unless the House refers the Bill to a "Select Committee". At this point, the Bill is considered in very close detail and amendments to the Bill may then be moved and voted upon. A Bill may not be rejected during the committee stage, as this power is reserved for the House.

Report Stage:

After the committee stage, there is the "report stage", when the Speaker reports what has happened to the Bill in committee, whether there have been amendments or not.

Third Reading:

No amendments of a substantial nature may be made at the "third reading"; a Bill may be accepted or rejected by means of a vote. When a Bill is first passed by the House of Representatives, it is sent to the Senate, where it goes through the same procedure as one which originated in the "Lower House". If the Senate disagrees with any aspect of the Bill and makes an amendment, the Bill is sent back to the House of Representatives for consideration. If the House disagrees with the Senate's amendment, it informs the Senate, which is then asked to reconsider the Bill.

When an agreement is reached and the Bill has been passed through all its stages in both Houses, it requires only the Royal Assent to make it law. The Royal Assent is given by the Governor-General.

Source: adapted from Jamaica Information Service website

Exercise

1. Name the three branches of government in Jamaica.
2. Write your own definitions of the Legislature, the Executive and the Judiciary.
3. Carry out research into the current Governor-General. What policies have the implemented? Create a time line of the past five Governor-Generals of Jamaica.

Did you know...?

The idea of having three branches of government dates back to the time of the ancient Greeks.

The Executive

The Executive is made up of Members of the Cabinet. The **Cabinet** consists of the **Prime Minister**, or head of government, and his or her ministers.

The Jamaican Coat of Arms.

The Cabinet

The Cabinet controls the government and provides direction and leadership. It is the main body responsible for initiating policies and programmes through which the government operates and guides the country. However, the Cabinet is responsible to Parliament and cannot carry out actions that are not approved by Parliament.

The Cabinet has to consist of the Prime Minister and not less than 11 other ministers. Not more than four ministers must be appointed from the Senate, and they may have specific responsibilities. The other Cabinet Ministers are selected from the House of Representatives.

Cabinet Ministers may be assisted by Ministers of State and Parliamentary Secretaries.

Cabinet ministers are usually assigned what is called a portfolio and have responsibility for a particular ministry. A ministry is a government department with special responsibility for an area of the society such as health, education, justice or finance.

Each minister conducts the day to day business of his ministry without referring to any other Minister. However, important matters, especially those which may become the subject of discussion in Parliament, are brought to the whole Cabinet for discussion and decision.

Executive Agencies

Each ministry has a number of agencies to assist in carrying out its functions. Some of these agencies are called executive agencies.

An Executive Agency is an agency that can act in the ways it sees fit. It remains a part of government but has more responsibility for its own management and performance. The aim is to reduce central control and pass some authority to the Chief Executive Officers in the various government institutions. Another aim is to improve the quality and quantity of services provided by Government agencies.

An example of an Executive Agency is the Passport, Immigration and Citizenship Agency (PICA). It falls under the Ministry of National Security.

The Judiciary

The Judiciary is the branch of government that ensures that the laws are interpreted and applied fairly. These functions are the responsibility of the court system, which maintains law and order. It decides whether a person accused of breaking the law is innocent or guilty.

The legal system of Jamaica is based on British common-law. In Jamaica justice is carried out through a network of courts. The courts of Jamaica are:

- The Judicial Committee of the Privy Council, which is the final court of appeal, is based in London, England. It hears appeals on criminal and civil matters from the Jamaican Court of Appeal.
- The Court of Appeal consists of the President of the Court of Appeal, the Chief Justice (who sits at the invitation of the President) and six judges of the Court of the Appeal. A person who is dissatisfied with a decision of one of the other courts, except Petty Sessions, can appeal to this court. Petty Sessions appeals are heard by a judge in chambers.
- The Caribbean Court of Justice (CCJ) is one of the primary institutions of the Caribbean Community (CARICOM). The CCJ has two core functions – to act as the final appellate court for the CARICOM member states and as an international court ruling on matters relating to the foreign policy coordination of the Revised Treaty of Chaguaramas (2001) that outlines terms.

Checks and balances

As well as the separation of different functions of the legislature, executive, and judiciary, a number of checks and balances have been set up by the Constitution to limit the power of the executive.

These include the offices of Leader of the Opposition, Auditor General and Director of Public Prosecutions and the institution of the three services commissions with responsibilities relating to the appointment and disciplinary control of public servants. This helps to make sure that the government is run fairly and its actions are transparent.

Project

As a class, agree on a local issue that you would like to raise with your Member of Parliament. Write a letter to your MP and ask whether they would be willing to come to your school and talk about their role and the work they do.

Research

Use a search engine to find local newspaper articles about the roles of the branches of Jamaica's government, the functions of the opposition and the civil service. In groups, use Canva or another graphic software to create a graphic organiser that shows what you find out.

Exercise

4 Which branch of government makes the policies that guide the actions of the government?

5 The Minister of Finance is part of the Cabinet. Research and name other ministers in the Cabinet. Discuss your findings as a class.

6 Work in groups and make a short presentation to the class on the structure of the government in your country. Use a diagram to illustrate your presentation.

Key vocabulary

bicameral

bicameral system

Cabinet

democratic

Executive

Governor-General

House of Representatives

Judiciary

Legislature

Parliament

power

President

Prime Minister

representative

Senate

Senator

system

unicameral system

Structure of local government

We are learning to:

- explain the composition of each branch of government
- evaluate the role of each branch of government.

According to the Ministry of Local Government and Rural Development, local government is the public administration of towns, cities, counties and districts. In Jamaica, local government operates at the parish level and in some cases, a **municipal** level. An example of a municipality is Portmore in St Catherine.

Portmore is a municipality in St Catherine.

Specific responsibilities of local government include:

- developing, managing and maintaining roads, and public facilities such as water supplies, drains and gullies, parks, recreational centres, markets, abattoirs, pounds, cemeteries, transportation centres, public sanitary conveniences and public beaches
- ensuring that local services run, such as poor relief, public cleansing, public health and street lighting
- the regulation of building and planning approvals and development control, licensing of trades and businesses, street parking, control of public vending
- coordinating non-governmental organisations (NGOs), community-based organisations (COBs) and government agencies which operate in the parish and are set up to run local services or in local development
- support of national policies/development programmes at the local level
- to implement plans and initiatives for the orderly, balanced and sustainable development of the parish as a whole, and major towns in particular, and for the boosting economic activity and local wealth creation within the parish.

Local authorities in Jamaica are referred to as Parish Councils or Municipal Corporations. A local authority has two parts, the political and the administrative. The political arm is made up of councillors, headed by the Mayor who chairs the Council and is responsible for shaping and deciding upon policies. The administrative arm is headed by a manager who advises and puts into practice policies. Some key positions include the Chairman and Deputy Chairman along with the Chief Engineer Officer and Disaster Coordinator.

Local authorities are able to make **by-laws**, regulations and rules for the good **governance** of the parishes over which they have jurisdiction.

Overview of the different agencies that work with local authorities

1. Disaster Preparedness and Emergency Management (ODPEM)

   This agency works to identify disaster threats and risks throughout the country and to help formulate plans to create a state of readiness to meet the needs of victims when a disaster strikes. It also has responsibility for taking action to reduce the impact of disasters and emergencies on the Jamaican population and its economy. It plays a coordinating role in the execution of emergency response and relief operations in major disaster events.

2. The Social Development Commission (SDC)

   This is the main community organisation agency working with Jamaica's 775 communities. Positioned in the Ministry of Local Government & Community Development works to directly or indirectly serve the advancement of sport, social, cultural & economic development – for the people of Jamaica and workers in particular. It aims for citizens of Jamaica to be involved in activities which results in good governance, economic prosperity, sustainable environment and social well-being.

3. The National Solid Waste Management Authority

   Since it began, this agency has been serving the entire island of Jamaica and its people, providing timely, efficient waste management services across the island in order to the safeguard public health while helping to create an environment for all to enjoy and preserve. This agency has helped to set up disposal sites for the proper disposal of solid waste to ensure environmental protection, solid waste disease and pest or nuisance control.

Source: adapted from Ministry of Local Government & Community Development

Queen Elizabeth II with the mayor of Montego Bay in 2002.

Exercise

1. Look up the following words and write their definition.
   - **a)** municipal
   - **b)** by-laws
   - **c)** governance
   - **d)** jurisdiction
2. Find out what your local government area is.
3. Carry out research into one of the agencies that works alongside the government. Explain its role in detail, giving examples of how that work improves your local community.

Key vocabulary

by-laws

governance

municipal

Functions of central and local government

We are learning to:

- evaluate the role of each branch of government
- describe the extent to which the Members of Parliament are carrying out their functions.

The functions of central and local government

Central government helps to make laws, enforce order, create economic policies, provide services like health and education, national security, and leadership at home and abroad. Local government provides the basic services that we need for small geographic areas, such as a city, town, county or state. Local government receives grants from central government to provide services.

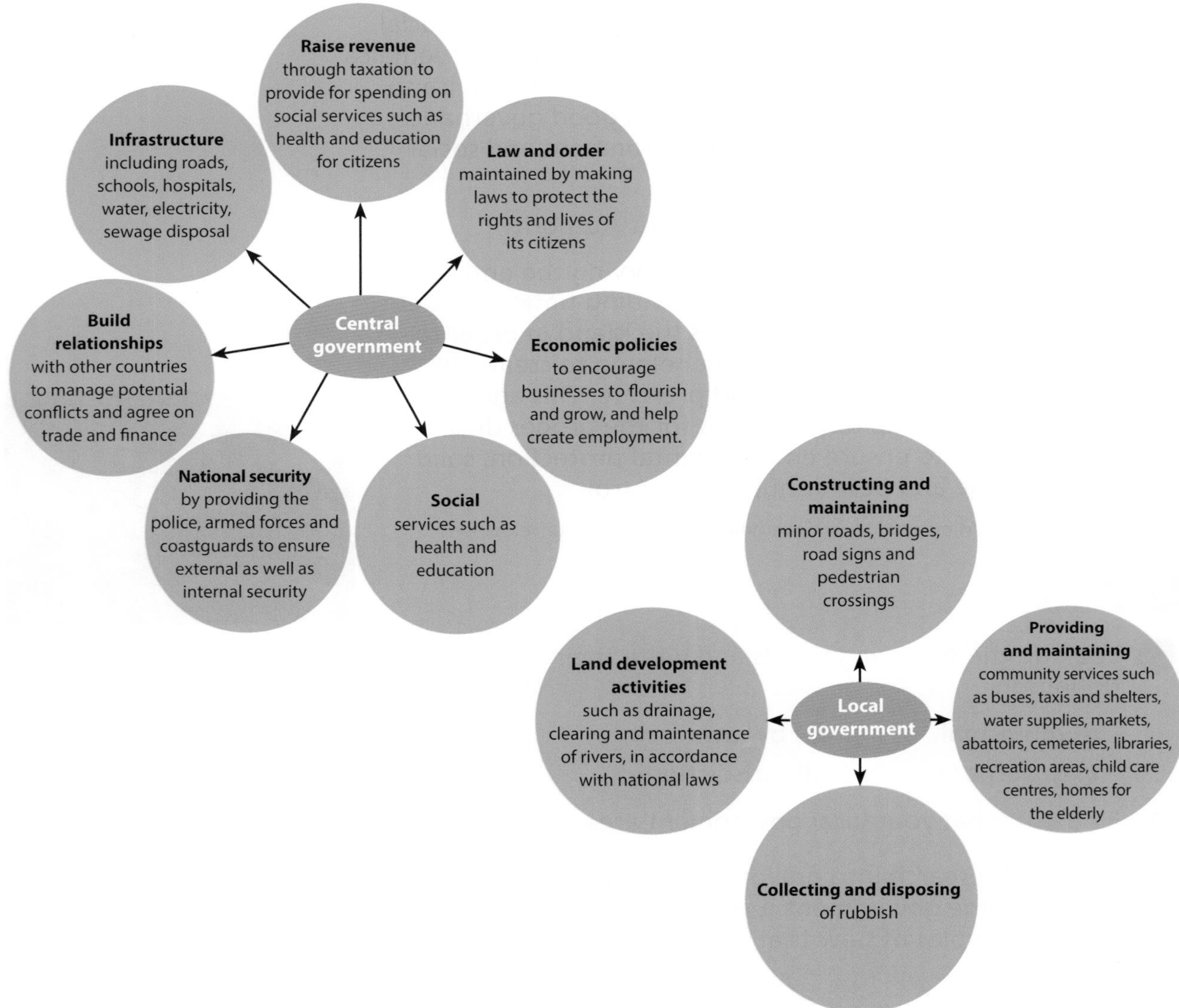

Good governance

The governance of a country relates to the way that a country is governed, how public affairs are conducted and how public resources are managed by those in power and authority.

Good governance depends on a number of factors:

- its citizens taking part in deciding how the country is run through voting and knowledge of the political system of the country
- making sure the judicial system remains independent and fair
- assuring government is run in an open fashion and is seen to be above the abuse of power and authority
- seeing that the government of a country is held **accountable** and their decision making is checked for corruption or wrongdoing
- making sure the needs of the citizens are met by government – if they fail to do so, they will be voted out at the next election
- ensuring that citizens should be given access to information by government under freedom of information laws as to how resources and money are allocated and how decisions are made
- seeing that the government makes good use of its natural, human and financial resources for the benefit of the country
- making sure the functions of government are carried out efficiently
- ensuring that a country's constitution recognises that its citizens have basic human rights.

Project

Find letters in the local newspaper which comment on the central or local government's performance. Decide if they are happy with their performance or unhappy with it. Then, write a letter to the editor of the newspaper either praising or criticising the government's performance.

Exercise

1. In your own words outline the functions of central and local government.
2. Why do you think governments should be held to account?
3. Research things that central or local governments do that are not part of their normal activities; for example, giving assistance to victims of natural disasters.

Key vocabulary

accountable

Questions

See how well you have understood the topics in this unit.

1. Match the key vocabulary word with its definition.
   - **i)** government
   - **ii)** constitution
   - **iii)** democracy
   - **iv)** secession
   - **v)** anarchy
   - **a)** the principles and laws by which a country is governed
   - **b)** when a country, or a group, separates from a larger group
   - **c)** a group of people, usually elected, who have the power and authority to manage the affairs of a country
   - **d)** a system of government in which a country's citizens choose their rulers by voting for them in elections
   - **e)** when the absence of a government causes a breakdown of law and order in a society
2. Which of these is a characteristic of a democracy?
   - **a)** unable to question government decisions
   - **b)** the rights of a country's citizens to choose their own government representatives at regular periods
   - **c)** that elections are closed to the public
3. Name two reasons why we need a government. Write 50 words.
4. Name five services that we would not have if we had no government.
5. Name the three branches of government in Jamaica.
6. Identify whether the following are functions of central or local government:
   - **a)** providing services such as buses, taxis and shelters, water supplies and markets
   - **b)** infrastructure including roads, schools, hospitals, water, electricity, sewage disposal
   - **c)** constructing and maintaining minor roads
   - **d)** collecting and disposing of rubbish
   - **e)** law and order is maintained
   - **f)** social services such as health and education

7. What is meant by the 'Westminster model'?
8. What does the word 'bicameral' mean. Explain in your own words.
9. Who is the current Governor-General of Jamaica?
10. Correct this statement: Everyone can vote in elections.
11. When was the last referendum in Jamaica? What was is about?
12. When was the Constitution of Jamaica written?
13. Give three examples of ways to bring about change in the law that are peaceful and non-confrontational.
14. What is the role of the head of state?
15. How many MPs are there in Jamaica?
16. What Parish and constituency do you live in?

Grade 9 Unit 5 Summary

Democracy and government

In this chapter, you have learned about:

- What is meant by the terms government and democracy
- The functions of a democratically elected government
- What the terms constitution, referendum, secession and anarchy mean
- The characteristics of a democracy
- What the main difference between a direct and a representative democracy is
- The characteristics of a representative democracy
- The non-confrontational ways to bring about change in government
- The reasons governments are necessary.

The structure and functions of central government

In this chapter, you have learned about:

- The structure of the central government of Jamaica
- What is meant by a Head of State
- What the Legislature is and how it works
- The process of making a bill into a law in Jamaica
- The Executive and how its made up
- What the Cabinet is and what Cabinet ministers do
- Executive Agencies and examples of them
- The checks and balances in the Jamaican system of government.

The structure and functions of local government

In this chapter, you have learned about:

- The responsibilities of the local government
- The agencies that work with local authorities
- What good governance means.

Checking your progress

To make good progress in understanding the structure of the Jamaican government, check that you understand these ideas.

- [ ] Explain and use correctly the terms *democracy* and *government.*
- [ ] Describe the structure of government in Jamaica.
- [ ] Explain the differences and similarities between democracies and other types of governments.
- [ ] Explain and use correctly the terms *Westminster System* and *bicameral*.
- [ ] Name the parishes of Jamaica.
- [ ] Explain the role of the monarchy in Jamaican government.
- [ ] Explain and use correctly the term *judiciary*.
- [ ] Name three reasons we need government.
- [ ] Explain how local government is organised in Jamaica.
- [ ] Explain and use the term *secession*.
- [ ] Describe the role of the legislature.
- [ ] Explain the role of the constitution in Jamaica.

SOCIAL STUDIES

Unit 6: The Electoral Process

Objectives: You will be able to:

The electoral process in Jamaica

- outline the major steps of the electoral process in Jamaica.

Constituents and constituencies

- define and use appropriately relevant terms and concepts: constituency, constituent, campaign, manifesto.

Nomination Day

- describe the preparations which political parties make before an election
- outline the major steps of the electoral process in Jamaica.

Ballots

- explain the steps to be taken in casting a vote
- discuss the factors that influence the outcome of elections
- appreciate the work of election day workers.

Voting systems

- define and use appropriately relevant terms and concepts: floating voters, first-past-the-post system, Election Day, hung parliament
- explain the process to be followed on Election Day.

Preparing for an election

- explain the steps to be taken in casting a vote
- discuss the factors that influence the outcome of elections
- appreciate the works of election day workers
- recognise the importance of a free and fair election process.

The electoral process in Jamaica

We are learning to:

- outline the major steps of the electoral process in Jamaica
- define and use key concepts.

The system of government in Jamaica is a representative democracy. This means that people are elected by voters to serve in the government.

Elections are held regularly to choose who will serve in national and local government. Candidates are chosen according to an electoral process, which is described in the constitution of the state.

Political rallies are a major part of elections around the world.

The Electoral Commission of Jamaica (ECJ)

The Electoral Commission of Jamaica (ECJ) oversees and manages the electoral process in Jamaica. It is an independent body established by the Constitution of Jamaica and operates separately from the government. The key functions of the ECJ are to:

- ensure free and fair elections
- maintain an accurate list of people who are eligible to vote
- promote public understanding of the electoral process.

It has eight members appointed by the the Governor-General. Four of the members are selected jointly by the Prime Minister and Leader of the Opposition. The other four members are **nominated**, two each by the Prime Minister and the Leader of the Opposition. Two of the eight members are then nominated to be:

1. The Chairman of the ECJ whose role is to oversee the conduct of the Commission.
2. The Director of Elections whose role is to manage the electoral process.

The Electoral Office of Jamaica is the administrative arm of the ECJ.

Mission Statement of Electoral Office of Jamaica

To conduct national elections so that no advantage is given to any party or individual, and ensuring that the objective of 'one man one vote' is met under six principles:

THE VOTE IS UNIVERSAL

THE VOTE IS FREE

THE VOTE IS SECRET

THE VOTE IS DIRECT

THE VOTE IS PERSONAL

THE VOTE IS NON-TRANSFERRABLE

Source: Electoral Commission of Jamaica website

Exercise

1. In your own words, explain the difference between the role of the chairman of the Electoral Commission and the Director of Elections.
2. Why do you think the Electoral Commission of Jamaica is independent and operates separately from government?
3. Explain why each of the principles of the Electoral Office of Jamaica is important.

The structure of the Electoral Commission of Jamaica

The Electoral Commission of Jamaica is structured into different parts, as follows:

- Chairman
- Commissioners
- Director of Elections
- Legal and Compliance Division
- Voter Registration and Identification Division
- Electoral Office Operations Division
- Communication and Public Relations Unit
- Monitoring and Evaluation Unit

Activity

Carry out research to find out the purpose of each part of the Electoral Commission of Jamaica. Use a graphic organiser to outline the composition/structure of the Electoral Commission of Jamaica and how it promotes an environment for free and fair elections.

Exercise

1. Think about what you would like to find out and write some interview questions to ask personnel from the Electoral Commission.
2. Write an email or a letter to the Electoral Commission of Jamaica inviting personnel to come and speak at your school and explaining what you would like to find out from them.

Did you know...?

One way of organising information so that it's easy to read is by using a graphic organiser. Here are some examples of ways to show information graphically:

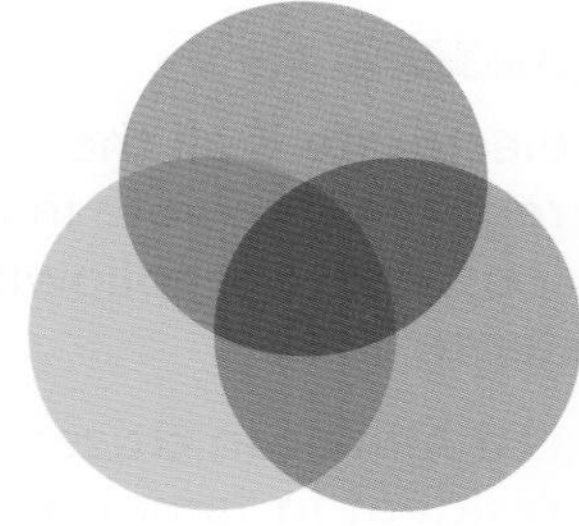
A Venn diagram

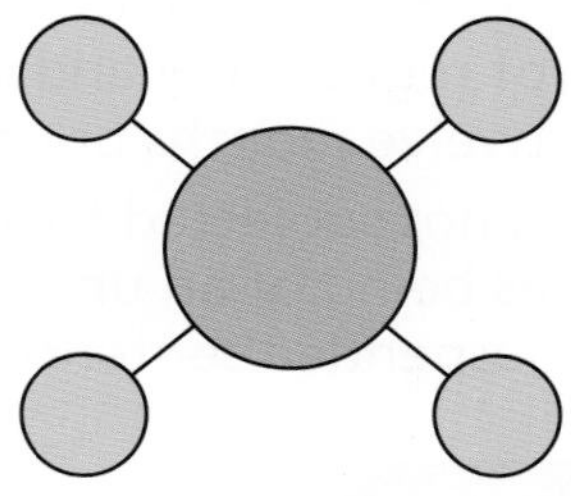
A bubble organiser

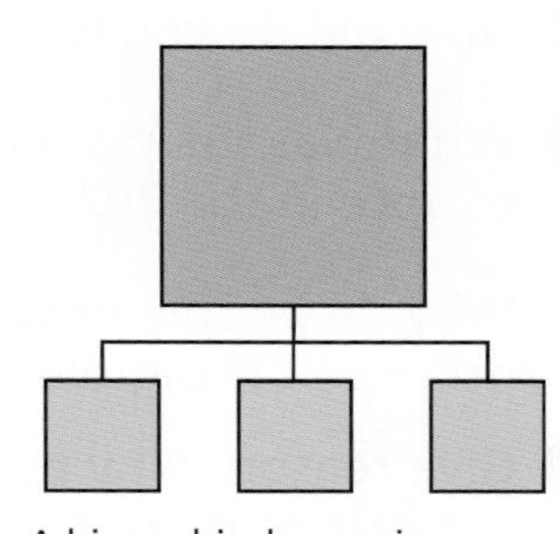
A hierarchical organiser

Elector

An **elector** is a person who has the right to **vote** in an election. In order to have the right to vote, you have to be eligible and you must also be registered as a voter.

You need to have a **National Identification Card** in order to register as a voter.

The Electoral Commission of Jamaica (ECJ) publishes two voters' list each year. One list is published on 31 May and the other six months later on 30 November. Registration takes place on a continuous basis and anyone who wants to vote, can visit their ECJ Constituency Office and apply.

> **Did you know...?**
>
> General elections were held in Jamaica on 3 September 2020.

> **Did you know...?**
>
> Due to the Covid-19 pandemic and the Dengue Fever epidemic, the voter turnout of 37% was the lowest in a general election since 1983.

Electorate

The **electorate** is all the people in the country who are eligible and registered to vote in an election. Every Jamaican citizen who possesses the following qualifications is entitled to register to vote:

- is a Jamaican citizen of eighteen years or over and resident in Jamaica or
- is a Commonwealth citizen who is eighteen years of age or older and who is resident in Jamaica at the date of registration and who has been a resident for at least twelve months prior to the date of registration
- is not subjected to any legal incapacity to vote such as being of an unsound mind, convicted or under a suspended sentence.

Exercise

1. How old do you have to be in order to vote?
2. What was the percentage of people who turned out to vote in the 2020 election?
3. Why do people need to be citizens of a country in order to be eligible to vote?
4. Give reasons why people who are able to vote sometimes do not.

Candidates

A **candidate** in an election is a person who seeks to be nominated or elected to a position in the national or local government.

If the candidate gets enough votes and is elected, he or she **represents** the people who have voted. This is a principle of **democratic government**.

Candidates in elections in Jamaica have to:

- be aged 21 years or older
- have been born in Jamaica or have lived in the country for 12 months immediately before nomination
- be able to speak English, to allow them to take part in the proceedings in the House
- be **nominated** by at least six registered electors
- be registered with an established political party or stand as an independent
- register and pay a deposit before they can start their campaigns to win **supporters** who will vote for them.

Candidates can be members of political parties or they can be **independent candidates**. You have to be 18 years old to be eligible to vote in most democratic countries around the world. Some countries, for example Brazil, Argentina, Cuba and Austria allow citizens to vote from the age of 16.

Source: adapted from Electoral Commission of Jamaica website

The red mark on the finger shows that these people have voted in the election. This is to prevent people having more than one vote.

Discussion

Why is it important to get a National Identification Card? Why do you think that registered voters do not always cast their votes in an election? Discuss these questions in class.

Research

You are going to carry out research into the electoral process. Find out about the process people have to go through in order to be nominated as a candidate in Jamaica.

Exercise

5. What is the difference between a candidate and an elector?
6. In one sentence, describe what is meant by 'the electorate'.
7. Would you be allowed to nominate a candidate for your government? Give a reason for your answer.
8. Are you, or members of your family, eligible to vote? Why/why not?
9. Write a paragraph explaining the qualities of a good candidate for national government.

Key vocabulary

candidate
democratic government
election
electorate
elector
independent candidate
National Identification Card
nominated
represent
supporter
vote

Constituents and constituencies

We are learning to:

- define and use appropriately relevant terms and concepts: constituency, constituent, campaign, manifesto.

Constituents and constituencies

According to the Electoral Commission of Jamaica, Jamaica is divided into a number of areas known as **constituencies**. The people who live in this area, the **constituents**, vote for who they want to represent them in local and national elections.

The person who receives the majority of votes from that area is the winner. He or she then represents that constituency at local or national level in government.

Gerrymandering is when a political group tries to change a voting district to create a result that helps them or hurts the opposing group.

Discussion

What ideas would you like your elected representatives to include in their manifestos? Think about issues that affect your life or the lives of your families and friends. Make a list of five ideas.

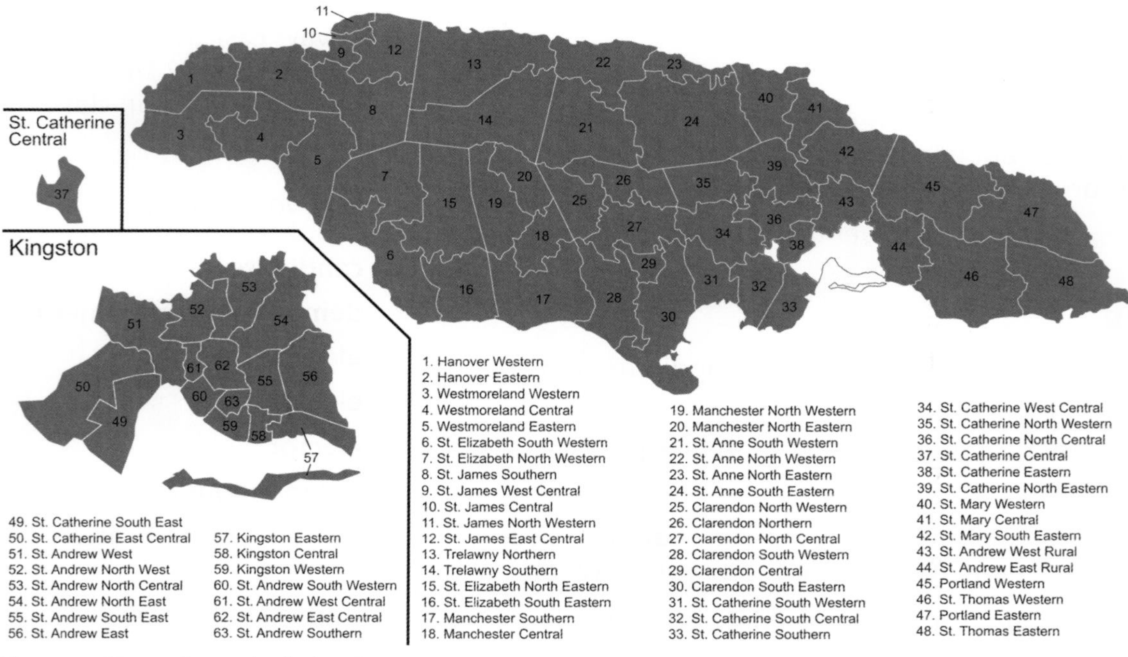

There are 63 constitutencies in Jamaica.

There are 63 constitutencies in Jamaica. Each constituency elects one Member of Parliament (MP) to sit in the House of Representatives, which is part of the national government.

Campaign

A **campaign** is a series of events that are organised to help a candidate get elected. During a campaign, candidates try to convince voters about why they should get their votes.

Candidates present their ideas about matters that concern the people of the constituency and the country as a whole. They use the media as well as personal appearances to get their messages across to voters.

Manifesto

All candidates put together a **manifesto** before they begin their campaigns. A manifesto states publicly what the candidate's views are on certain issues and explains the policies they support or will introduce if they are elected. The manifesto will reflect the policies of the political party that the candidate represents. Manifestos are very important to the electoral process in all countries.

Source: adapted from Electoral Commission of Jamaica website

Did you know...?

You can also make a personal manifesto in which you publicly declare what you would like to achieve. Here are some things that people have written in personal manifestos:

- Live up to my potential!
- See the world!
- Work out regularly.

Exercise

1. In your own words define the terms 'constituency', 'constituent', 'campaign' and 'manifesto'.
2. How many constituencies are there in Jamaica? Name five of them.
3. Who do constituents vote for?
4. Name five types of campaign activity that a candidate could engage in while running for election to national or local government.
5. Explain what you would expect to see in a manifesto.
6. Find out the name of the constituency in which you live.
7. Choose five constituencies in your country. Find out who has been elected to represent these constituencies in national government as an MP. Find out which political party each MP belongs to.

Research

Work in pairs and find out the meaning of the expression 'to be on the campaign trail'. Find examples of what happens on the campaign trail, then report back to the class with your ideas.

Key vocabulary

campaign
constituency
constituent
manifesto

Nomination Day

We are learning to:

- describe the preparations which political parties make before an election
- outline the major steps of the electoral process in Jamaica.

Franchise

To have the **franchise** means to have the right to vote. People who have the right to vote are enfranchised. In most modern democracies all adult citizens are enfranchised.

Jamaica was granted full adult suffrage on 20 November, 1944.

Adult suffrage

Adult suffrage is the right that adults (people over a certain age) have to vote in political elections. Until the 1920s adult suffrage was a privilege that was reserved for some people only. In most countries, only wealthy men were allowed to vote. People who did not own land, and women, were not enfranchised.

Today suffrage is seen as a right, and most democracies allow all adult citizens over the age of 18 to vote. Adult suffrage was granted to all the British colonies in the Caribbean in the 1940s and 1950s. Jamaica was granted full adult suffrage on 20 November, 1944.

Discussion

Why should electors nominate candidates? Why should candidates have to pay a deposit in order to be officially declared a candidate? Discuss these questions with your teacher.

Exercise

1. Explain in your own words what the terms 'franchise' and 'adult suffrage' mean.
2. Make this statement accurate: All adults in Jamaica have been enfranchised since the 1920s.
3. How did voting change in the 1940s and 1950s in the Caribbean?
4. What effect do you think the granting of adult suffrage has had on the people of Jamaica?

Did you know...?

In the 19th and 20th centuries in the UK, women, known as suffragettes, fought for their right to vote in elections.

Nomination and Nomination Day

6.3

Before they can stand for election, all candidates who represent political parties, as well as independent candidates, have to gain formal **nomination** as candidates.

Nomination means that candidates have to follow a certain procedure in order to be able to stand for election. These procedures take place on **Nomination Day**.

Read the following newspaper article about Nomination Day in a recent general election.

Case study

Nomination Day

The process begins at 7 a.m. and ends at 5 p.m. Each candidate must make a statutory declaration that indicates that they are a person who is properly qualified to be nominated as a candidate in Jamaica. Anyone who wishes to stand for election must be nominated on an official nomination paper.

Candidates are expected to present themselves to returning officers in their respective constituencies and should be recommended by six electors from their constituencies in order to be nominated. Candidates can stand either for an established political party or as an independent.

Additionally, each candidate is expected to make a deposit of $3000, which at the end of the day is deposited into the treasury. Candidates lose their deposit if they do not secure a specified number of votes in the election.

When all the documents are in order, the information is then sent to the Electoral Office, where the process of printing the ballot papers with the names of those who have been properly nominated takes place.

Questions

1. List three things that you have to do if you wish to become a candidate in an election in Jamaica.
2. To whom do candidates have to apply for nomination?
3. What does the Electoral Office do?
4. Who can nominate a candidate?
5. What happens to the nomination fees collected?
6. What happens to the candidate's fee if they do not get a reasonable number of votes?

Research

Find out more about Nomination Day and how nominations work in your country. Create a document which explains the process, using images.

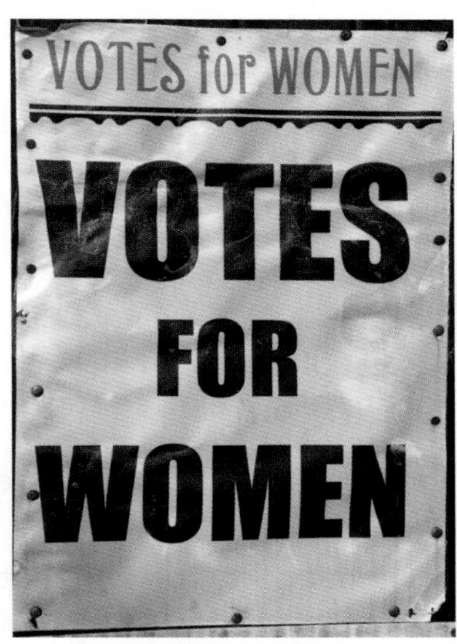

In the UK, suffragettes were women who fought for the right to vote.

Key vocabulary

adult suffrage
franchise
Nomination Day
nomination

Ballots

We are learning to:

- explain the steps to be taken in casting a vote
- discuss the factors that influence the outcome of elections
- appreciate the works of election day workers.

Ballots

A **ballot** is a vote or a piece of paper on which a person records his or her vote. When people talk about winning 'the ballot', they mean the total number of votes cast in an election.

Ballot papers are counted carefully and behind closed doors.

Ballot paper

A **ballot paper** on which you cast your vote has the names of the candidates and the political parties with which they are associated.

In some countries there are also photographs of the candidates on the ballot papers. In order to cast your vote, you make a cross next to the name of the person for whom you are voting.

Ballot boxes are sealed so that people cannot tamper with them.

The candidate

The candidate in an election is the person who seeks to be nominated or elected to a position in the national or local government. Voters have to decide who they are going to vote for. Their choice may depend on a number of factors, such as:

- what party the candidate belongs to
- if they are currently in national or local government, and are doing a good job
- whether they agree with the candidate's policies, for example their economic, education and health policies
- whether they have the necessary qualities to be a leader, for example, are they honest or a good communicator?
- if the voter likes the candidate.

Discussion

In groups, discuss the reasons why you would vote for someone in an election. Make a list and then share them in a class discussion.

Exercise

1. Define the term 'ballot'.
2. What would you expect to see on a ballot paper?
3. What do you do with a ballot paper?
4. What does it mean if a candidate wins the ballot?

Key vocabulary

ballot
ballot box
ballot paper
secret ballot

Ballot box

Once you have chosen the candidate for whom you wish to vote, you place your ballot in a **ballot box**.

A ballot box is a special box which is sealed so that people cannot tamper with it. Voters put their ballot papers in the ballot box. The box is only opened when the votes are to be counted.

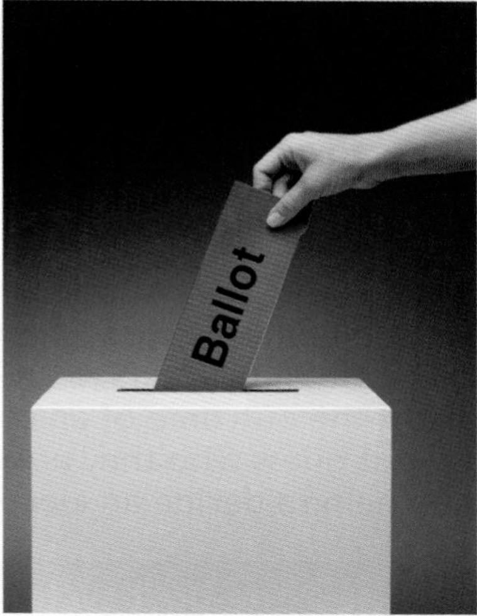

Voting in elections in Jamaica has to be by means of secret ballot.

Secret ballot

When you vote or cast your ballot in an election, you do so in secret. You do not have to tell anyone who you have voted for and nobody should watch you while you make your cross on the ballot form.

The Jamaican constitution states that voting in elections has to be by means of a **secret ballot**.

Secret ballots allow people to vote anonymously and freely. This helps to make sure that you have a real choice when you vote, as it stops other people from intimidating or bribing you to vote for someone else. This helps to prevent electoral fraud.

Did you know...?

The word ballot comes from an Italian word *ballotta*, which means 'a small ball'. It refers to an old system of voting in which people cast their ballots by placing small coloured balls in a container.

Show of hands

Another way of voting is by means of a show of hands. This method is sometimes used in schools or clubs. People are asked to raise their hands to vote for a person or to agree with a proposal.

This method is not secret, as everyone can see how you vote. It is not appropriate in general elections, as it would be difficult to check votes afterwards and it could also lead to corruption and voter intimidation.

Exercise

5 Write a sentence explaining what a secret ballot is.

6 Why does a ballot box have to be sealed?

7 What are the advantages of a ballot by show of hands? Are there any disadvantages?

8 Which of the following are advantages/disadvantages of a secret ballot?

- **a)** You can vote for whom you choose without fear of intimidation.
- **b)** It makes it difficult to bribe people to vote for a certain candidate, because you cannot be sure who they will really vote for.
- **c)** Some people may be anxious about having to complete the process by themselves.
- **d)** You don't have to tell others who you have voted for.

Voting systems

We are learning to:

- define and use appropriately relevant terms and concepts: floating voters, first-past-the-post system, Election Day, hung parliament.

Floating voters

Some voters always support one political party, while others are sometimes unsure who to vote for. These voters are called **floating voters** in an election. Floating voters can affect the outcome of an election, because political parties cannot guess who they are going to vote for. Their votes can also help to decide an election that is closely contested.

Floating voters can be influenced by party political advertising.

First-past-the-post system

There are two types of electoral system: the **first-past-the-post system (FPPS)**, and the **proportional representation (PR)** system. The difference between the two relates to how votes are counted and the way candidates win elections.

The first-past-the-post system is used to elect Members to the House of Representatives in Jamaica. In this system, one candidate is elected for each constituency. The candidate who wins is the candidate who gets the most votes in that constituency. In some systems, candidates have to win a **majority** of the votes – in other words, more than 50% of the votes. The winning candidate becomes the constituency representative in the House of Representatives, and wins a seat in Parliament.

The party that wins the majority of seats in Parliament wins the overall election and therefore forms the government. The Prime Minister is selected from the winning party and the leader of the opposition is selected from the party with the second-highest number of seats.

Proportional representation

In some countries, like Guyana, candidates are elected through a system of proportional representation (PR). In a PR electoral system, voters vote for a political party. Each party draws up a list of candidates for an election. The number of candidates elected from each party is directly proportional to how many votes were cast for that party.

Research

Work in groups. Find out:

- on which date the last general election was held in Jamaica
- which political parties contested the election
- which political party won the election
- the names of five candidates who were elected to serve in the House of Representatives.

Key vocabulary

Election Day

first-past-the-post-system (FPPS)

floating voter

hung parliament

majority

proportional representation (PR)

Election Day

Candidates who are elected to serve in the House of Representatives serve for four to five years at a time. This means that new elections have to be held at least every four to five years.

The Prime Minister, Premier, President or Chief Minister can call for elections before the five years have been completed. This sometimes happens when one party does not have a clear majority or when there are important issues that need to be resolved.

A country may have an Electoral Department, Electoral Office or Elections and Boundaries Commission, which along with the government will notify voters when elections will occur. On that day, **Election Day**, people cast their votes. The votes are counted and the results are usually announced the following day, as counting the votes can take a long time.

In Jamaica the Electoral Commission of Jamaica (ECJ) is the body responsible for election procedures. It was established to make sure that elections are fair and conducted correctly. The ECJ is also responsible for maintaining the register of electors; verifying the identity electors; approving political parties to receive state funding and overseeing electoral funding requirements.

Activity

Your cousin in another Grade 9 class has asked you to explain the terms 'first-past-the-post' and 'proportional representation'. Use a graphic organiser to demonstrate the similarities and differences between them.

Hung parliament

A **hung parliament** is when no party has gained the overall majority of seats in Parliament to take control and to form a government. When this situation occurs, two (or more) parties may join forces to create a government. Alternatively, the election may be held again.

Exercise

1. Research the electoral systems used in the following Eastern Caribbean countries: Anguilla, Antigua and Barbuda, Barbados, Dominica, Grand Cayman, Grenada, Guyana, Montserrat, St Kitts and Nevis, St Lucia, St Vincent and the Grenadines.

   What do you notice about these countries' electoral systems? Add the information you have found to your portfolio.
2. In your own words, define 'floating voter'.
3. What is Election Day?
4. Explain the term 'hung parliament'.

Preparing for an election

We are learning to:

- explain the steps to be taken in casting a vote
- discuss the factors that influence the outcome of elections
- appreciate the work of election day workers.

Differences between politics and government

It is important to understand the differences between politics and government. Politics refers to the beliefs or theories people hold about the way a country should be run, while government is the body, or institution, that runs the country. This is why we have different political parties, which have different ideas as to how a country should be run.

Steps in preparation for an election

There are a number of legal steps involved in setting up a national election before polling day in Jamaica.

- The government announces the intention to hold an election and Parliament is dissolved.
- Electoral registration – the electorate (voters/electors) check that they are registered to vote.
- The dates for Nomination Day and the election are set.
- Political parties nominate their candidates on Nomination Day. Candidates have to be nominated by at least six people.
- Venues for polling stations are identified. The buildings must be safe, a public or community-owned building with facilities for the disabled and elderly voters, and located within the electoral district.
- A notice about the polling stations is published in a newspaper, detailing the date of the election, hours when the polling station is open, its address and station number, and information about the candidates.
- Poll cards are sent out. These contain the details of the elector, date of the election and location of the elector's polling station.

Following Nomination Day, the candidates and parties begin their campaign. First they decide their policies and publish their manifesto. The campaign that follows typically has public meetings and rallies, **house-to-house canvassing** and **opinion polls**.

Activity

In groups, imagine that you are a youth officer with a political party. Brainstorm a five-minute speech in which you aim to encourage people to vote for your party. Outline your manifesto and say why people should vote for you. Then one member of your group presents your speech to the rest of the class.

Activity

Review the steps in preparing for an election, then write a list of questions for the Electoral Commission of Jamaica. For example, what barriers were encountered in previous elections and how were they corrected? Then write a letter to the ECJ inviting a member of staff to talk to Grade 9 students at your school.

Key vocabulary

house-to-house canvassing

opinion poll

The Political Ombudsman

Office of the Political Ombudsman.

The Office of the Political Ombudsman (OPO) was established to conduct investigations into any action taken by a political party, its members or supporters, where there has or may have been a breach of the Code of Conduct of political activities.

The Ombudsman is an official appointed by the Governor-General after consultation with the Prime Minister and the Leader of the Opposition. The Ombudsman is independent from the government and represents the interests of the public by investigating reported complaints.

Source: adapted from Office of the Political Ombudsman Jamaica website

Factors influencing a political choice

In Jamaica, all citizens aged 18 and over can vote in a national election. In Jamaica and different parts of the Caribbean, there are many different factors that determine the party or candidate a voter may choose to vote for.

- Gender – men and women sometimes vote differently based on certain issues, as particular things will be more important to men or women. A party's manifesto may contain promises that appeal particularly to men, or more to women.
- Race/culture – voters from a particular ethnic group may choose to vote for a candidate from the same ethnic group; in countries that are dominated by one ethnic group, the party that has the support of that group often wins the election.
- Religion – some religious denominations do not allow people to vote in elections, but when they do they often vote for a candidate or political party that shares their religious views.
- Emotions – people may be biased by responding emotionally to a particular candidate's or party's campaign. They may not like the other candidates, not agree with a political party's view or feel unhappy with the performance of the government.
- Family – family members often vote for the same party that their family has voted for across several generations, as they often share the same value systems and outlook on life.
- Political socialisation – political parties attract loyal followers, who will always vote for a particular party.
- Tolerance of different political views to your own.
- The media have a responsibility to give accurate, balanced and unbiased coverage of an election, allowing all parties equal access to advertising opportunities. However, newspapers, television and radio can influence public opinion. Sometimes they can present a biased view of a certain political party, either in a positive or negative way, and in some countries governments own particular media outlets.

Activity

Write a paragraph to describe why someone might change their mind about which political party to vote for.

Discussion

As a class, your teacher will lead a discussion on why people give support to different political parties.

Exercise

1 Draw a flow diagram that outlines the steps in preparation for an election.

2 Why do you think people from the same ethnic and/or religious groups often vote for the same party?

The process on Election Day

We are learning to:

- explain the process to be followed on Election Day.

Before Election Day

It is important before polling day that voters do the following:

- make sure that they have registered to vote – if they are not registered they cannot vote
- make sure that they know where their polling station is – voters are usually given these details
- make sure that they know what time the polling station opens and the time it closes – voters have to be in the queue to vote before closing time to be allowed to vote
- make sure that they take something with them to prove their identity (for example some countries have a National Identification Card), otherwise they will not be able to vote.

The police are often at polling stations to make sure voting is fair and peaceful.

The process on Election Day

Polling stations open at different times in different countries, for example in Barbados it is from 6 a.m. to 6 p.m. and in Jamaica the times are 7 a.m. to 5 p.m. Voters are allowed to go and cast their vote at any time during those hours. If a voter is still queuing to get in the polling station at the final hour they are allowed to vote, but no one who joins the queue after this time is allowed to vote.

The voting process: Jamaica

- The presiding officer shows those at the polling station the empty ballot boxes to prove they are empty, before sealing and locking the boxes.
- Voters are directed to provide their name to the presiding officer or polling clerk who checks their name against the **voter list** (or register).
- The voter is given an official ballot paper which is marked by an official mark to show it is genuine.
- The voter enters a private voting booth. The ballot lists the candidates in alphabetical order. An X is placed next to the candidate selected and the ballot paper folded and put into the ballot box.

- Ballot boxes are taken to a central place in the constituency where each ballot is counted in the presence of the candidates.
- When all the votes are counted the results are announced by the Returning Officer.

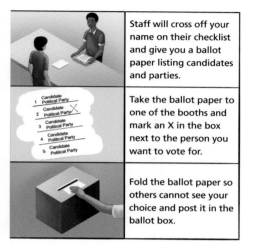

Staff will cross off your name on their checklist and give you a ballot paper listing candidates and parties.

Take the ballot paper to one of the booths and mark an X in the box next to the person you want to vote for.

Fold the ballot paper so others cannot see your choice and post it in the ballot box.

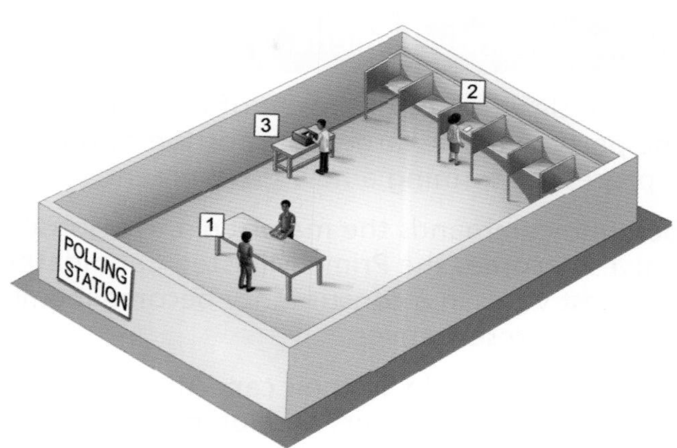

The illustrations above show what happens once you are inside the polling station.

The voters are supervised by a number of staff at the polling station:

- the presiding officer – responsible for the running of the polling station
- poll clerks – who are responsible for managing the queue, asking the elector for his or her ID card, checking the documents to determine that the elector is entitled to vote and ticking off the elector's name to say they have voted
- officers in charge of the ballot box
- information officer(s) (where considered necessary) – who help to give general information to the electors and answer questions.

Exercise

1. Does Election Day occur before or after Nomination Day?
2. Between what times are you allowed to vote?
3. What should you bring with you to the polling station?
4. What are the roles of the presiding officer and poll clerks on Election Day?
5. Draw a flow diagram that outlines what happens on Election Day.

Project

In groups, role-play the steps involved in a general election. Include the selection of candidates, the campaign, the casting of ballots, the declaration of a winner and the victory and losing speeches.

Key vocabulary

polling station

voters list

A new government

We are learning to:

- discuss the activities following an election in the formation of a new government.

Formation of a new government

Following the declaration of the result of the general election, the party with the largest proportion of the vote begins the process of forming a new government.

The member who commands the majority in the House of Representatives becomes the Prime Minister. Candidates who get the most votes in a constituency become members of the House of Representatives.

It is the Prime Minister's role, in their capacity as head of government, to appoint ministers and junior ministers to the Cabinet. If they feel it is necessary, he or she can restructure the ministries in the government.

The Opposition

The Opposition to the government is led by the largest party that did not form the government after a general election.

The role of the Opposition is to hold the government to account for the decisions that it makes and to scrutinise their policies.

Exercise

1. Explain how senators are selected in Jamaica.
2. After a general election, who appoints the new Cabinet?
3. What is the role of the Opposition?
4. Write a short paragraph describing how a new government and Opposition are formed after a general election.

Activity

Use the internet to research the current Senate in Jamaica. Do the senators have expertise in particular areas? How do you think having appointed members of government and elected members benefits your country?

The role of the citizens

People who are elected to national and local government in a democracy have a responsibility to carry out the duties and services for which they have been elected.

The citizens who have elected these representatives also have a responsibility to make sure that these representatives do their jobs correctly.

There are several ways in which citizens can be involved.

- When Parliament is discussing new proposed bills, which may later become laws, members of the public are invited to comment and to give their views.
- Government representatives also hold meetings from time to time, which citizens can attend.
- There are websites from which citizens can get information freely and through which they can contact government representatives.

If government officials do not do their work in a satisfactory manner, there are ways of removing these officials from their jobs:

- Elected officials will not be re-elected if they have not performed well.
- Officials who are found to be corrupt can be removed from office.

All government officials, including the Prime Minister, are subject to the laws of the country, like any other citizen.

Jamaican Prime Minister Andrew Holness, in 2016.

Exercise

5. Name two ways in which citizens can scrutinise the role of the government.
6. How can government officials be removed from office if they are not doing their job satisfactorily?
7. Do you think the Prime Minister can be removed from office? How and why?
8. Research, compare and contrast the roles of:

   a) The Governor General

   b) The Prime Minister and Opposition Leader.

Free and fair elections

We are learning to:

- define and explain relevant terms and concepts: free and fair elections, universal suffrage
- recognise the importance of a free and fair election process.

Universal suffrage in Jamaica

Originally, the ability to vote in Jamaica, as in other British colonies, was only granted with ownership of land or the payment of taxes above a specific level. However, the franchise was restricted to White men, age 21 years and above. In 1830, free Black men were granted the right to vote followed by Jewish men in 1831.

After the end of enslavement in 1838, and the burst of enterprise by the newly emancipated, White people were outnumbered in the electorate by 1849. Ironically, where Jamaica abolished race as a disqualification for voting, race was used by the British to hinder Jamaica's advancement in democracy.

Jamaica was granted full adult suffrage on 20 November, 1944. Before that, the right to vote was determined by the amount of wealth or property a man held, and women were not allowed to vote at all. The new system extended voting rights to adults irrespective of their race, sex, or social class.

Within a month, on 12 December, Jamaica became only the third state in the British Empire to conduct elections on the basis of universal adult suffrage, preceded only by New Zealand and the United Kingdom. Among the countries in 1944 that conducted elections on the basis of universal adult suffrage, Jamaica was the only colony, the only state with a Black majority and the only small state with an economy based largely on agriculture. The election was won by the Alexander Bustamante-led Jamaica Labour Party (JLP), which claimed 22 seats; the Norman Manley-led People's National Party (PNP) and the Independents won five seats each.

Did you know...?

Women first voted in Jamaica in 1920 but were subjected to higher age and property requirements.

Exercise

1. In your own words, define the term 'universal suffrage'.
2. What three points differentiated Jamaica from the UK and New Zealand in 1944?
3. What were the terms of the limited franchise in Jamaica before universal suffrage was applied? Were these terms good for the nation's citizens?

Research

Using the internet, research situations around the world where elections have not been free or fair. For example, you could research occasions in the past when people have been excluded from voting or other countries around the world that are not democracies. You could use the search phrase 'unfair elections in history'.

Write an essay of 200 words outlining your findings. Add any consequences for countries that have not had fair elections.

Free and fair elections

An election should adhere to the principles of universal adult suffrage and has to be **free and fair**.

A free and fair election occurs when the parties taking part in the election do not try to persuade citizens to cast their votes in their favour by using force or intimidation. It should also ensure that the counting of the votes is accurate and not open to abuse.

Elections, at both national and local level, also require the following conditions to make them free and fair:

- universal suffrage for all eligible men and women
- freedom to register as a voter or as a candidate
- freedom of speech for candidates, their parties and the freedom to hold political rallies and campaigns
- polling stations accessible to everyone and supplying a private space for people to cast their vote.

Discussion

In groups, discuss this statement: 'Elections should be free, fair and free from fear.' Do you agree with this? Discuss as a group, then outline your conclusions to the rest of the class.

Importance of free and fair elections

It is in the interests of all political parties to make sure that general elections are **transparent**:

- to avoid voters being persecuted or prevented from voting, by threats of violence or attacks on polling stations
- to avoid voters being intimidated or bribed to vote for a candidate or a party
- to avoid voters being excluded from voting based on race, sex, beliefs, wealth or social status
- to ensure that the counting of votes is transparent and independent and not tampered with
- to ensure that ballot papers are not deliberately miscounted, lost or destroyed.

Key vocabulary

free and fair

transparent

Case study

Citizens Action for Free and Fair Elections (CAFFE) has now successfully monitored eight Island-wide elections, the national general elections of 1997, 2002, 2007, 2011, 2016 and 2020 the local government elections of 1998, 2003, 2007, 2012 and 2016 as well as every single by-elections and re-runs. CAFFE's reputation as an election watchdog and for its contribution to the development of sound electoral practices was further enhanced by its performance during the 2016 and 2020 elections.

CAFFE has faithfully pursued its mission to promote free and fair elections and advocate good governance. The organisation is now respected nationally and internationally as a symbol of patriotic endeavour, civic volunteerism, and citizen participation.

Source: adapted from Caffe Jamaica website

Exercise

4 List four scenarios that would make an election unfair.

5 Do you think it is fair that people should be excluded from voting because of their race, sex, beliefs, wealth or social status? Explain why/why not.

Activity

In groups, recap the factors that determine who wins an election. Create a mock-up of a Wikipedia page with the information.

Questions

See how well you have understood the topics in this unit.

1. Match the key vocabulary word (**i–viii**) with its definition (**a–h**).

i) election	**a)** the ballot of voting papers on which you choose your candidate in an election
ii) elector	**b)** a person who lives in a constituency
iii) electorate	**c)** a process during which voters choose candidates by voting for them
iv) candidate	**d)** proposed as a candidate
v) votes	**e)** a voter or person who has the right to vote in an election
vi) nominated	**f)** people who are registered to vote in an election
vii) constituency	**g)** an area in a country where voters elect a representative to a local or national government body
viii) constituent	**h)** a person who seeks election

2. Explain the difference between a ballot and a secret ballot.
3. What is Nomination Day?
4. How often does a general election happen in Jamaica?
5. In your own words, explain the terms first-past-the-post and proportional representation.
6. Name five factors that can affect how a person chooses to vote.
7. Who forms a new government after an election?
8. Explain why a general election should be free and fair.
9. Read the results in the table from an imaginary parliamentary election. Answer these questions:

Results
Candidate A (Blue party): 14 780 votes
Candidate B (Green party): 17 890 votes
Candidate C (Red party): 11 301 votes
Total number of votes cast: 43 971 votes

   a) Which political party won this seat in Parliament?
   b) Did any candidate win a majority of the votes?
   c) Which system was used to declare the winner of this election?

10. Write a short paragraph explaining what is meant by a 'first past the post' system.

11. What is the purpose of the Universal Declaration of Human Rights?

12. Describe the role of each of the following:

    a) Presiding officer

    b) Voter

    c) Poll clerk

13. Look at the diagram and describe what is occurring at each location (1–3).

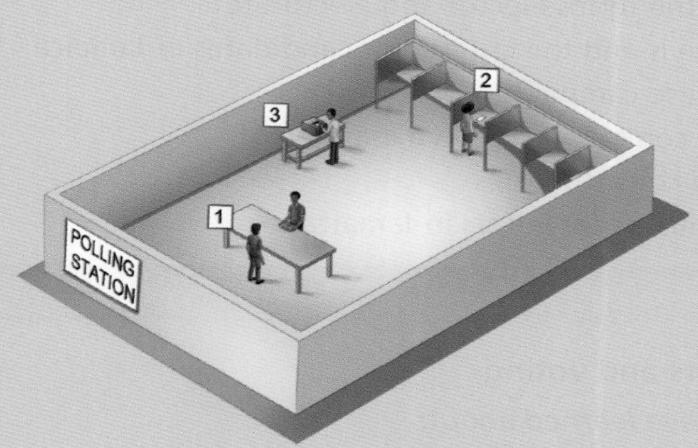

Grade 9 Unit 6 Summary

The electoral process in Jamaica

In this chapter, you have learned about:

- The purpose and structure of the Electoral Commission of Jamaica
- The meaning of the terms elector and electorate
- What a candidate is and the criteria for candidates in Jamaica
- Why candidates use campaigns
- How policies are communicated in a manifesto
- Constituents and constituencies
- What franchise means for voters in Jamaica.

Nominations, ballots and voting

In this chapter, you have learned about:

- The events on Nomination Day in Jamaica
- Ballots and the steps to be taken in casting a vote on Election Day
- The differences between first-past-the-post system and proportional representation
- How politics is different from government.

Preparing for an election

In this chapter, you have learned about:

- The steps in preparing for an election
- The role of the Political Ombudsman
- The factors that influence political choice
- The Election Day process
- The formation of a new government
- The role of the Opposition
- The roles and responsibilities of citizens
- The significance of universal suffrage for voters in Jamaica
- The importance of free and fair elections.

Checking your progress

To make good progress in understanding the electoral process in Jamaica, check that you understand these ideas.

- Explain and use correctly the term *elector*.
- Describe the function of the political ombudsman.
- Explain the differences between the role of the Chairman of the Electoral Commission and the Director of Elections.
- Explain and use correctly the term *gerrymandering*.
- Name the types of elections held in Jamaica.
- Explain the preparations made before an election takes place in Jamaica.
- Explain and use correctly the term *first past the post*.
- Name the time period for elections in Jamaica.
- Explain the role of the returning officer.
- Explain and use correctly the term *adult universal suffrage*.
- Describe the steps taken in casting a vote in Jamaica.
- Explain the factors that influence the outcome of elections.

End-of-term questions

Questions 1–7

See how well you have understood ideas in Unit 4.

1. Explain natural and human resources of Jamaica.
2. Define the following terms: **a)** sustainable urban **b)** rural development **c)** Human Development Index **d)** climate change.
3. Explain what is meant by a population pyramid, and outline what changes have occurred in the population of Jamaica over the past 50 years.
4. Briefly describe the goals of Vision 2030.
5. Explain the progress being made on each goal.
6. Match these terms to their definitions:

   1) on-the-job training
   2) mentorship (or coaching)
   3) succession training
   4) tuition assistance

   a) where the employee's skills and abilities are developed to prepare them for promotion
   b) training whilst working, to help develop skills within a job
   c) an employee can go on additional training courses to help build up their knowledge and skills
   d) another more experienced employee gives advice and support to someone less experienced
7. Complete these sentences.

   _________ resources come from the natural environment, for example wood, water and soil.
   _________ resources are other tangible resources made by man, such as buildings and equipment.
   _________ resources are people and their various skills, talents and abilities.

Questions 8–14

See how well you have understood ideas in Unit 5.

8. Explain how Jamaica has the Westminster model of government.
9. What is a democratic government and what are the strengths of a democracy? Write a short paragraph to explain.

10. Write a short essay of three paragraphs in which you explain the role of the **a)** judiciary **b)** executive **c)** legislative.

11. Explain how laws are created in Jamaica.

12. Create a spidergram showing the structure of Jamaican government, including all key roles.

13. State whether the following are functions of central or local government:

a) Responsible for social services
b) Raise revenue through taxation
c) Responsible for the disposing of rubbish
d) Responsible for maintaining roads and bridges
e) Responsible for law and order
f) Build relationships with other countries
g) Responsible for providing services such as buses and libraries
h) Responsible for drainage and river maintenance
i) Responsible for the infrastructure

The write a short text of about 100 words explaining why central and local government are responsible for those functions.

14. Match these terms to their definitions:

1) Democracy
2) Government
3) Constitution
4) Referendum
5) Anarchy

a) An opportunity for eligible people to vote on a particular issue.
b) A form of government in which all eligible citizens have an equal say or participation in the decisions that affect their lives.
c) A group of people who manage the affairs or goals of a country.
d) When law and order break down in a country.
e) A written document that sets out the laws by which a country is governed.

Questions 15–16

See how well you have understood ideas in Unit 6.

15. Find out information about the last general election in your country and write a report about the outcome of that election. Add the report to the information you have already gathered.

16. Write an information leaflet in which you explain why elections should be free and fair, and why general elections need to be transparent. Write about 150 words.

SOCIAL STUDIES

Unit 7: Environmental Problems and Green Solutions: Green Technology

Objectives: You will be able to: 

Types of green technology and how they are used in Jamaica

- analyse and assess the claims of each type of green energy
- formulate questions about how green technology can help to sustain the environment and human health on planet Earth, and gather evidence to answer questions
- identify organisations that are certified as being environmentally friendly, assess their operations, gather information from other sources and then develop guidelines for other organisations to become environmentally friendly.

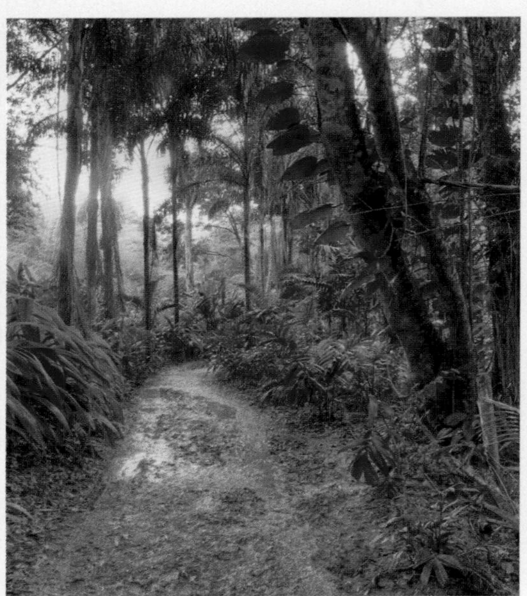

Environmental issues in Jamaica

- create and interpret statistical maps and diagrams showing environmental problems and solutions
- make predictions about the possible impact of a variety of continued and combined unsustainable practices on different types of environment and the health of different people.

Deforestation

- understand the importance of forests and the reasons for deforestation and its effects
- identify strategies that are in place to prevent deforestation.

Pollution and land degradation

- identify the primary sources of pollution in Jamaica
- understand the effects of pollution in our country
- define land degradation, understand the causes and consequences, and the ways in which it can be slowed or reversed
- create and interpret statistical maps and diagrams showing environmental problems and solutions.

Preservation and conservation of the environment

We are learning to:

- differentiate between preservation and conservation of the environment
- justify the need for the sustainable use of physical resources to protect the environment.

We often refer to preservation, conservation and sustainability when we talk about the environment. The natural environment needs to be protected so that future generations can enjoy its benefits as much as we do today.

Coral on a Jamaican reef.

Preservation

Preservation of the environment means protecting areas at risk with strict laws and regulations that prevent them from being damaged. Countries might do this by declaring them national parks or nature reserves, where any activity that will damage the environment is prohibited. In addition to the Blue and John Crow Mountains National Park, Jamaica has three marine parks and more than 200 protected areas, which include forest reserves and fish sanctuaries.

Did you know...?

In 1990, Blue and John Crow Mountains National Park was declared Jamaica's first national park.

Conservation

Conservation is concerned with managing the use of natural resources. Conservation regulations state that people can use these natural resources as long as some of them are left for future generations.

A good example of this would be fossil fuels such as oil and gas. These are a non-renewable resource, which means that once they are used up they cannot be replaced. Across the Caribbean there are several conservation strategies designed around the use of the tropical forests.

Sustainability

Sustainability is concerned with the use of natural resources in such a way that their quantities are maintained. If sustainability is practised, the resource will be available for future generations.

It is often possible to replace renewable resources, such as trees, as they are used. For example, if a forest is deforested, more trees can be planted in its place.

Activity

In groups, discuss the difference between preservation, conservation and sustainability. Give examples of each one and share your ideas with the other groups.

Case study

Using and protecting our natural resources

Our planet has many resources that humans have enjoyed for thousands of years. There are amazing landscapes that should be protected, wildlife and plant species that need to be protected and natural resources that must be maintained.

You are going to choose an area in your country and examine the positive and negative effects of the way the land is used. You will decide whether the land is being used well, and give recommendations on what else could be done. Then you will share your ideas in a presentation to the class.

Follow these steps:

1. Choose a place in Jamaica that is rich in natural resources.
2. Decide whether the resources are renewable (they can be replaced) or non-renewable (they can never be replaced).
3. Do some research to find out how the land is being used. For example:
   - Are the resources being used? If so, what for?
   - Are the resources being preserved by the government? If so, how? What laws exist to protect the area?
   - Are there any conservation strategies in the area? If so, what are they?
   - If the resources in the area are renewable, are they being used with sustainability in mind?
4. Conduct field observations, interviews and surveys to help with your project.
5. Decide whether or not you think the use of the land you have chosen is acceptable. Why?
6. Create a PowerPoint presentation to share information on your chosen place.

Your presentation must include the following:

- location of study
- the way in which the land is used
- positive and negative effects of land use
- evidence of primary and secondary sources of information – for example, library and internet sources, articles from newspapers, magazines, journals
- proper citation of sources.

Planting new trees helps combat the effects of deforestation.

Key vocabulary

sustainable/sustainability

What is green technology?

We are learning to:

- analyse the goals of green technology
- gather information from multiple sources on types of green technology (innovation) used in various sectors of society.

Green technology refers to a type of technology that is considered environmentally friendly based on its production process or the way that it is supplied. It can also refer to clean energy production; the use of alternative fuels and technologies that are less harmful to the environment than fossil fuels.

Green energy refers to any type of energy produced in a sustainable way that does not negatively affect the environment.

Examples of green technology include the technology used to recycle waste, purify water, create clean energy, and conserve natural resources. The demand for green technology is relatively recent. However, it is receiving a lot of interest due to increasing awareness about the impacts of climate change and the depletion of natural resources.

Green technology offers alternative energy sources to traditional sources such as logging.

What are the goals of green technology?

- To protect the environment and, in some cases, to even repair past damage done to the environment
- To make sure that similar, affordable levels of energy are provided to non-renewable sources
- To use green technology to produce goods that are recyclable and/or reusable
- To reduce waste and create energy efficiency
- To move towards a more sustainable lifestyle.

According to a 2018 report by the United Nations, global investment in green technology was more than $200 billion in 2017; $2.9 trillion has been invested in sources like solar and wind power since 2004. The U.N. report also stated that China was the largest global investor in the sector, with approximately $126 billion invested in 2017.

The benefits of Green Technology

Recycling – green technology helps manage and recycle waste material. It allows it to be used for beneficial purposes. This technology is used for waste management, waste incineration, and more. A lot of recyclable material has allowed individuals to create plant fertiliser, sculptures, fuel, and even furniture.

Purifying water – green technology involves the purification of water. The scarcity of pure drinking water is a major concern. Through the use of various technologies a lot of campaigns have been successful in providing people with clean drinking water.

Purifying the air – dealing with carbon emission is another focus. While humans are improving in terms of developing various technologies, cars, factories and other forms of machinery are emitting a lot of carbon that is damaging to the planet. Green technology helps to reduce carbon emission and purify the air. This allows people and other animals and plants to survive healthily.

Conserving energy – alternatives to devices that use a lot of electricity or fuel are being introduced to the public. The use of electric cars is on the rise, for example. People using environment friendly devices and appliances is encouraged. While installation of such devices, namely solar panels, might be expensive for some people the benefits it offers with regards to reducing bill expenses are tremendous.

Rejuvenating ecosystems – green technology is also being used to improve ecosystems that have sustained a lot of damage due to human involvement. Through the use of this technology trees are replanted, waste is managed and recycled. This ensures that the affected ecosystem is able to start again, and this time remain conserved.

Source: adapted from US Green Technologies website

Factories and other forms of machinery are emitting a lot of carbon which is damaging to the planet.

Activity

Create a PowerPoint explaining the benefits of green technologies. Use images and examples.

Activity

Find out about an entrepreneur in green energy technology in your area. Carry out research into their business. How does their business offer a good alternative to other forms of technology?

Solar panels are an example of an energy conserving device.

Exercise

1. Explain what is meant by **a)** 'green energy', and **b)** 'green technology', using your own words.
2. Why is there more interest in green forms of energy at the moment?
3. Write an essay explaining why green technology is beneficial, including examples from Jamaica.

Key vocabulary

green energy

green technology

Types of green technology and how they are used in Jamaica

We are learning to:

- analyse and assess the claims of each type of green energy
- formulate questions about how green technology can help to sustain the environment and human health on planet Earth, and gather evidence to answer questions.

Recycling

Green technology is used in the recycling process, as well as in waste incineration. Recyclable material can be used when manufacturing plastics, fertiliser, and fuel. Green technology can also be a part of the production process, such as processes to recycle water or waste in the manufacturing process.

Recycling is an important form of green technology.

According to the National Environment and Planning Agency (NEPA), Jamaica produces an average of 8 657 tonnes of solid waste per day. Not all of this waste has been properly disposed of with figures showing that between March 2014 and March 2017, 3.3 million pounds of plastics – or well over 100 million bottles – have been recovered from the environment in Jamaica.

Here are some ways in which recycling helps us and the environment:

Recycling

1. Recycling reduces the amount of garbage in landfills. This helps to conserve valuable land space.
2. Recycling conserves natural resources such as trees, oils, and minerals which are depleted less rapidly when material derived from them such as paper, glass, and metal are recycled.
3. Over time, waste in landfills leaks harmful toxins into the earth and greenhouse gases, such as carbon dioxide and chlorofluorocarbons are released into the air. Recycling helps to reduce this pollution.
4. Compared to the energy needed to extract resources to make new materials, recycling uses less energy. For example, recycling paper and glass uses 40% less energy, and recycling metal uses 95% less.
5. Recycling helps to conserve the natural habitats of wild animals, thus also helping to protect their lives.

Source: adapted from jis.gov.jm/information/get-the-facts/get-the-facts-why-recycle/

The Jamaican government encourages persons to recycle by making simple changes, such as the ones below:

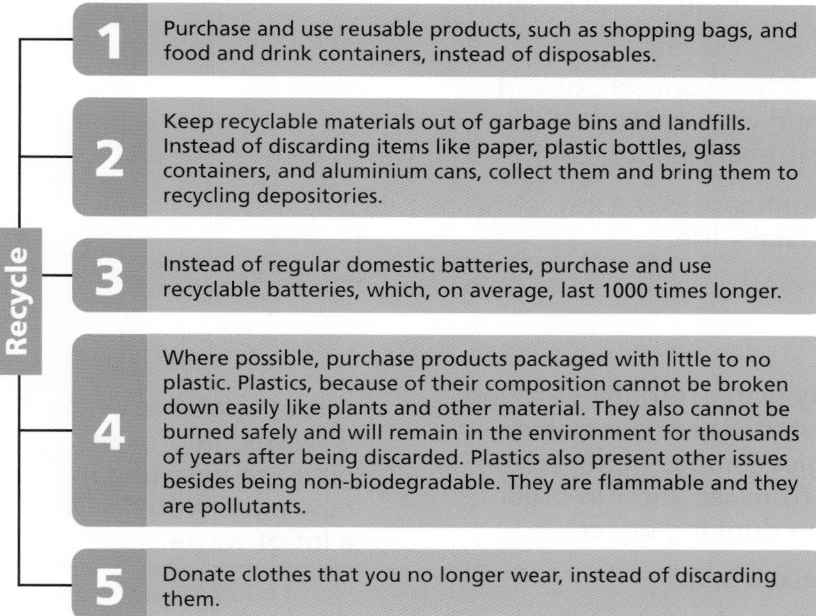

Recycle
1
Purchase and use reusable products, such as shopping bags, and food and drink containers, instead of disposables.
2
Keep recyclable materials out of garbage bins and landfills. Instead of discarding items like paper, plastic bottles, glass containers, and aluminium cans, collect them and bring them to recycling depositories.
3
Instead of regular domestic batteries, purchase and use recyclable batteries, which, on average, last 1000 times longer.
4
Where possible, purchase products packaged with little to no plastic. Plastics, because of their composition cannot be broken down easily like plants and other material. They also cannot be burned safely and will remain in the environment for thousands of years after being discarded. Plastics also present other issues besides being non-biodegradable. They are flammable and they are pollutants.
5
Donate clothes that you no longer wear, instead of discarding them.

Case study

Single-use plastic bags

From 1 January 2019, the Jamaican Government introduced a ban on single-use plastic bags, straws and polystyrene. The ban includes the importation, manufacture and distribution of these materials. The plastic bags to be banned are known as 'scandal bags' or other bags with dimensions of 24 inches by 24 inches or less, typically used for shopping.

According to the government, bags that are used for packaging and maintaining public health or food safety standards will not be banned. This applies to plastics that are essential for the maintaining food and safety standards, including plastics used to package raw meat, flour, sugar, rice and baked goods, such as bread.

In some cases, the use of plastic bags will be permitted. However, manufacturers will have to apply to the National Environment and Planning Agency (NEPA) for exemptions.

The polystyrene ban applies to those that are used as food and beverage containers. Regarding drinking straws, the ban will not apply to those that are used in medical facilities like hospitals or care homes for patients.

Activity

In what other areas could single-use plastics be replaced with recyclable materials? Make a list of these suggestions and discuss how you can implement one change in your school.

Jamaican Environment Trust (JET) notice.

Exercise

1. Remember your three 'R's from Grades 7 and 8. What do they stand for?
2. Carry out research into recycling in your school and home. What are you doing and what more could be done to make sure you recycle everything possible?
3. Produce a wall display that summarises the key ways that recycling can be done in daily life.

Clean water

Green technology is used to purify water resources around the world. In parts of the world where there are scarce water resources, green technologies can be employed to purify dirty water or remove salt from seawater in order to increase the availability of clean drinking water.

What are Jamaica's main water resources?

- Surface water is water from river, rainwater, lake or freshwater wetland, which can be treated using different methods, such as filtration systems.
- **Desalination** takes water from the ocean or sea and treats it using desalination systems to remove the salt from the water.
- Groundwater or brackish water is from water located in the pore space of soil and rock (borehole well), which can be treated using purification systems, filters, chemical treatments or UV sterilisers.

Did you know...?

A lot of potable water is wasted in broken pipes, so investing in new pipes would save a lot of waste.

Exercise

1. Find out what is meant by 'potable water'.
2. Explain what is meant by 'desalination'.
3. Carry out some research to find out how much water is estimated to be lost through broken or leaking pipes in Jamaica.

Clean air

Green technology is used in processes that purify the air by reducing **carbon emissions** and gases that are released into the air from manufacturing plants, causing air pollution. These are mainly currently focussed on reducing emissions released by planes, cars and lorries. For example:

- switching to electricity powered cars
- driving fuel efficient cars
- having cars where the engine turns off when the car is stationary
- avoiding using a car or plane where possible
- keeping tyres properly inflated.

Did you know...?

The global **aviation** industry produces around 2% of all human-induced carbon dioxide (CO_2) emissions.

Exercise

1. How can air pollution be reduced in your day to day life?
2. Using your own words, explain what is meant by carbon emissions.
3. What kinds of health problems does air pollution cause? Carry out research and create a poster highlighting the key dangers.

Energy efficiency

Green technology can be used in processes intended to conserve energy, such as:

- energy-efficient light fixture
- green technology is also used to create alternative fuel sources that are more environmentally friendly than fossil fuels. Fossil fuels typically create waste as a by-product of their production
- solar, wind, and hydroelectric dams are all examples of green technology because they are safer for the environment and don't produce fossil fuel waste by-products.

An energy-saving lightbulb.

Solar power

Solar energy works by capturing the sun's energy and turning it into electricity for your home or business.

- Our sun is a natural nuclear reactor. It releases tiny packets of energy called photons, which travel the 93 million miles from the sun to Earth in about 8.5 minutes.
- Every hour, enough photons impact our planet to generate enough solar energy to theoretically satisfy global energy needs for an entire year.
- More than 20 000 Jamaican homes are expected to be powered by clean, affordable, renewable energy to be generated from the US$61 million solar electricity plant, being built in Content District, Clarendon.
- Solar technology is improving and the cost of going solar is dropping rapidly, so our ability to harness the sun's abundance of energy is on the rise.

Solar power is becoming more widely available in Jamaica.

How do solar panels work?

- When photons hit a solar cell, they knock electrons loose from their atoms.
- If conductors are attached to the positive and negative sides of a cell, it forms an electrical circuit.
- When electrons flow through such a circuit, they generate electricity.
- Multiple cells make up a solar panel, and multiple panels (modules) can be wired together to form a solar array.
- The more panels you can use, the more energy you can expect to generate.

What are the disadvantages of solar power?

- It is expensive to set up.
- It is weather dependent. Although solar energy can still be collected during cloudy and rainy days, the efficiency of the solar system drops.
- Solar energy storage is expensive.
- Solar panels use a lot of space.

4 Extra electricity may be used by the grid

2 An inverter converts electricity from DC to alternating current (AC)

INVERTER

SUNLIGHT PHOTONS

1 Solar panels convert sunlight into direct current (DC)

SOLAR PANEL

3 The AC powers your home

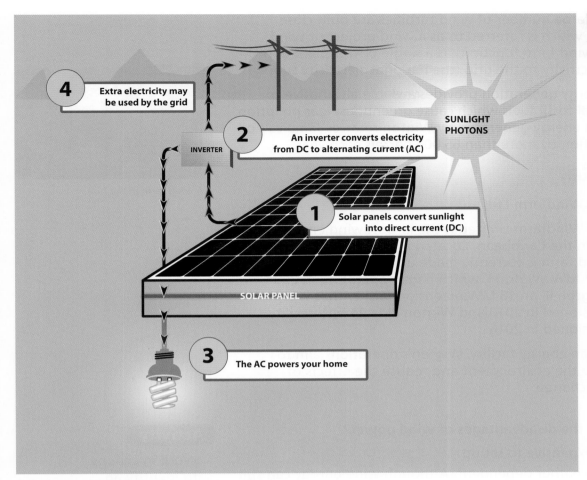

A diagram explaining how solar energy is produced.

Wind power

Wind energy (or wind power) refers to the process of creating electricity using the wind, or air flows that occur naturally in the Earth's atmosphere. Modern wind turbines are used to capture potential or **kinetic energy** from the wind and generate electricity. These are either on land or offshore.

Wind turbines.

How wind turbines work

When the wind blows past a wind turbine, its blades capture the wind's kinetic energy and rotate, turning it into mechanical energy. This rotation turns an internal shaft connected to a gearbox, which increases the speed of rotation by a factor of 100. That spins a generator that produces electricity.

Often, a large number of wind turbines are built close together, which is referred to as a wind project or **wind farm**. A wind farm functions as a single power plant and sends electricity to the **grid** (the national electricity supply).

Wind energy generation provides a viable alternative to traditional fossil fuels which cause greenhouse gas pollution. The clean energy generated by Wigton reduces Jamaica's oil consumption by more than 65 000 barrels each year.

A wind farm in the hills.

Case study

Wigton Windfarm Ltd

Wigton Windfarm Limited is the largest wind energy facility in the Caribbean. Located in Rose Hill, Manchester, the wind farm is currently made up of three plants, the 20.7 MW Wigton I, which began operating in 2004 and Wigton II, an 18 MW extension facility that was commissioned in 2010 and Wigton III, a 24 MW facility commissioned in 2016.

As a clean energy facility, Wigton's operations aim to preserve the environment and reduce the effects of climate change.

What are the disadvantages of wind power?

- It is expensive to set up.
- It is weather dependent. Although wind energy can still be collected during less windy days, the efficiency of the system drops.
- Some people object to the appearance of wind farms
- Wind turbines use a lot of space.

Exercise

1. Explain what is meant by 'kinetic energy'.
2. Explain how wind turbines work, using your own words.
3. Summarise the strengths and disadvantages of wind power in two paragraphs.

Activity

Work in groups to identify an environmental problem in your community. Carry out a survey with local people to find out how they think it affects the environment and how they would like it to change in the future.

Share your findings to the rest of the class in the form of a presentation which should include data from your research.

Hydroelectric dams

Hydroelectric power is generated using flowing water to spin a turbine which turns a shaft that is connected to an electric generator. Often, hydroelectric dams are used to direct the water downward through the turbine in a way which can be controlled to maximise energy production.

There are many hydroelectric dams in Jamaica.

What are the advantages of hydroelectricity?

- Water is a renewable source of energy.
- Hydro can be a very predictable and consistent form of electricity which works well with other forms of renewable energy to match demand.
- Hydroelectric power can be turned on and off very easily to meet demand.
- Hydroelectric generators also have long lives when compared to other forms of electricity generation. A hydroelectric generator can still be in service after 50 to 100 years and requires very little labour with low maintenance costs which makes a lot of economic sense.

What are the disadvantages of hydroelectricity?

- You need to have very specific conditions and elements available in order to generate electricity using this type of system.
- The initial cost to develop and build a project can be very high. Large-scale hydroelectricity projects require significant investment in order to be built. Even then, there can be other permissions that are required which can slow can and even halt development.
- While certain methods like tidal power are extremely predictable, river run hydro power depends on a constant flow of water which relies on rainfall.

The expansion of the Maggoty Falls hydropower project began in 2012 and was completed in 2014. It was the first new hydro facility implemented in Jamaica in the past 30 years.

Reggae falls, St Thomas, Jamaica.

Great River, St James, Jamaica.

Exercise

1. Draw a diagram explaining how hydroelectric dams work, labelling all the different parts of the process.
2. Carry out research into a hydroelectricity plant nearby you. How much energy does it supply?
3. In your opinion are there more strengths or disadvantages of this green technology?

Key vocabulary

aviation
carbon emission
desalination
grid
hydroelectric power
kinetic energy
wind energy
wind farm

Green technology in businesses

We are learning to:

- identify organisations that are certified as being environmentally friendly, assess their operations, gather information from other sources and then develop guidelines for other organisations to become environmentally friendly.

One way to move from traditional forms of energy and technology to green or clean forms is to encourage businesses to develop alternative forms that can be sold or marketed to the public or other businesses, by showing their benefits. Jamaica has many excellent examples of entrepreneurial ideas and business in green technology, in an area which is growing all the time.

Case study

National Baking Company

Gary 'Butch' Hendrickson, current Chief Executive Officer, has recently introduced green technology into his business. These include:

- Solar-powered lamps are used in all parking lots.
- Cardboard boxes and recycled plastic trays are used for carrying bread and buns during deliveries.
- Propane replaced diesel fuel in all ovens, for cleaner emissions.
- National's delivery trucks use a combination of diesel and biodiesel. Recycled cooking oil from local restaurants and leftover vegetable oil used to prepare products such as peanuts and cashew are used to create biodiesel. The company has been recycling leftover cooking oil since 2007.
- National has its own fuelling station at the St Andrew location and processes the biodiesel on site.
- The fuelling system is equipped with sensors that indicate if there is a leak to prevent contamination of the underground water supply.
- All the plastic used for bread and roll bags are 100% biodegradable and are stamped with the biodegradable seal. These bags break down within nine months to five years after being discarded.

Did you know...?

The 'polluter pays' principle is the idea that those who produce pollution should bear the costs of managing it to prevent damage to human health or the environment.

Businesses are looking for ways to use green technologies.

Discussion

Which alternative source of energy is most suitable for Jamaica? Discuss the strengths and weaknesses of each, justifying your final decision.

Activity

Carry out research into a company that has developed its use of green technology to ensure that the environment is protected through its activities. Create a presentation, explaining the strengths and weaknesses of the company's environmental strategy.

Case study

The Jamaica Public Service (JPS) has commissioned the first desalination plant of its kind in the Caribbean at its Rockfort Power Station. It is predicted to save US$35 000 in annual operating costs, while reducing the water demand by 20% on the Hunts Bay aquifer.

This plan is linked to the company's 'Clean and Green' programme which is linked to their ambition to reduce any negative environmental impact from its day to day operation.

In the past, water was drawn from a well at another of the company's power stations – the Hunts Bay Plant. However, the desalination plant makes pure distilled water from saline (sea) water by removing the natural salts. The generator, which is the first of its kind in the Caribbean, produces over 30 000 litres of purified water daily.

"The implementation of this element of the JPS's Clean and Green programme demonstrates the company's commitment to being PowerSmart – by improving the efficiency of the company's operations through the use of technology while preserving the environment," the JPS said.

Source: adapted from Jamaica Gleaner website

Case study

Shelly-Ann is one of Jamaica's youngest female farmers and a Jamaica Broilers Group (JBG) champion farmer. She represented Jamaica as one of four speakers who shared their challenges and breakthroughs on a World Bank's panel discussion entitled: 'Future Harvest: Who Will Grow Tomorrow's Food?' — from using solar power to lower the costs of poultry farming in Jamaica to growing fresh greens for a small café in Kampala, Uganda as well as making farming viable for young women in remote Western Australia.

Source: adapted from forbes.com/sites/jamesellsmoor/2019/02/07/jamaican-renewable-energy-entrepreneurs/?sh=35f3b4fd6d4a

Activity

Using the case studies, identify the green practices and their outcomes. Use this information to develop a set of guidelines other organisations can use to develop and implement green technology in their operations.

Exercise

1. Explain how green businesses are different to other forms of business.
2. Why might products from green businesses appeal more to customers?
3. Carry out research into a green business in your area and write a report summarising the main benefits of that business.

Environmental issues in Jamaica

We are learning to:

- create and interpret statistical maps and diagrams showing environmental problems and solutions
- make predictions about the possible impact of a variety of continued and combined unsustainable practices on different types of environment and the health of different people.

There are several environmental problems in Jamaica. You have already encountered some of these in Grades 7 and 8. Here we look in more detail at these issues as well as looking at what is being done to address the problem.

The Jamaican Iguana, an endangered species.

Endangered species

Many Jamaican animals can be found in Jamaica and nowhere else in the world. We describe these as being **endemic**. Unfortunately, many of these animals are **endangered**, having been the victims of natural and human interference. These species include:

- The Jamaican Iguana, found only in the Hellshire Hills, is one of the two lizards in the world closest to extinction. It was classified by the International Union for the Conservation of Nature as critically endangered and was ranked among the world's 100 most endangered species in 2012.
- The endangered manatee enjoys shallow brackish coastal waters, especially where rivers flow into the sea, providing a source of drinking water. These large gentle creatures, often known locally as sea cows can weigh 1000 lbs and measure one to four meters in length. Small in number, they are protected by law and closely monitored.
- The sea turtle is an endangered species in Jamaica. The leatherback sea turtle comes ashore on Jamaica's north coast to the east of Ocho Rios in order to lay their eggs.
- The Jamaican Boa is more commonly called the yellow snake, or sometimes called 'Nanka'. It is endemic to Jamaica and is another endangered species.

The manatee is an endangered species.

Sea turtles, an endangered species.

What are the causes of declining species?

- Wildlife exploitation: Food, clothing, medicine, souvenirs, pets, and building supplies are just some of the uses that have led people to rely on wildlife. We overfish rivers and oceans and poach endangered animals.

The Jamaican Boa, an endangered species.

- Human land use competing for space with wildlife: habitat degradation and change have resulted in a 31.4% loss of wildlife. This includes deforestation.
- Pollution: Waterways are polluted with runoff from manufacturing facilities, factory farms, and the gas and oil that collects on roadways. Mining practices discard unusable heavy metals and minerals into groundwater sources. Air is polluted by the fumes from traffic and burning fossil fuels. Pesticides sprayed onto crops inadvertently kill other plant species. Garbage and litter fills the land with non-biodegradable plastics that are consumed by animals both on land and in sea.
- Invasive species: Humans increased movement around the world has allowed for the spread of non-native plants and animals into new areas. Non-native wildlife is referred to as invasive species and are responsible for the loss of 5.1% of all wildlife and for threatening 42% of all endangered species. Invasive species move into an area and quickly reproduce and spread. They outnumber native species, preying on them and competing with them for food. This decreases the biodiversity and changes the structure of the ecosystem.

What are the solutions to the loss of biodiversity?

- Educating the public to work at a local level to promote small-scale conservation efforts.
- Business owners need to be held accountable for the environmental degradation that their work causes and forced to reduce and offset this destruction.
- Policy makers at an international level need to tackle wildlife trade and poaching concerns. National governments should focus on converting their nations to renewable energy sources.
- Individually people need to focus on reducing, reusing, and recycling products. This problem is large, it cannot be fixed by one person. Action is necessary across boundaries and cultures.

The mongoose has been linked to one of the causes of extinction in five endemic species: a lizard, a snake, two species of birds and a rodent.

Did you know...?

Globally, biodiversity has declined by more than a quarter in the last 35 years. The Living Planet Index (LPI) shows a decline of 52% between 1970 and 2010.

Research

Carry out research into the endangered birds of Jamaica. Focus on three species, explaining how many are left, how they are protected and how they became endangered.

Exercice

1. Name four endangered species.
2. Explain what is meant by 'biodiversity'.
3. Write a short essay on the causes of species becoming endangered.

Key vocabulary

endangered

endemic

Deforestation

We are learning to:

- understand the importance of forests to our environment
- understand the reasons for deforestation and its effects
- identify strategies that are in place to prevent deforestation.

According to NEPA, in their State of the Environment Report 2013 deforestation, the removal of trees and forests, is a serious problem in Jamaica. The World Wildlife Fund states that deforestation is a leading environmental concern in Jamaica.

Why are forests important?

Forests are made up of natural ecosystems which carry out many important functions. These include:

- Forests act as a watershed. Rainfall is captured and channelled underground into aquifers, which then appear as springs and rivers. If deforestation occurs, the result will be reduced humidity and a generally hotter climate, lower rainfall, less productive or dry wells, rivers having reduced flow or drying up, as well as soil erosion that results from rainfall washing away topsoil. Reduced groundwater and surface water in turn lead to less water available for agricultural, industrial, or domestic use, which may lead to a national crisis. Water shortages can be a threat to public health and can slow down or even reverse economic growth.
- Forests provide a home to animal and plant biodiversity, including birds, reptiles and insects.
- Trees and forests produce oxygen, without which human animals cannot survive.
- Forests extract carbon dioxide (a greenhouse gas causing global warming) – from the air.
- Forests are an important source of firewood and charcoal, timber for furniture and construction.

Deforestation is a really important issue which needs careful management in Jamaica.

Why deforestation is occurring?

In Jamaica the main reasons for deforestation are:

1. **Bauxite mining**
   Bauxite is extracted by open cast mining, which requires the complete removal of vegetation and topsoil. Bauxite mining also leads to deforestation through the opening of access roads into forests. Once access roads are built, loggers, coal burners and yam stick traders move in, taking the trees in and around the designated mining areas.
2. **Clearing land for new buildings and tourism**
   As the population grows, the economy has also grown. Tourism has become a major part of the Jamaican national income. As a result, tourist resorts and infrastructure such as roads have been built which result in deforestation.

3. **Cultivation**
   As the population grows, so does pressure on the land to produce foods and goods for locals and for export. This includes farming of coffee, sugar, bananas and other products which involves deforestation.

4. **Hurricanes**
   In 1988 Hurricane Gilbert, (the worst hurricane in Jamaica since 1951) occurred, causing much damage to trees and forests. The hurricane led to some 32.4 inches of rain falling in the mountainous interior of the island, resulting in wide-scale flash flooding, ripping many trees out by their roots.

Cultivated land.

Flooding and damage caused by Hurricane Gilbert.

What are the effects of deforestation?

According to the WWF, deforestation causes 'massive soil erosion and the quality of the land deteriorates rapidly. Water-courses leading from the mountains become heavily laden with sediment and water flows decrease and become more erratic. This results in water shortages alternating with floods at lower altitudes. Until recently, interior forests were very inaccessible, however, continued road construction into these areas will inevitably lead to increased deforestation and selective cutting'.

Source: World Wildlife Fund website

What strategies are in place to prevent deforestation?

In order to respond to these problems, in 2010, the Forestry Department published its forest-management plan: Strategic Forest Management Plan 2010–2014. One of their aims was to 'maintain and restore forest cover'. However, according to The National Forest Management plan, the reforestation targets were not achieved and strategies to reduce the effects of climate change were not introduced.

Source: The University of the West Indies website

Did you know...?

Forest and woodland in Jamaica decreased 7% annually between 1990 and 1995.

More recently, The Forest Policy for Jamaica (2015), has tried to address the challenge of reducing deforestation. This policy was designed to work alongside the national sustainable development goals of Vision 2030 Jamaica and attempts to continue successful aspects of the Strategic Forest Management Plan 2010–2015. At the centre of the 2015 Forest Policy is a commitment to encourage and involve the Jamaican people in the protection, conservation and management of Jamaica's forests.

Exercise

1. Name three reasons for deforestation.
2. Explain why forests are so important.
3. Write a paragraph explaining how deforestation affects Jamaicans.

Pollution and land degradation

We are learning to:

- identify the primary sources of pollution in Jamaica
- understand the effects of pollution in our country
- define land degradation, understand the causes and consequences, and the ways in which it can be slowed or reversed.

According to The National Report on Integrating the Management of Watersheds and Costal Areas in Jamaica (2001), pollution is a major environmental issue. Pollution is the introduction of harmful materials into the environment.

What are the primary sources of pollution in Jamaica?

- Sewage effluent – disposed of in large absorption pits without septic tanks, or latrines. Pollution problems occur when these absorption pits are located close to river systems or shallow aquifers which feed nearby river flows. Poorly situated pit latrines can also be a source of pollution. In some areas of Jamaica, there are pit latrines located at river heads and springs, which feed major river systems, which are major sources of drinking water to several communities. Sometimes sewage effluent is not absorbed by the earth and instead flows laterally towards a river or spring system causing contamination.
- Industrial waste – when stored in unlined holding ponds, can lead to seepage into limestone rocks, which often leads to contamination of groundwater.
- Solid waste – if not collected this presents problems, for example, if garbage is thrown in natural and man-made gullies, and along riverbanks. The result is the pollution of rivers, streams and ultimately the coastal waters into which these rivers drain.
- Urban and agricultural runoff – often contains elevated levels of nutrients from fertilisers and other agricultural chemicals applied to the fields. These chemicals are carried with rainfall runoff into rivers and streams, reservoirs and coastal waters, polluting water bodies and changing water based habitats.

Waste water.

Industrial waste.

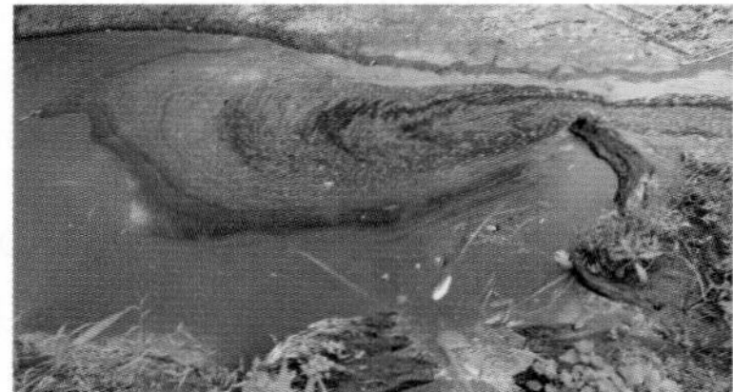

Blue-green algae grows due to agricultural runoff.

What are the effects of pollution in Jamaica?

- Drinking water becomes contaminated or high in pollutants.
- Wildlife habitats are affected, leading to a change in animals that can live in the new habitat or the death or reduction of animals or plants living in that habitat.

Did you know...?

There are seven different types of pollution. These include air, water, land, radioactive, thermal, light, and sound pollution.

- Swimming and fishing activities become reduced as water contains contaminants that make the water dangerous or unpleasant.
- Long-term exposure to air pollution, can lead to chronic respiratory disease, lung cancer and other diseases.
- Toxic chemicals that accumulate in animals and fish can make some species unsafe to eat.
- Pollution can lead to a lack of clean water and sanitation, placing people at risk of contracting deadly diseases.

Case study

A marine scientist has warned that the Kingston Harbour has high levels of contamination that could pose serious health risks for people who visit popular parts of the coastline for recreational swimming and fishing. The level of pollution from faeces and harmful chemicals is so high that Professor Mona Webber, director of marine sciences at The University of the West Indies (UWI), says the water should not come in contact with human skin. Other Marine ecologists have reported that that marine life in Kingston Harbour has long been ingesting heavy metals resulting from industrial run-off.

Source: adapted from Jamaica Gleaner website

Fishing in Kingston Harbour.

Exercise

1. Explain what 'pollution' means in your own words.
2. Identify the main causes of pollution.
3. Produce a poster highlighting the main effects of pollution on people's lives in Jamaica.

Activity

In groups, identify one example of an environmental problem from the categories you have studied so far. Create a video to depict the environmental problem and to suggest how green technology can provide a sustainable solution.

Land Degradation

Land degradation is a process where the value of the land is affected by a combination of manmade processes acting upon the land. This is usually seen as a change or reduction in quality of the land.

According to the World Health Organization, land degradation has accelerated during the past two centuries due to increasing and combined pressures of agricultural and livestock production (over-cultivation and overgrazing), urbanisation, deforestation and extreme weather events such as droughts and coastal surges.

What causes land degradation?

The factors **responsible** for degradation of land include:

Causes

Physical causes include water shortages as a result of drought. This can lead to a drop in the water table meaning many plants die as their roots cannot reach the water. This leads to desertification (where fertile soil turns into desert land) as roots can no longer anchor the soil which in turn is easily blown away. Flash floods also wash away the exposed top soil.

Human causes include population growth, which in turn means an increased demand for food. This results in farming on land that may not be as fertile and also farmers decreasing the time they rest the soil between crops. This means the land does not have time to recover or regenerate. Increased demand for firewood also leads to deforestation.

Frequent water shortages lead to the need for more wells, meaning the water table falls. Overgrazing destroys the vegetation cover, leading to soil erosion and poor irrigation methods lead to the evaporation of stagnant water, leaving behind a salty infertile cruSt

What are the consequences of land degradation?

Environmental – as vegetation dies or is removed the roots are no longer able to bind the soil together and the soil becomes at risk of wind erosion. The fertile topsoil is then easily blown away. The land becomes infertile, turning to desert, a process known as desertification.

Social – people are unable to farm the land or live in particular areas, and are then forced to migrate, with many people - young men in particular, leaving to work in cities and towns, placing more pressure on already limited urban resources. Land disputes can erupt between herdsmen and farmers. Food shortages may then result.

Economic – as the land becomes less fertile, farm income decreases, which leads to widespread poverty and more need to rely on overseas aid.

How can land degradation be reversed or slowed?

Land degradation requires careful management. Strategies to prevent or reverse land degradation may include the following:

- restore natural vegetation cover, over time
- improve and increase small-scale irrigation projects
- plant drought resistant shrubs and grasses to help bind the soil and prevent further soil erosion
- plant more trees, and a variety of tree species
- control grazing of animals
- build more dams
- practise crop rotation to allow soil to recover.

Controlled animal grazing can help reduce land degradation.

Case study

Water supply for the 660 000-plus people in the Kingston Metropolitan Area, served in part by Hope River in St Andrew and Yallahs River in St Thomas, should improve over the next five years. The two rivers provide 42% of the water for the region, but not unlike several of the country's 26 watersheds, they are in a state of severe degradation and if left unchecked, could result in more severe water restrictions than were experienced during last year's long dry spell.

In a move to remedy the situation, Government, with support from the Inter-American Bank and the Global Environment Facility, on Monday launched the Integrated Management of the Yallahs and Hope River Watershed Management Areas project which is expected to improve the amount and quality of the water supply in both watersheds. A spokesperson for the project stated: "As we seek to provide food and housing, our habitats have become threatened by deforestation and degradation and this has decreased the productivity of our soil due to, in some instances, improper agricultural practices and when you have degradation of the land, degradation of the water resources is going to follow."

Referring to data collected under the project preparation phase, the environment minister said soil erosion, waste water disposal and the use of chemicals in hillside coffee farming were among the major causes of land degradation.

Source: adapted from Jamaica Observer website

Project

Download some images from the internet or use your smart phone to capture human activities showing production and consumption. Then use the pamphlet or brochure feature on your device or, Canva, to create an information brochure for sharing digitally with your friends, family and community members.

The brochure should distinguish between the sustainable and unsustainable practices and provide some guidelines about how to reduce or halt unsustainable practices and how to improve on the sustainable ones.

Exercise

1. What is 'land degradation'?
2. Why has land degradation increased in the past century?
3. Create a leaflet describing the main ways to slow or reverse land degradation.

Key vocabulary

responsible

Sea levels rising

We are learning to:

- create and interpret statistical maps and diagrams showing environmental problems and solutions
- make predictions about the possible impact of a variety of continued and combined unsustainable practices on different types of environment and the health of different people.

Global sea levels have been rising over the past century, and the rates have increased in recent decades. The two major causes of global sea level rise are **thermal expansion** caused by warming of the ocean (since water expands as it warms) and increased melting of land-based ice, such as glaciers and ice sheets. Global warming is set to increase over coming years, so this is a problem that is becoming more urgent.

Tide gauge records all over the world show this trend. The rate of rise varies slightly from place to place due to the differing reactions of the adjacent landmasses, but in this part of the world, it averages about 2 millimetres annually.

What are the effects of water levels rising in Jamaica?

- Rising sea levels are also a result of rising sea temperatures. Increasing ocean temperatures affect marine species and ecosystems. Rising temperatures cause the loss of breeding grounds for marine fish and mammals.
- Rising sea temperatures has also led to **coral bleaching**. Coral bleaching occurs when **coral polyps** expel **algae** that live inside their tissues.
- After a series of natural and manmade disasters in the 1980s and 1990s, Jamaica lost 85% of its coral reefs and fish catches hugely declined. Many scientists thought the reefs had been permanently lost but today the corals and tropical fish are slowly reappearing, thanks to the work of local and national projects.
- One effect of water levels rising is loss of beaches and properties along the coaSt Some examples of affected communities include Alligator Pond, Hellshire and Negril.

Coral Bleaching leads to the death of some coral.

A diagram showing sea levels rising over time.

Exercise

1. Explain the reason why sea levels are rising, using your own words.
2. What is 'coral bleaching'?
3. Explain in your own words the effects of sea levels rising.

Case study

Ridge to Reef Watershed Project

The Ridge to Reef Watershed Project (R2RW) was a five-year, $8 million initiative undertaken by the Government of Jamaica's National Environment and Planning Agency (NEPA) and the United States Agency for International Development. The Project aimed to address the degradation of **watersheds** (an area or ridge of land that separates waters flowing to different rivers or seas) in Jamaica by improving and sustaining the natural resources in targeted watershed areas that are both environmentally and economically significant. R2RW had three strategies:

1. Working with local-level organisations to promote sustainable environmental management practices
2. Identifying and supporting solutions that encourage better enforcement of existing environmental regulations and policy
3. Enhancing the Jamaican government agencies and private-sector and public organisations to create and manage watershed programs in Jamaica.

NEPA projects aim to address environmental projects.

Jamaican coral reefs are protected by the work of the Ridge to Reef Project.

What are the solutions to rising water levels?

- National and international strategies such as Ridge to Reef
- Choosing more sustainable renewable energy sources rather than relying on fossil fuels
- A reduction in the production of carbon dioxide, reducing pollution and rising temperatures
- You can help slow global warming and ocean acidification by reducing your **carbon footprint**; the amount of carbon dioxide released as you go about your daily activities. Making little changes in the way we live can go a long way to reducing energy use and carbon emissions.

REDUCE YOUR CARBON FOOTPRINT

Reducing our carbon footprint helps tackle rising water levels.

Exercise

1. Explain what a 'watershed' is.
2. What did the Ridge to Reef project aim to do?
3. How are rising pollution levels linked to rising sea levels?

Key vocabulary

algae
carbon footprint
coral bleaching
coral polyps
thermal expansion
watershed

Questions

See how well you have understood the topics in this unit.

1. Explain what is meant by the following:
   a) preservation
   b) conservation
   c) sustainability.
2. Explain why fossil fuels are more damaging than alternative fuels for the environment.
3. Write a paragraph explaining how recycling helps the environment.
4. Complete the following diagram by adding the correct labels.

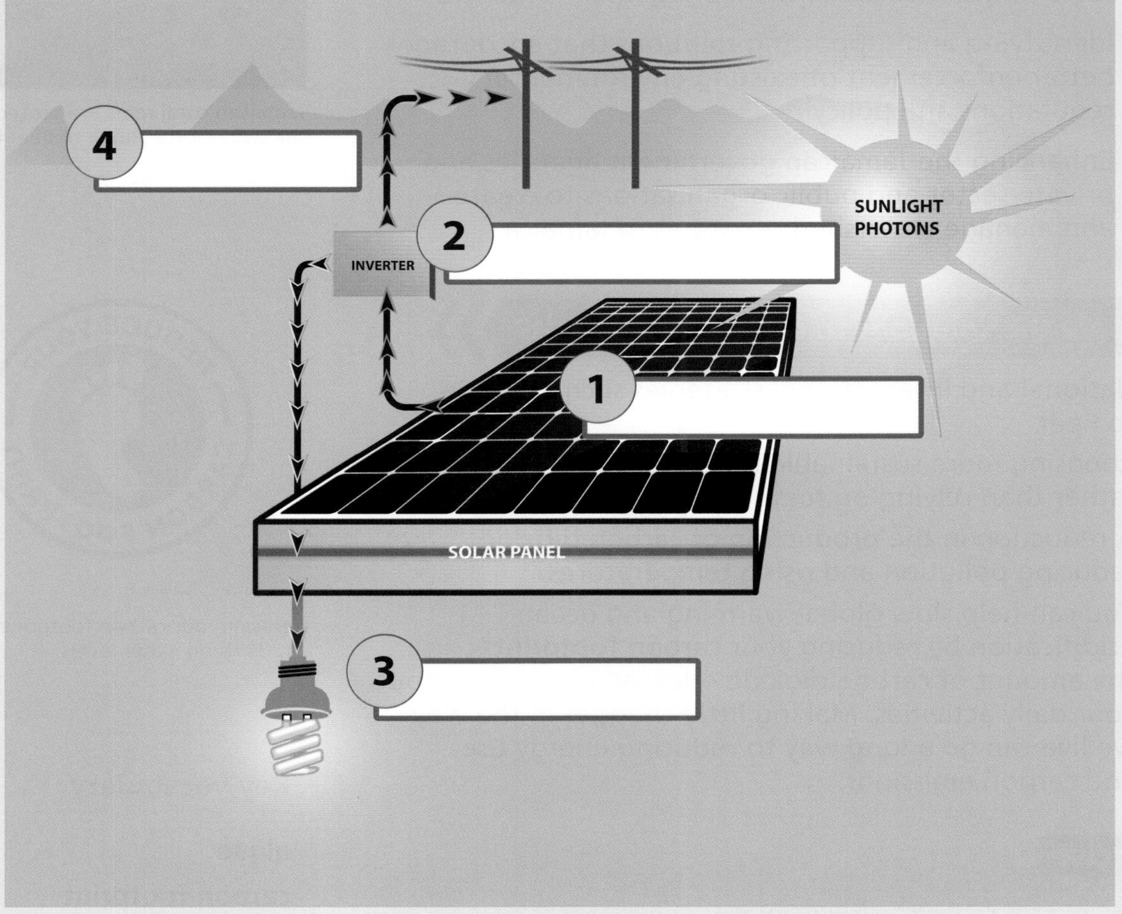

5. Decide which alternative source of energy is most useful, explaining why.
6. What are the main environmental issues facing Jamaica?
7. Write a list of endangered species in Jamaica, suggesting reasons why they have become endangered in recent years.
8. Do you think the 'polluter pays' principal works? Explain your answer.
9. Produce a poster explaining the work the government does to protect the environment. Explain the role of each agency.
10. Using your own words, define the following:
    - **a)** carbon emissions
    - **b)** sustainable development
    - **c)** green technology
    - **d)** invasive species.

Grade 9 Unit 7 Summary

Green technology in Jamaica

In this chapter, you have learned about:

- The importance of preservation, conservation and sustainability
- The meaning and goals of green technology
- Recycling in Jamaica and the efforts to increase it
- How green technology can be used to provide clean water for citizens
- Ways in which green technology and sustainable practices can reduce carbon emissions
- Using green technology to conserve energy
- How solar power works and the factors that hinder its extensive use
- The green technology of wind power and the factors that prevent its widespread use
- What hydroelectric dams are, and their advantages and disadvantages
- The use of green technology in businesses in Jamaica.

Environmental issues

In this chapter, you have learned about:

- Environmental issues such as endangered species and declining species in Jamaica
- Possible solutions to the loss of biodiversity in Jamaica
- The importance of forests to the human and physical environment
- The factors that cause deforestation
- The effects of deforestation and the implementation of strategies to prevent further damage.

Pollution and land degradation

In this chapter, you have learned about:

- The primary sources of pollution in Jamaica and their effects
- What the causes and consequences of land degradation are
- How land degradation can be slowed or reversed
- The effects of rising water levels in Jamaica
- What the solutions to rising water levels are.

Checking your progress

To make good progress in understanding environmental problems and green solutions, check that you understand these ideas.

- [ ] Explain and use correctly the term *sustainable development*.
- [ ] Describe how Green Technology works.
- [ ] Explain the difference between sustainable and unsustainable development.

- [ ] Explain and use correctly the terms *pollution* and *carbon emissions*.
- [ ] Name three types of alternative energy.
- [ ] Explain the strategies to rebuild biodiversity.

- [ ] Explain and use correctly the terms *preservation* and *conservation*.
- [ ] Name three types of green technology.
- [ ] Explain how green technology is being used.

- [ ] Explain and use correctly the term *invasive species*.
- [ ] Describe sea level rise.
- [ ] Explain the effects of land degradation.

Unit 8: Individuals in the Workplace

Objectives: You will be able to:

Why people work and types of job

- state reasons why people work
- explore the types of jobs that are available in Jamaica
- identify jobs which no longer exist
- explore types of jobs in the hotel industry in Jamaica.

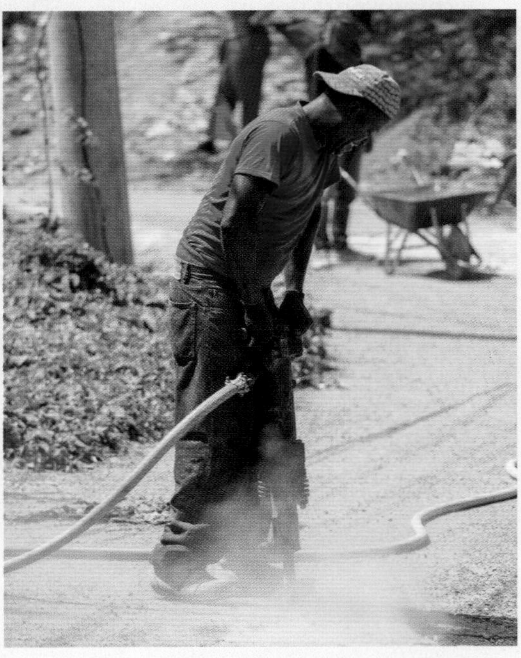

Personal development and choosing a career

- recognise the skills and knowledge needed to pursue specific careers
- writing a résumé, cover letter and preparing for an interview.

Issues and problems in the workplace

- identify issues employers and employees may face in the workplace
- identify what constitutes sexual harassment
- discuss how employees and employers should handle workplace problems.

Work ethics

- examine expected work ethics at places of work
- assess the importance of having rights and protective laws for workers.

Role of the trade unions

- examine the role of the trade unions in Jamaica.

The world of work

We are learning to:

- define relevant terms and concepts: employment, career, occupation, employer, employee, lifelong learning, entrepreneurship.

Introduction to the world of work

'What do you want to do when you grow up?' is a question many children hear. As you grow into a young adult, you may also be asking yourself: What are my passions and interests? How do I like spending my time? What are my talents and abilities? What would I like to achieve in my future?

A career can be defined as an **occupation** undertaken for a significant period of a person's life.

A profession is a paid occupation, one that usually means having gained particular qualifications.

Types of work

The world of work has changed dramatically since the twentieth century. The types of **employment** available have changed. People have also changed how they work.

You have already learned about workers in the **primary**, **secondary** and **tertiary** industries. Remember, primary workers extract or harvest resources, for example farmers, fishermen, miners. Secondary workers process or manufacture products, such as factory workers or builders. Tertiary workers provide services, like doctors, teachers or advertisers.

Construction worker carrying out an inspection.

In the past, there were fewer **career** possibilities. The opportunity to study for a professional occupation did exist, for example as a doctor/nurse, lawyer, accountant, architect or teacher. Although these occupations are still available now, there is greater **choice** open to young people.

The development of technology has created many new **jobs** – from computer programmers, software developers and technicians, to people who run successful businesses using digital technology, social media and the internet.

Exercise

1. **a)** Look at the photos on these pages. Find other pictures in magazines of people doing different jobs.

   b) Describe what you can see in each picture and the jobs that these people do. Use the terms in the key vocabulary box.
2. In your own words, define career.
3. Which careers do you see as traditional occupations? Which would you describe as more modern ones?

Architects discussing a plan in the office.

How people work

In the past, many people stayed in a single career for most of their lifetime. A person might get their first job with an employer and gradually work their way up in the company over many years. Today, this is very different.

Employment is the state of having paid work to do. The average employee stays in the same job for around three to five years. People have also started to value **lifelong learning**. They may continue education, training and acquiring new skills throughout their lives, which can lead to a change in career.

Some people are **self-employed** and they hire out their time in return for payment, for example in construction or retail, while some people become **entrepreneurs**.

Entrepreneurs are people who have started up their own business – a clothes shop or an internet business, perhaps – and have taken on the challenge of building a business.

Activity

Look at this population distribution. Why might this lead to a shortage of jobs?

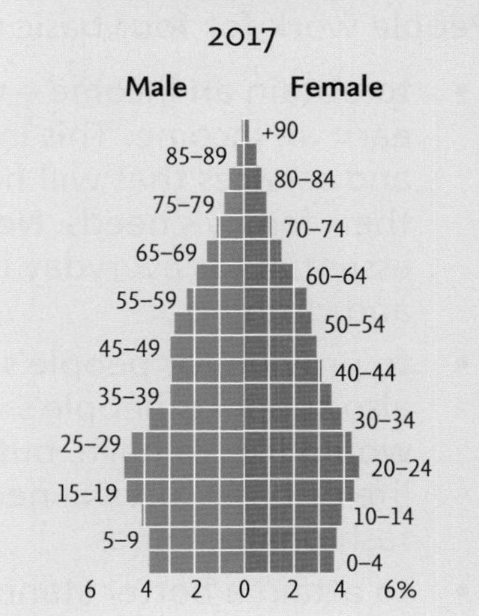

Challenges

The 21st century workplace also brings its own challenges. In some industries, new technologies can replace particular job roles. This can cause **unemployment**.

People also live longer today than in the past, meaning that workers need to save more money for their retirement. A person who retires at age 65 may live for another 30 years or more, and will need to meet their needs when retired.

Exercise

4 What difference do you understand between the words occupation and career? If necessary, use a dictionary to help you come up with definitions.

5 In your own words, define the terms 'employer', 'employee', 'self-employed' and 'entrepreneur'.

6 What challenges exist for 21st century workers?

7 What do you understand by the term lifelong learning?

8 Study the employment listings in your local newspaper. What does this tell you about the jobs that are available in your local area? Write a paragraph explaining which of these jobs you would like to do, and why.

Key vocabulary

career
choice
employment
entrepreneur
job
lifelong learning
occupation
primary industry
secondary industry
self-employed
tertiary industry
unemployment

Why people work

We are learning to:

- state reasons why people work.

Reasons why people work

Why do people spend so much time working? Why do we spend so much time thinking and talking about what work we will do after we have left school?

People work for four basic reasons:

- to obtain an income – working in a job allows people to earn an income. This in turn allows them to buy goods and services that will help themselves and provide for their family's needs. **Needs** are those things that are essential for everyday living, such as food, water, shelter and clothing
- to provide for people's **wants** – income from work also supports people's wants – items that a person would like to have, but are not essential for everyday life or basic survival needs, such as a cell phone or fashionable shoes
- to attain a better standard of living – income that helps to provide for our needs and wants also helps to improve our standard of living. The more income someone has, the more opportunities they have to improve their own and their family's lives
- to use our skills and **qualifications** – being a productive part of the wider economy provides **self-esteem** for the individual, as well as a sense of feeling fulfilled and reaching their potential by using their skills, knowledge and creativity.

One other very important reason why people work is to contribute to the overall economy. They are contributing to society by applying their skills and knowledge to their job; and by paying tax they contribute money, which helps to provide goods and services the whole community needs.

Exercise

1. Why does earning more income help to improve someone's standard of living?
2. Explain the difference between a need and a want.
3. Write 150 words on the topic 'Why do people work?'

Discussion

In groups, discuss the four reasons why people work. Can you think of any others? Of the reasons given, which do you think are the most important?

Project

In groups, create a questionnaire asking people why they work. Choose five questions for your questionnaire, for example:

- What is your job?
- Why did you choose your job?
- Did you need qualifications to get your job?

When you have agreed on your questions, ask your parents, neighbours and teachers. See if you can find common reasons or a pattern to their answers. Write a paragraph outlining your findings, then share with the class.

Benefits of work

Look at the diagram below, and read some of the reasons that people give to explain why they work. Then answer the questions.

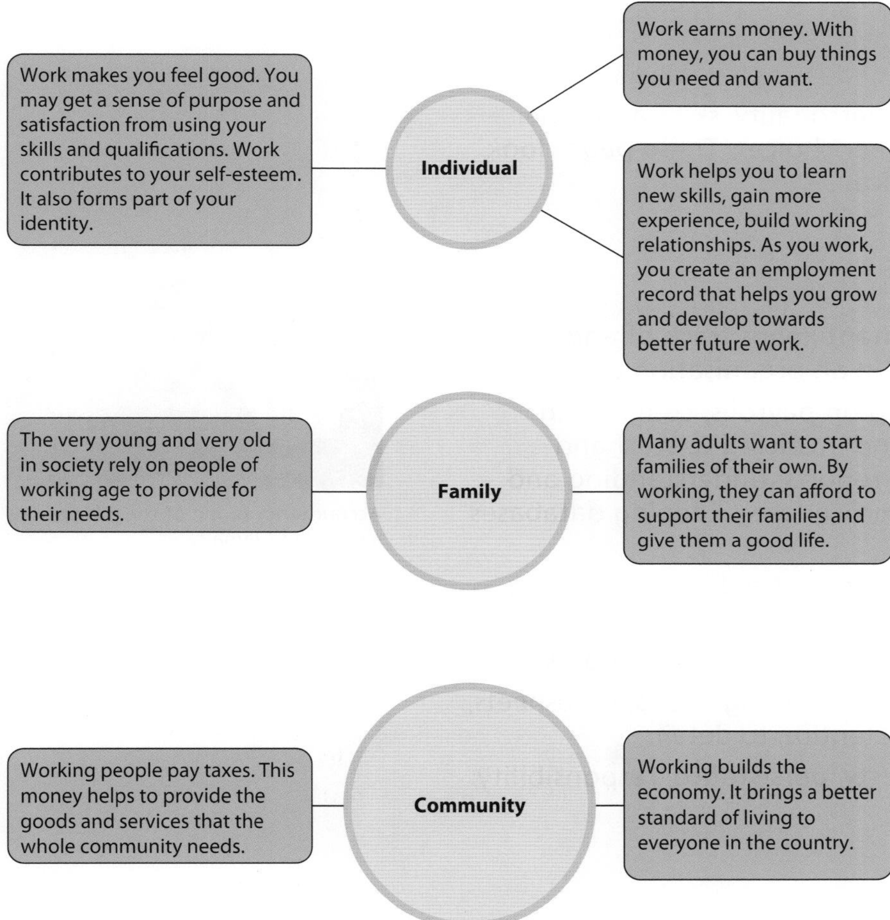

Individual
Work makes you feel good. You may get a sense of purpose and satisfaction from using your skills and qualifications. Work contributes to your self-esteem. It also forms part of your identity.
Work earns money. With money, you can buy things you need and want.
Work helps you to learn new skills, gain more experience, build working relationships. As you work, you create an employment record that helps you grow and develop towards better future work.
Family
The very young and very old in society rely on people of working age to provide for their needs.
Many adults want to start families of their own. By working, they can afford to support their families and give them a good life.
Community
Working people pay taxes. This money helps to provide the goods and services that the whole community needs.
Working builds the economy. It brings a better standard of living to everyone in the country.

Exercise

4. Name the three sectors of society that benefit from people working.
5. Why does working make a person feel good?
6. Why do you think working contributes to a person's self-esteem?
7. Which age groups in a family rely on other members of the family for income?
8. How does paying taxes contribute to the wider society?

Key vocabulary

needs
qualification
self-esteem
wants

Types of jobs

We are learning to:

- explore the types of jobs that are available in Jamaica
- identify jobs which no longer exist.

Career options

We have looked at how our personality, skills and other factors can influence our career choices. These pages look at some job options in Jamaica.

Job profile

Accountant

Job description: An **accountant** keeps track of and records the flow of money in an organisation or business.

Work may include: Working on payrolls, completing audits; explaining billing and invoicing to staff and clients; budgeting; writing reports; understanding and implementing accounting procedures; keeping databases and records in order.

Qualifications: Business degree; specialised accounting certificate.

Interests: Finances, business, working with numbers.

Skills needed: Computer skills, working with spreadsheets, mathematical skills, logic, attention to detail.

Values and attitudes: Honesty, **persistence**, responsibility.

Accountancy is one of the job options available in Jamaica.

Job profile

Insurance agent

Job description: An **insurance agent** sells **insurance policies** for an insurance company.

Work may include: Understanding and explaining policies; identifying and contacting new clients; helping clients choose policies that suit them; analysing clients' existing policies in order to advise about possible changes; keeping records and handling renewals of policies; helping clients settle claims.

Qualifications: High school diploma; additional qualifications such as business courses are optional. Agents may have to take courses to keep up to date with tax laws and regulations.

Skills needed: Communication skills; interest in others.

Values and attitudes: Planning ahead; honesty; empathy; good service skills.

Job profile

Teacher

Job description: A teacher works with students, presenting classes, lectures and assignments, and helping students to develop skills and knowledge.

Work may include: Preparing and presenting lessons, lectures and assignments; grading tests; preparing assessments; keeping records; counselling students and parents; enforcing rules; accompanying classes on outings or trips.

Qualifications: Teaching degree or diploma.

Skills needed: Communication skills, listening skills, ability to work with people; sensitivity to feelings; interest in specific subjects and flexibility.

Values and attitudes: Lifelong learning, reflection, patience, appreciation, service, responsibility, curiosity and empathy.

A teacher works with students, just like yourself.

Job profile

Data analyst

Job description: A Data Analyst is someone who studies information using IT-based data analysis tools.

Work may include: Drawing information from raw data to help their employers or clients make important decisions by identifying various facts and trends. Typical duties include: using advanced computerised models to extract the data needed.

Qualifications: High school diploma, mathematics qualifications or programming qualifications at degree level.

Interests: Problem solving, an interest in statistical data, programming.

Skills needed: The ability to work to deadlines, a methodological approach, accuracy and attention to detail, confidence with computer software and programming, a good knowledge of statistics.

Values and attitudes: Honesty, persistence, teamworking skills.

Job profile

Web designer

Job description: A web designer is responsible for creating the design and layout of a website or web pages.

Work may include: creating webpage designs, meeting with clients to discuss requirements, demonstrating web pages and receiving feedback, developing skills and expertise in programming.

Qualifications: High school diploma and relevant computer skill training and on the job training.

Skills needed: Communication skills; an ability to realise the needs of the client. Good networking social skills, being friendly, organised and calm under pressure.

Values and attitudes: Hard working, good listening skills, being adaptable and flexible.

Job profile

Business Process Outsourcer

Job description: A Business Process Outsourcer (BPO) is responsible for the process of contracting business functions to parties outside the company.

Work may include: Helping businesses to run more efficiently by finding specialists to take particular tasks outside the main company. For example, working in a call centre involves working as a vocal communication channel that customers use to report requests or complaints to a business.

Qualifications: High school diploma; BPO training course.

Skills needed: Communication skills; interest in others.

Values and attitudes: Planning ahead; honesty; **empathy**; good service skills.

Exercise

Work in groups. Choose one of the occupations shown on these pages.

1. Read through the information with your group.
2. Read through the values and attitudes under each career. Explain what you understand by each term and why it might be important for that job.
   - **a)** Discuss the job description. Does it sound accurate to you? What else might you include in this job description?
   - **b)** What hours does this occupation involve: ordinary office hours, or does it involve after-hours work? Are there any advantages or disadvantages to the hours?
   - **c)** Brainstorm any other skills or interests that might draw someone to this occupation.
   - **d)** Would this job appeal to you? Why, or why not?
3. Choose another job that interests you. Write up a similar fact file, giving a brief job description, a list of what the work may include, and necessary qualifications and skills. You may do research on the internet or interview adults in your community to find the information you need.

Key vocabulary

accountant
empathy
insurance agent
insurance policy
persistence

Which jobs no longer exist due to developments in technology?

Today, technological advances have meant that some jobs are obsolete, or no longer needed. These include:

Switchboard operator

Switchboard operators were an essential part of a telephone network's operation before modern technology made them unnecessary. They would connect short- and long-distance calls among other things that are now done digitally.

Switchboard operators used to be essential.

Lamp lighter

Today we don't give much thought to streetlights being turned on/off, but before electricity was commonplace, lamplighters were in charge of lighting and extinguishing street lamps in the morning and evenings.

A lamplighter at work.

Computer

"Computer" used to be somebody's title. Before electronics were developed, these workers, who were usually women, would convert figures by hand; they literally computed. They worked in a variety of fields until they were replaced in offices by what we know today as computers, beginning as early as the 1970s.

Daguerreotypist

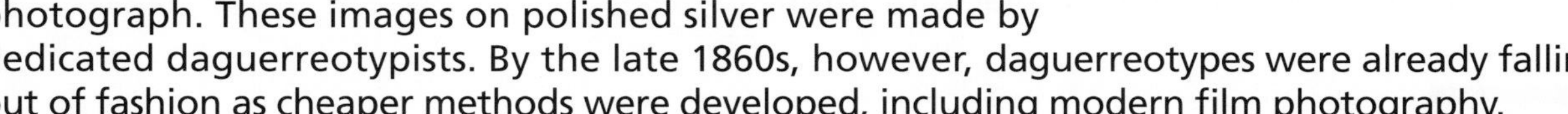

Before we had digital photography or even negatives, we had daguerreotypes, the earliest kind of publicly available photograph. These images on polished silver were made by dedicated daguerreotypists. By the late 1860s, however, daguerreotypes were already falling out of fashion as cheaper methods were developed, including modern film photography.

Quarryman

A quarryman would extract stone from the earth that may be used for various construction purposes, like a kitchen counter.

The job was often dangerous, involving intense manual labour and occasional maiming or death due to accidents like runaway railway wagons or falling stone.

Exercise

4. What does it mean when a job has become 'obsolete'?
5. Provide two more examples of jobs that no longer exist today due to increasing technology.
6. Write a paragraph explaining how technology will replace currently existing jobs in the future, giving examples.

Discussion

What are the advantages and disadvantages of technology replacing particular roles or jobs in society? Discuss.

The hotel industry

We are learning to:

- explore the types of jobs that are available in the hotel industry in Jamaica.

One of the biggest industries in Jamaica is the hotel industry. There are a wide range of career opportunities in this industry:

- A hotelier (or hotel manager) supervises and manages the running of a hotel.
- In bigger hotels, there are department **managers** in charge of different divisions, such as front desk, reservations, sales and marketing, conventions, restaurants, human resources, entertainment and accounts.
- An **events planner** organises events such as weddings, conferences, parties and other functions.
- **Marketing staff** find ways to advertise and promote the business.
- The housekeeping staff keep all areas of the hotel clean, tidy and fresh, and may also be responsible for providing services such as washing, sourcing equipment that guests need and maintenance.
- The reception staff welcome new guests, give advice and information and assist with requests and enquiries.
- The kitchen staff may include chefs, bar staff, sommeliers, waiters and cleaning staff.
- Tour guides arrange tours to places of interest.

The hotel industry is one of the biggest industries in Jamaica.

Activity

As a class, make a list of the careers or jobs held by your parents or relatives. Organise a 'work-shadow day', when you can spend a day at a parent's or relative's workplace. Report back on your work-shadow day with a short oral presentation to the class.

Exercise

1. The first members of staff you meet at the front desk of a hotel are the:
   - **a)** reception staff
   - **b)** marketing staff
   - **c)** housekeeping staff.
2. The number of staff in a large hotel resort is likely to be:
   - **a)** about 10 people
   - **b)** about 20 people
   - **c)** more than 100 people.

Case study

Caterer

Read this interview with Philip, whose job is as a caterer. Then answer the questions below.

Q: What does a caterer do?

A: I meet with clients to work out what they need for their event. We work out a menu and a budget, then arrange to prepare, cook and deliver the food for the event.

Q: How did you start out?

A: I did a full-time course at the HEART College of Hospitality Training in Runaway Bay, St Ann. As a student, I had some part-time work helping in restaurant kitchens. After my diploma, I worked as a chef at a hotel for two years.

Q: Why did you become a caterer?

A: I wanted to run my own business, and I enjoy working with people. I also like the challenge of making different menus for different clients.

Q: What is the hardest part of the work?

A: Each event has its own challenges. You have to transport the food to the venue. Sometimes we are preparing and presenting food in outdoor places that don't even have running water or electricity. You have to plan ahead carefully for each event!

Questions

1. How is catering different from working as a chef? Explain at least three differences.
2. Which college did Philip attend? Suggest some other careers that might be open to someone who studied at the same college as Philip. Then check their website to see if you were correct.
3. Suggest three kinds of events that a caterer might work at.
4. How could someone interested in the hotel or catering business gain experience and earn extra money while they are still at school? Come up with at least three suggestions.

As a caterer, you can be your own boss.

Project

Create a directory of job vacancies that are advertised in newspapers and magazines in Jamaica. Create an A–Z list of the job types, listing the job title, role, wages/salary, qualifications/experience needed and where it is located. When you have finished your directory, choose three of the jobs you would like to do and explain why.

Discussion

As a class, discuss some different careers you are interested to hear more about. Arrange a guest speaker to come to your class to talk to you about their career.

Key vocabulary

events planner

manager

marketing staff

Personal development

We are learning to:

- recognise the skills and knowledge needed to pursue specific careers
- define relevant terms and concepts: résumé.

Knowledge and skills

Although computers and machines can do many different kinds of work, we still need people to process resources into products, and to provide services. People bring their skills, knowledge, ideas, creativity and experience into their work.

- Knowledge is what we know and learn about a particular subject, and often we are able to pass it on to someone else. For example, you might know the rules of cricket and you pass that knowledge on to someone who is just learning the game.
- A skill is an area of expertise or the ability to carry out activities or job functions involving ideas, things and/or people. Skills are abilities (or talents) we have acquired through learning. They help us to do things well, and we develop our skills through new experiences and by practising them.

In order for a country to prosper, its people need to develop their skills and knowledge so that they can carry out the work that uses their talents in the best way.

Qualities needed for careers

We can each evaluate our own qualities, academic capabilities and potential to help work out our career paths.

Personal qualities: your personality, what you enjoy and what you are interested in.	**Academic capabilities:** your ability to study, read and understand, and do well in examinations and courses.	**Potential:** what you might be able to become in the future; even if you are not a strong student now, perhaps you could become one if you followed a course of study that really interested you.

Exercise

1. In your own words, define 'knowledge' and 'skills'.
2. List other factors to consider when choosing a career, including the effect it will have on family life.
3. What personal qualities do you think that you have that make you suited for a particular job?

Qualifications

Education is the main way that a country develops its human resources. Education takes place at many levels: in the home, at school, at institutions such as colleges and universities, and in the workplace.

At school, children learn the subjects set out in the national **curriculum**. Schools also teach skills that prepare children for life as a part of society, including communication, listening, problem solving, cooperation and fitting in with expectations. School may also teach values and attitudes, such as respect for rules and for their peers and elders.

Research

Think of five different jobs and research which qualifications and skills are needed for each. You should also research which institutions offer these qualifications in Jamaica.

Institutions

Once students have graduated from secondary school, they may further their training at institutions such as:

- community colleges – such as Montego Bay Community College and Portmore Community College
- teacher training colleges – such as Shortwood Teacher's College and Sam Sharpe Teachers' College
- technical institutes and colleges – for example, Heart Trust/NTA and the Vocational Training and Development Institute (VTDI)
- universities – including the University of the West Indies at Mona, University of Technology (UTech) and Northern Caribbean University – or overseas colleges
- nursing schools – for example, the University of the West Indies School of Nursing.

Activity

Write a reflective journal entry about the kind of work you would like to do in the future, and how you see your work fitting in with your personal values.

Governments spend hundreds of millions of dollars each year on **tertiary education**, for example National Development Scholarships, Student Revolving Loan Schemes and Scholarships for attending the University. Governments also run On-the-Job Training Programmes, which provide opportunities for nationals between the ages of 16 and 35 to gain practical experience in companies. For example, the Hope Programme, set up by the Jamaican government continues to recruit young people between the ages of 18 and 24 years for training and apprenticeship experience. Participants will be trained and certified in several areas including digitisation, general construction, customer service, GIS mapping, hospitality among others.

Source: Youth Jamaica website

Exercise

4. What is the main way a country can develop its human resources?
5. What skills do we learn in school to prepare us for work?
6. Name three types of further training institutes we can go to after mainstream schooling.
7. Name two government programmes that offer tertiary education funding or training.

Key vocabulary

curriculum

tertiary education

Choosing a career

We are learning to:

- describe the factors one must consider when choosing a career.

Factors to consider when choosing a career

There are a number of factors to consider when thinking about your chosen career. Some of them are outlined below.

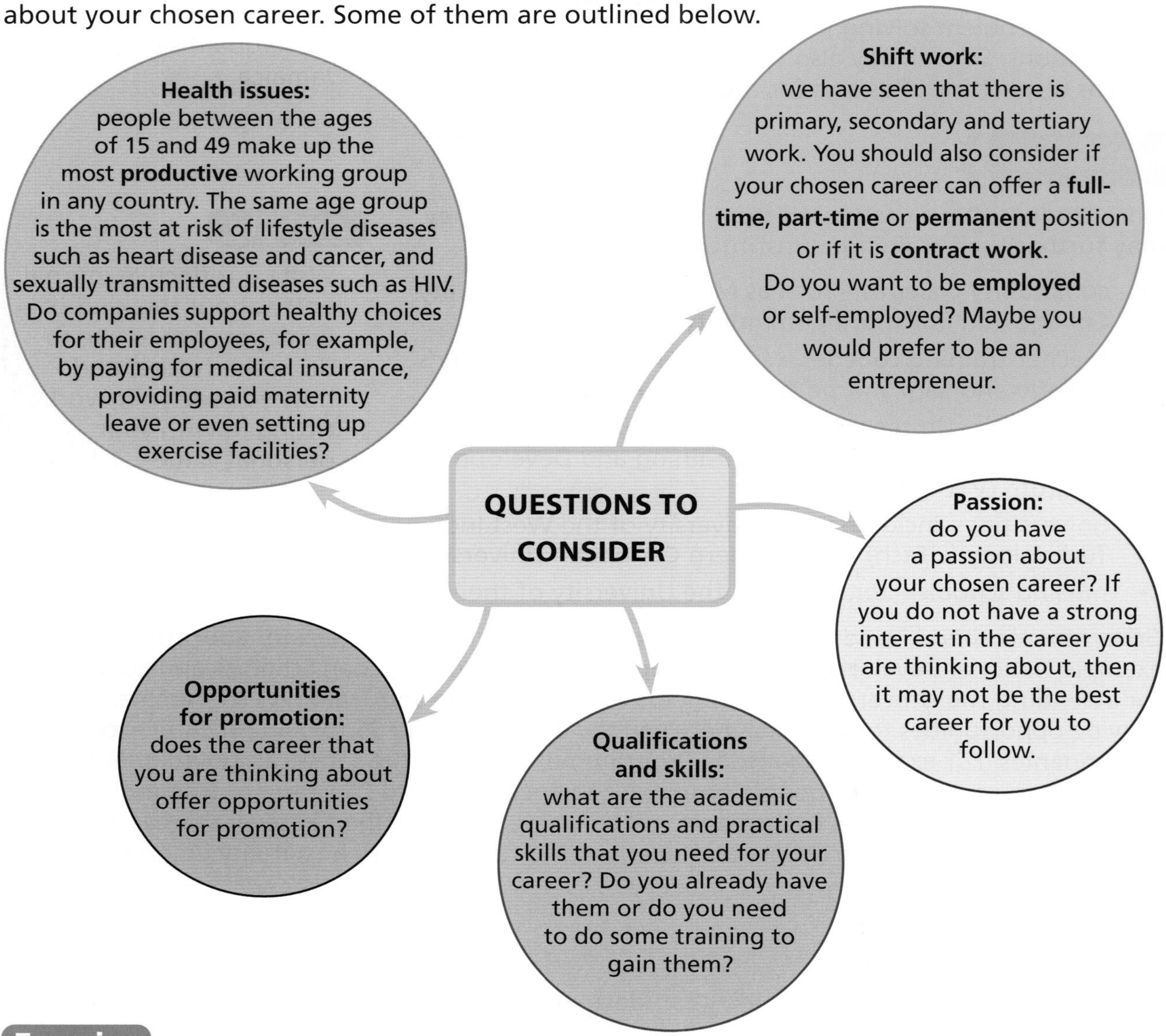

QUESTIONS TO CONSIDER

Health issues: people between the ages of 15 and 49 make up the most **productive** working group in any country. The same age group is the most at risk of lifestyle diseases such as heart disease and cancer, and sexually transmitted diseases such as HIV. Do companies support healthy choices for their employees, for example, by paying for medical insurance, providing paid maternity leave or even setting up exercise facilities?

Shift work: we have seen that there is primary, secondary and tertiary work. You should also consider if your chosen career can offer a **full-time**, **part-time** or **permanent** position or if it is **contract work**. Do you want to be **employed** or self-employed? Maybe you would prefer to be an entrepreneur.

Passion: do you have a passion about your chosen career? If you do not have a strong interest in the career you are thinking about, then it may not be the best career for you to follow.

Qualifications and skills: what are the academic qualifications and practical skills that you need for your career? Do you already have them or do you need to do some training to gain them?

Opportunities for promotion: does the career that you are thinking about offer opportunities for promotion?

Exercise

1. Which of the factors above do you consider to be the most important when thinking about a career?
2. Which of the factors would you consider to be least important?
3. Why do you think it is important to think about issues such as these before you choose your career?

Factors to consider

Some of the other things to think about when choosing a career include:

- needs and wants – Can the career you would like to follow provide the income you need for yourself and your family? How much are you likely to earn? Will your chosen career allow you to earn more money in the future?
- values and attitudes – What is important to you? For example, do you want to earn a lot of money, help others, look after the environment, work with animals, be creative? Would you like to be self-employed, employed, work for a large multinational company or work as a volunteer?
- interests – What do you enjoy doing? For example, do you like doing creative projects, helping others, teaching, working alone, solving problems, designing things, fixing things and so on? Are you able to turn your interests into your career? For example, if you like to make things would you like to be a carpenter? If you are interested in music, would you like a career as a musician?
- potential – What do you want to do or achieve in your life? Who would you like to become? What are your dreams?
- talents – What are you good at? What are your special talents? For example, are you good at working with numbers, do you have good communication or writing skills or are you a good problem solver?
- social factors – What influences you? For example, what do your parents, friends, teachers or peers think you should do?

Other practical things to consider include:

- Will you be able to earn more as your skills and training develop?
- What type of environment is it to work in? Is it safe?
- How far would you have to travel every day? If your chosen career is not close to you, would you be willing to move closer to the workplace?

Exercise

4 Look at the factors listed above. Which one is most important to you? Which one is least important?

5 Why do you think your personal interests are important when thinking about a career?

Some people like to work in a busy and noisy atmosphere.

Project

Identify a career that you would like to follow. In about 100 words, discuss three factors that have influenced your choice of career. Share with the rest of the class.

Key vocabulary

contract work
employed
full-time
part-time
passion
permanent
productive

How to write a résumé

We are learning to:

- learn how to write a résumé and understand its importance.

Résumé writing

A **résumé** (or **curriculum vitae**, CV) is a document that summarises your skills, experience and education, and which you present when you apply for a job or for a course of study. Your résumé creates an impression of you that can determine your career opportunities.

Elements of a résumé

A résumé should include key information, including:

- a summary outlining what you can offer the employer
- contact information – include your name, address, email, phone number
- experience – in reverse order, list your job title, name of employer, dates of employment and positions held
- education – school name, location, qualifications
- training and qualifications – related information
- skills and abilities – for example, computer skills
- interests and hobbies – for example, clubs you belong to, sporting activities, community activities
- references – two people who can vouch for your skills, character and qualifications.

A résumé, or CV, is an important document that is used by employers when they are interviewing candidates for jobs in their company.

Presentation of a résumé

Your résumé should be neatly presented and printed out on clean paper. Never crumple or fold it – instead, present it in a folder or envelope. Employers receive many résumés, so they prefer the document to be short and easy to read. Don't go over two sides. Carefully check your résumé to make sure that there are no errors in the language and spelling.

Ethics associated with résumé writing

When writing a résumé, you may be tempted to over-state things to improve your chances of getting the job. Ensure you avoid this, as you may get asked to back up the facts you present in your résumé. Avoid exaggerating things such as:

- more qualifications than you actually have
- changing job titles so they look more impressive
- claiming that you have done something at your present employer, when in fact someone else did it.

Did you know...?

It is important when writing your résumé that you write information that is true and honest. If an employer finds out that you have included false information, they will not offer you the job. Word may get around that you are dishonest. Therefore, always write the truth.

Case study

Look at the résumé below, which is for someone applying for a new teaching positon.

PATRICK BARROW

3 Lodge Road, 95 King St, Kingston, Jamaica; tel. no.: 0111 222 3333; email: **pbarrow@email.com**.

SUMMARY

It is my mission to inspire students to pursue academic and personal excellence whilst striving to create a challenging and engaging learning environment in which students become lifelong scholars and learners. I use innovative teaching methods as well as effective use of multimedia teaching tools.

EXPERIENCE

1. St Stephen's Primary School in 2002. This was a temporary appointment for two months (September and October) due to the assigned teacher being ill.
2. St Winifred's School for the period November 2002 to July 2005.
3. Lester Vaughan Secondary School for the period September 2005 to present. I am currently teaching Economics, Principles of Business and Social Studies.

EDUCATION

Bachelor: BSc Economics from the University of the West Indies, Mona for the period 2015–2018.

TRAINING AND QUALIFICATIONS

Skills: Teaching, Microsoft Office

Interests and hobbies: Cricket, reading, volunteer work

References: Available on request

Exercise

1. What is the writer of the résumé passionate about?
2. Look at the list of key information that a résumé should contain and then at the résumé above. What is missing from the résumé? Why would this be a problem?
3. Do you think his key skills will enable him to be a teacher?
4. What are the two likely places you would submit a résumé?
5. Why is it important to have a well-presented résumé?
6. Explain why you should not give false information on a résumé.

Discussion

Discuss what kinds of achievements you would like to list on your résumé at the end of secondary school:

- What will your educational qualification say?
- Which interests do you currently have, and how are you following them?
- What activities would you be able to list on your résumé?
- What qualities would you use to describe yourself? Are there any adults you could list for references?

Activity

Draw up your own résumé. You can use the example on this page as a guide.

Key vocabulary

résumé/curriculum vitae

Applying for a job

We are learning to:

- write an application letter and résumé and complete job application forms
- demonstrate how to prepare for an interview.

When you are looking for a job, usually online, you will find job descriptions which outline the role, qualifications needed, other qualifications or interests and skills that are desirable as well as details of the conditions of the job.

CUSTOMER SERVICE PROFESSIONALS

Location: Kingston and St Andrew / St Catherine

Company name: Retrice

Position: Permanent full-time

Type of Job: Human Resources

Description
Immediate opening for Customer Service Representatives to join the call centre.

JOB SUMMARY
Your mission is to provide quality services to customers via phone.

About us
At Retrice, our aim is to make lives better, one interaction at a time. As a global leader in customer service and experience, we serve the world's biggest brands. We offer the financial stability and growth potential to provide a solid foundation for early career development. This comes with technologically advanced work spaces and a positive working environment. Our team spans locations around the globe, and we employ over one hundred thousand employees. We are looking for enthusiastic hard working individuals to join our team.

Why should you join our company?
As a member of our call centre team, you'll have the opportunity to work in an exciting and collaborative environment, with a diverse group of experienced professionals that will help you advance your career. As an employee of our company, you'll also enjoy additional benefits which include:

- Full-time work (no short-term contracts)
- Transportation

- Performance bonuses
- Health Insurance
- Life Insurance
- Professional Development opportunities
- Discounts on local products and services
- Fun cultural and community outreach activities

KEY JOB RESPONSIBILITIES

- Provide excellent customer service experience
- Maintain a high level of professionalism.
- Provide prompt resolution to customer enquiries by providing appropriate and accurate information.
- Maintain diplomacy when addressing escalated matters.

JOB REQUIREMENTS

Minimum

- Education: 3 CSEC® passes inclusive of English A
- Language: strong oral communication skills
- Demonstrate problem-solving skills
- Have the ability to troubleshoot customer issues
- Demonstrate strong familiarity (and aptitude for learning); Critical Thinking ability, be conversational & persuasive.
- Excellent accurate data entry skills
- Typing speed of 25 words per minute
- Candidates must have originals and copies of a valid government issued ID, NIS and TRN

Preferred

- Customer Service experience is a plus (training is provided if necessary)
- Able to navigate different internet tabs at the same time (ability to multi-task).
- Demonstrate strong familiarity (and aptitude for learning) of Microsoft Windows and browser applications.
- Ability to deal with stress & work pressure in fast-paced environment.
- Ability to work in a team-fostered environment.

Writing a cover letter

When you apply for a job, you will often be expected to write a cover letter. A well-written cover letter is essential for the majority of job applications to accompany your CV. A good cover letter gives you the chance to successfully sell your skills, knowledge and abilities to prospective employers. Below is an example of a cover letter.

JOZELLE HARDING

35 Main St., Ochos Rios, Saint Ann, Jamaica

Mrs Wendy Smith
Retrice Call Centre
35 Young Street, Ochos Rios, Jamaica

13 January 2021

Dear Mrs Smith

I am writing to apply for the role in the call centre currently advertised on the Career Jamaica website. Please find enclosed a copy of my CV.

As you'll see, I have valuable experience working as a call centre agent. In my previous role I was responsible for answering calls, assessing customer needs, redirecting calls to the relevant department, answering customers via emails and ensuring they had a good customer experience.

I am an enthusiastic and hard-working person with excellent communication skills, both written and verbal. I have plenty of experience when it comes to taking calls and informing the customer of products and services best suited to their needs. I have a clear and communicative phone manner, and am well-equipped at handling any issues that might arise. Finally, I know how to deal with a high volume of calls and to work under an immense amount of pressure.

With my experience and expertise, I strongly believe that I would be an asset your team at Retrice Call Centre.

Thank you very much for considering my application. I look forward to hearing from you.

Yours sincerely

Jozelle Harding

Contact phone number 984-2562

Activity

Carry out some research into a job that you would like in the future. Prepare a cover letter for the job, following the structure of the letter above.

Did you know...?

On a cover letter you finish by saying 'Yours sincerely' if you know their name or 'Yours faithfully' if you do not know their name.

How to prepare for an interview

If your application is successful the next stage in getting a job usually involves a face to face or online interview. You will usually receive a letter or an email explaining the structure of the interview. It is very important that you prepare for the interview in the following ways:

- research your employer – you need to show that you understand the business beyond the basics. What job sector does it operate in? What challenges does it face? Who are its competitors? What major projects has it recently completed? What are its culture and values? This kind of knowledge demonstrates a genuine interest and shows that you are an informed and serious applicant.
- role – read the job description again and, if you completed an application form, go over it to refresh your memory of how your skills and qualifications match the role you are applying for. It's vital that you can explain why you want the job, that you understand the role and, even more importantly, why the employer should choose you over other candidates.
- interview panel – if you can, find out who will be interviewing you. The email inviting you to the interview may include this information. Use websites, especially the 'About us' section of the company website to find out more about their professional interests and experience. This may help you to connect with your interviewers and creative a positive impression during the interview.
- questions – you should consider how you'll answer questions that might come up as well as preparing some questions that you would like to ask the interviewer.
- practical things to plan – exactly when and where is the interview taking place? Have you planned your journey and checked the timetables for any public transport you need to take? What will you eat before the interview?
- a healthy breakfast – on the morning of your interview is important preparation. If your interview is scheduled for just after lunchtime, make sure you eat something even if you're feeling nervous – you won't put in your best performance on an empty stomach.

Exercise

1. What information does a job description contain?
2. What is the purpose of a cover letter?
3. Carry out research into the main job advertising websites, such as Youth Jamaica and search for 'Places to find jobs in Jamaica'. Explore the types of jobs that are described, and make notes on the jobs which appeal to you and the qualifications that they require.

Activity

In small groups, find a job you are interested in. One or more of you prepare questions and one of you prepare for the interview. Conduct the practice interview and afterwards give feedback to the interviewee about how well they did, and suggest areas to work on. Swap roles and repeat.

Issues in the workplace

We are learning to:

- identify issues employers and employees may face in the workplace.

Issues in the workplace

Most forms of work require us to work and interact with other people, in **workplace relationships**.

Many jobs require that we work with other people. Our workplace relationships are **formal** and **involuntary**. They have clearly described roles and functions, and we usually can't choose who we work with. Workplace relationships vary according to **hierarchy**:

- **senior** roles – employer, boss, manager, mentor and so on
- **junior** roles – for example, new employees, who have less experience and less responsibility
- **equals** – teammates.

Workplace relationships differ from other personal relationships.

However, in a workplace with many different positions you cannot always judge people based on office hierarchy. It is a good idea to treat everyone with politeness and respect.

Friendships may grow as people work together, get to know each other and do things together outside the workplace. As they trust each other and feel a sense of connection to one another, they may share their personal or work problems more openly than in an ordinary work relationship.

Some work friendships develop further, into **intimate relationships**. Most employers discourage romantic or sexual relationships at work, as it can have damaging effects on the rest of the company.

Some workers get into conflicts with colleagues, and may even develop **enemies**. Having enemies at work can badly damage the cohesion of the group, and can reduce the job satisfaction of the people involved.

Exercise

1. What do you understand by 'office hierarchy'?
2. Describe three kinds of personal relationships that can arise at work.
3. What are the main differences between work relationships and personal relationships?

Case study

Building positive relationships at work

Read this case study, which outlines how to behave at work. Then answer the questions below.

COMMUNICATE! – communication includes all the ways you speak to co-workers, from talking as you walk into the office, to discussions in meetings, to emails and telephone calls. Colleagues aren't mind-readers! Give clear information. Ask questions if you need to. Listen without interrupting.

BE FRIENDLY – a positive, friendly attitude will help you work well with co-workers. Be friendly and encouraging to others.

NOT TOO FRIENDLY – your co-workers, especially your seniors, are not your friends. Stay polite. Remember to keep your communication and behaviour appropriate for the workplace.

NOT NASTY, EITHER – you can't always choose who you work with, and you may find that you don't always like all your co-workers. You don't have to be friends with everyone at work. However, you can be professional, respectful and friendly. You can also avoid co-workers that you find difficult or disruptive.

TAKE RESPONSIBILITY – always do the things you say you will do. If you cannot complete a task, communicate this to your co-workers as soon as possible.

Be considerate to others and be mindful in your speech – do not take part in office gossip. Have a positive attitude. Don't complain.

CONSIDER YOUR VALUES AND ATTITUDES – the following values and attitudes can help to ensure you maintain positive relationships with co-workers: understanding, reflection, empathy, cooperation, tolerance, discipline.

Questions

1. In your own words define communication in the workplace.
2. Why is it important to be friendly with co-workers?
3. What attitudes should you always show to co-workers, even if you don't get on with them?
4. Consider the values and attitudes listed on this page. In pairs or groups, choose one or more of these. Create a role play showing how to demonstrate this value/attitude in the workplace.

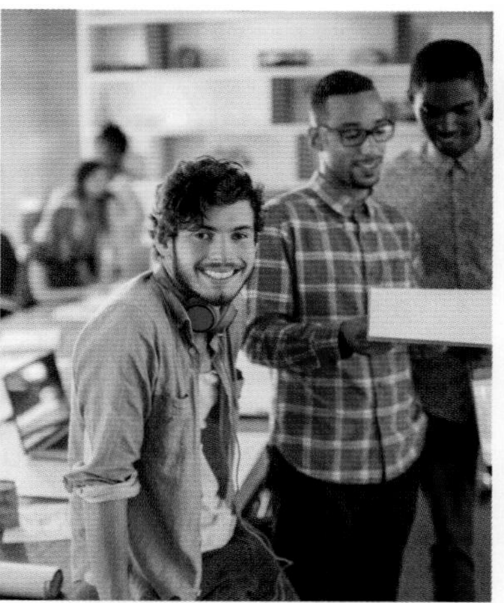

You should be professional, respectful and friendly at work.

Key vocabulary

enemy

equals

formal

hierarchy

intimate relationship

involuntary

junior

senior

workplace relationships

Problems in the workplace

We are learning to:

- identify what constitutes sexual harassment
- discuss how employees and employers should handle workplace problems.

Sexual harassment

Sexual harassment is any type of unwanted gesture or communication that has a sexual content. It may be:

- a sexual advance, such as trying to kiss, hug or touch a co-worker in a sexual way
- **obscene** or **suggestive** comments
- unwanted touching, such as brushing past someone too closely
- **inappropriate** emails, texts or phone calls
- **unsolicited** flirting
- unwanted comments such as general sexual remarks or **innuendoes**.

Although sexual harassment mostly affects women, it is not limited to men harassing women or bosses harassing their subordinates. An employer, employee, supervisor or client can harass a colleague, maybe making jokes and gestures that harass other workers. The harassment may be male to female, female to male, male to male or female to female.

Sexual harassment can be a big problem in the workplace.

Discussion

Brainstorm a mind map of issues in the workplace (and any others you can think of). Consider ways to deal with these issues – add them to the mind map.

What can you do about sexual harassment?

- Speak up – point out clearly that you are uncomfortable. Request that the harasser stops.
- Keep a record – if you notice harassment continuing, keep records of what happened. Note the date and time, what happened and what you said or did.
- Tell someone – a boss, manager or the police.
- Find work elsewhere – if you do not feel safe at work, you may feel that you need to leave the job.

Exercise

1. Define the terms sexual harassment and harassment.
2. If someone is being harassed, what type of behaviour could this be?
3. In your own words, explain why it is wrong for sexual harassment to happen in the workplace.
4. In your own words, explain the consequences of sexual harassment in the workplace.

Activity

Use newspapers or the internet. Find an example of a sexual harassment case reported in the news. Write a short news report or create a short radio report about the story.

Case study

Sexual harassment in the workplace

Sexual harassment has many damaging effects. According to recent news in a Jamaican Newspaper:

Not only does sexual harassment compromise safety and equality in the workplace, it can also affect a company's profitability. Sexual harassment leads to a stressful work environment. It increases illness and time taken off work. It reduces productivity and can even lead to increased employee turnover. Employers must therefore be made to create and uphold policies that allow us all to feel safe at work.

Other workplace issues

There are many other issues that affect workers in the workplace. Some of them are listed below.

- Poor wages – workers can be exploited by big companies by being paid a lower wage.
- Long hours – workers can also be exploited by having to work more hours in the knowledge that the worker can be easily replaced if they do not comply.
- Unsafe working conditions – this can involve working in dangerous or unsafe places, having to use unguarded machinery, exposure to chemical hazards (dust, fumes, gases), noise, bad lighting, high temperatures, badly designed facilities, having to use poorly maintained equipment, lack of training to use equipment and long work hours (which can cause loss of concentration and increase the likelihood of accidents).
- Unpunctuality of colleagues – this shows a lack of commitment to the job, lack of interest, and inability to do the job. It can lead to resentment by colleagues who do not consider someone a team player.
- Missed deadlines – this can lead to resentment by colleagues who are always on time; missing a delivery date for a job or client is not good business practice.

Exercise

5. Name three other workplace issues.
6. Name some of the health and safety issues that can occur in the workplace.
7. Why are punctuality and meeting deadlines important?

Research

In groups, create a questionnaire to ask a company's employers and employees about some of the issues they have faced at work. Compile a list of 10 questions. For example:

- Is there good communication in your company?
- Are people often late for work?
- Is there a sexual harassment policy at your workplace?

Present the findings from your questionnaire to the rest of the class.

Key vocabulary

inappropriate
innuendo
obscene
sexual harassment
suggestive
unsolicited

Rights and responsibilities of individuals in the workplace

We are learning to:

- identify at least five rights and five responsibilities of individuals in the workplace
- assess the importance of having rights in the workplace
- discuss at least three laws that protect the rights of employees.

What are rights and responsibilities of individuals in the workplace?

In any job there will be a range of risks that you encounter as well as responsibilities that all employees have in the workplace. It is therefore important that employers reduce risks associated with their specific workplace so that employees can fulfil their responsibilities. This is known as the employers' duty of care and is set out in the Occupational Health and Safety Bill which was introduced in Jamaica in 2017.

If an accident does occur, it is important for employers to be properly protected in case it results in injury, disability, or even death. If this happens, an employer may seek to ensure proper protection of his/her income through what is known as an employers' liability insurance policy, which a company is required to have.

Here are the basic rights that a worker has in the work place:

- The right to work in a safe environment where risks are reduced where possible
- The right to join a trade union
- The right to be given notice of redundancy (job being ended by the employer) and redundancy pay, in some circumstances, or notice of termination
- The right to paid holidays and paid sick leave
- The right to a minimum wage, which is set by the government
- The right to maternity benefits for women who are pregnant. This comes with particular conditions, such as having worked for a period of time before going on maternity leave.

Labour rights also include making sure that children are protected from working long hours, or working at all.

Did you know...?

In 2018, the government, on the advice of the National Minimum Wage Commission, announced a 12.9% increase in the national minimum wage from $6 200 to $7 000 per week.

Why are these laws important?

These laws are important as they protect workers' rights and the laws that set healthy working boundaries between the employers and the employees. They protect employees from being exploited, working in dangerous conditions or suffering health issues. They also make sure that workers are able to take proper breaks, have holidays and are able to take paid leave for medical issues. Many of these rights fall under the umbrella of international human rights.

Case study

The Occupational Health and Safety Act – introduced in Jamaica in 2017

The main objectives of the Act are:

- the prevention of injury and illness caused by conditions in the workplace
- the protection of workers from risks to their safety, health and welfare arising out of or in connection with activities in their workplace
- the promotion of health and safety in the workplace

Within this Act there are also responsibilities for the workers:

1. to wear or use safety equipment, protective devices or clothing required by employers
2. to work in line with the Act and its regulation
3. to report to the employer or supervisor any absence of or defect in equipment or protective devices which may endanger themselves or other workers
4. workers should not operate equipment in a manner that could endanger themselves or others.

Employers have a responsibility to provide the correct protective equipment and clothing.

Discussion

Either invite a trade unionist to speak at your school, or watch a recorded interview with one. Listen to what they say, then discuss the rights of employees in Jamaica and the laws that protect these rights.

As a follow-up, select the three rights that are most important to you as a future employee and and write a blog post on why they matter.

Exercise

1. Explain the difference between rights and responsibilities.
2. Explain why employees should be entitled to rights in their workplace.
3. Carry out research into the main employment legislation in Jamaica over the past 100 years. Describe how it has changed.

Appraisal of performance

We are learning to:

- evaluate ways of improving performance in the workplace
- define relevant terms and concepts: appraisal, self-appraisal.

Examining self and employer appraisal of performance

Today most employers conduct **appraisals** of an employee's performance at work. This is usually done on an annual basis (once a year) and reviews how the worker has performed over the last year, if they are happy in their role and if they met the standards required by the employer. It also includes a discussion of future training needs and aspirations.

Employees can also do self-assessment, or **self-appraisals**, for their employer. This involves a questionnaire and is used as part of the annual appraisal. The self-appraisal helps the employer to understand how the employee views their own performance and support over the last year.

Companies conduct appraisals of their employers at regular intervals, such as once a year, to find out how employees are getting on in their job.

Why are appraisals necessary?

There are a number of reasons why appraisals and self-appraisals are necessary. They:

- allow the employee to take an active part in an appraisal, rather than just get feedback
- help to give managers an insight into the employee's own view about their performance
- give the employee a chance to give their side of things
- help the employer to understand an employee's weaknesses and strengths
- help to decide what further training or help the employee would like, along with career development opportunities
- allow the employee to discuss proudly the things that they have accomplished in the last year.

Activity

Using the information on these pages, create role plays in groups of four to demonstrate how to improve performance in the workplace.

Exercise

1. In your own words define the terms 'appraisal' and 'self-appraisal'.
2. Draw a mind map to show why appraisals are necessary.

Alternative ways of getting the job done

The appraisal process is a good tool to find ways to improve performance at work. There are a number of simple ways in which performance can be improved at work, no matter what type of job (or career) you may have.

Be organised – make sure that you know what you have to do on the day you go into work, that you have everything you need to do the job (information, materials, contacts and so on). Write things down in a calendar or diary.

Emails and messages – people in office jobs can get lots of emails, and it takes time to look at them and reply, as well as interrupting other work. People often reply to emails straight after they have received them, thinking that an answer is needed immediately. One strategy is to set regular intervals during the day to check email.

Become a lifelong learner – this is gaining new skills and knowledge throughout life and not just while you are at school or university. The University of the West Indies Open Campus offers Continuing and Professional Education programmes which encourage lifelong learning. These programmes are designed to focus on pre-university knowledge and skill-sets and career-specific skill-sets so all can benefit.

Time management – a lot of people have problems with their time management skills, such as missing deadlines or being late for work or meetings. This can have a negative impact on people you work with and the company you work for. Set off for work earlier, set alerts to remind you about deadlines, and do a little bit every day, so that you are more likely to meet deadlines.

Work as a team – people often work on their own, when it would be more efficient to work as a team with someone or get someone to help them. Sometimes it is because they think they can do the job better on their own, they prefer to do the job on their own or they don't like their colleagues. By working as a team and being cooperative, both the worker's and the company's performance will improve.

Exercise

3 Name one regional institution that promotes lifelong learning.

4 Do you think some of the ways we have discussed are easy to implement in the work place? Why, or why not?

5 In about 100 words, explain how performance can be improved at work.

Key vocabulary

appraisal

self-appraisal

Work ethics

We are learning to:

- examine expected work ethics at places of work
- describe ways workers show dissatisfaction in the workplace
- explore solutions to resolve issues in the workplace
- define relevant terms and concepts: work ethic.

Work ethics

Ethics, involve your set of beliefs and principles about what is right and wrong. It also includes how you treat others and the choices you make when facing a moral dilemma.

Your **work ethic** is the same set of moral principles, but in the workplace.

An employer looks for good work ethics in their employees, such as:

- being **honest** in what you do and say at work
- showing **integrity**, or being **trustworthy**, for example being honest about meeting deadlines and not blaming other people for your mistakes
- being reliable and responsible enough and relied upon to do a particular job
- demonstrating knowledge about your work and being prepared to help others, who perhaps are just starting out
- being **self-motivated** – the ability to get on with your job or task without being supervised and to be trusted to finish the task
- being part of a team – working with your work colleagues to help solve problems and complete work quickly and efficiently, rather than doing it all on your own.

It is important to work as part of a team in whatever work you choose to do.

Exercise

1. In your own words, define 'work ethic'.
2. Why do you think an employer looks for good work ethics in their employees?
3. Define these terms: integrity, self-motivated, honest.
4. Create your own mind map that shows the work ethics required in the workplace.
5. Use newspapers, magazines and the internet to find reports of poor and/or unacceptable work ethics. Write your own short news report about the stories.

Discussion

In groups, discuss whether it is acceptable for workers to take industrial action. Then create a role play showing a dispute in the workplace. Split the group into two, where one half are the workers and the other half are the employers. Make sure that your dispute is resolved.

Ways workers show dissatisfaction in the workplace

- **Go slow** – this is when employees in an **industrial dispute** with their employer deliberately slow down their work rate. Soon, productivity drops, which causes profits to fall and results in losses for the company.
- **Work-to-rule** – there can be certain situations in the workplace where the employee works 'to rule'. This is where employees are in a dispute with their employer (usually about wages, safe working conditions or hours) and they do just enough at work so that they are within the terms of their job role or contract, and not so little that the employer can dismiss them.
- Protest/stay away from work – other ways workers can show dissatisfaction are to organise protests or simply to stay away from work (known as 'striking').

Workers showing their unhappiness with their employer.

Key vocabulary

arbitration
go slow
honest
industrial dispute
integrity
The Jamaican Court of Appeal
mediate
resign
self-motivated
trustworthy
work ethic
work-to-rule

Conflict resolution in the workplace

There are a number of ways in which work conflicts can be resolved:

- Have an informal discussion between the two parties to resolve their differences.
- If an employee has made a formal grievance against someone, usually a company has internal procedures to follow. If a grievance is found to be true, the person who has created the conflict will have to **resign** from their job.
- Get someone to mediate the conflict, using a process called **arbitration**. This is the use of an arbitrator to settle a dispute. They can listen to both sides impartially and come to an independent decision or suggest a solution.

If a dispute between an employer and employees cannot be settled and the employees are members of a trade union, an independent court **mediates** the case. The **Jamaican Court of Appeal** is an appeal court which also functions to mediate industrial disputes in countries which are under its mandate. The Industrial Disputes Tribunal was established under the Labour Relations (Industrial Disputes) Act as an arbitration (a kind of negotiation) panel to hear industrial disputes. The process of a tribunal depends on if a worker is part of a trade union or not. Jamaica has a history of working to settle industrial disputes.

Exercise

6. Define these terms: 'work-to-rule', 'dispute', 'go slow'.
7. What are the possible consequences of 'going slow'?
8. Describe how workplace conflicts can be resolved.

Role of the trade unions

We are learning to:

- examine the role of the trade unions in Jamaica.

Role of the trade unions in Jamaica

Trade unions started to become a feature of the labour movement in Jamaica at the end of the nineteenth century, long before the formation of political parties. Trade unions have played an important role in raising the standard of living amongst working people.

The main function of trade unions is to look after the interests of their members. This can involve strike action, or interaction and negotiation with employers on behalf of members, to bring about changes in conditions. Some important regional trade unions are:

The Bustamante Industrial Trade Union (BITU) and the National Workers Union (NWU) are two of the most important unions in Jamaica. Their aims are:

- creating unity among workers
- to plan and participate in joint trade union action where necessary
- protecting and defending the economic, social, educational, cultural and political interest of workers.

The Bustamante Industrial Trade Union (BITU) was formed in 1938 and built up a membership of 54 000 within 6 years. Its aims are:

- The BITU operates a credit union for its members. In this way members can benefit from the collective bargaining power of the union as well as its collective economic power. Another benefit for members is that a single trusted organisation handles both their labour and monetary affairs.
- Labour education is also promoted by the BITU, with plans for a labour college to be set up aimed at educating members about labour laws.
- The BITU maintains links with international unions such as the World Federation of Trade Unions (WFTU) and the International Union of Food, Agricultural, Hotel, Restaurant, Catering, Tobacco and Allied Workers' Associations (IUF).

The two largest trade unions in Jamaica are The Bustamante Industrial Trade Union (BITU) and the National Workers Union (NWU) respectively.

Trade unions help to organise workers to speak up with one voice.

Discussion

With your teacher, discuss the role of trade unions in Jamaica, and why they are important.

The Caribbean Union of Teachers (CUT) is affiliated to 2000 members. Its aims are to:

- agitate for the rights of teachers
- agitate for correct conditions and terms of service for teachers
- raise concerns regarding health and safety of teachers and students in the various schools
- organise professional development workshops for its members.

The Caribbean Union of Teachers represents about 2000 members.

Benefits of membership in a trade union

The main benefit of belonging to a trade union is **collective bargaining**. This is where the trade union will negotiate on behalf of the workers for more favourable working conditions and benefits, such as higher wages and better hours and working conditions. Collective bargaining by a union is for all its members, not just one. Trade unions can also help with:

- support, enabling the worker's voice to be heard
- equity and fairness in the workplace
- job security
- better training and promotion opportunities
- fair wages, housing assistance, death benefits
- legal advice/assistance when needed in connection with employment
- financial relief in sickness, accident, distress, unemployment, victimisation.

Research

Working in groups, identify a trade union in your country that interests you and has not been discussed so far. Find out:

- which industry they represent
- what their mission is
- the number of members registered
- their structure and activities.

Exercise

1. Explain, in your own words, the main function of a trade union.
2. When were trade unions first officially recognised in Jamaica?
3. Which trade union represents: forestry workers, teachers?
4. Outline the benefits of belonging to a trade union.

Key vocabulary

collective bargaining

trade union

Questions

See how well you have understood the topics in this unit.

1. Match the key vocabulary word (**i–vii**) with its definition (**a–g**).

   i) employment
   ii) occupation
   iii) job
   iv) employer
   v) employee
   vi) lifelong learning
   vii) entrepreneur

   a) type of job or the work a person does
   b) education that continues over a whole lifetime
   c) the state of having paid work
   d) someone who has a job with a specific company or employer
   e) a specific set of employment tasks at a particular workplace
   f) someone who runs their own business
   g) someone who offers employment

2. Name the four basic reasons why people work.
3. Fill in the gap to name these types of job:

   a) An ____________ keeps track of and records the flow of money in an organisation or business.
   b) An ____________ agent sells policies for a company.
   c) A ____________ works with students, presenting classes, lectures and assignments, and helping students to develop skills and knowledge.

4. Name the three qualities that you need to evaluate to help decide the career path you should take.
5. Complete the sentences:

   a) A ____________ industry is an industry that harvests raw materials.
   b) A ____________ industry is an industry that is mostly involved in processing and manufacturing.
   c) A ____________ industry is an industry that provides services.

6. Name five factors that you should consider when choosing a career.
7. Name five ways to behave and communicate while at work.
8. Name five issues that employers and employees may face in the workplace.
9. Write a short report discussing some of the ways performance can be improved on at work. Use around 150 words.

10. Fill in the gaps to show the type of information that you should show in a résumé.

______________: PATRICK **BARROW**

_________________: 95 King St, Kingston, Jamaica; email: **pbarrow@email.com**.

_________________: It is my mission to inspire students to pursue academic and personal excellence whilst striving to create a challenging and engaging learning environment in which students become lifelong scholars and learners. I use innovative teaching methods as well as effective use of multimedia teaching tools.

_________________:

1. St Stephen's Primary School in 2002. This was a temporary appointment for two months (September and October) due to the assigned teacher being ill.
2. St Winifred's School for the period November 2002 to July 2005.
3. Lester Vaughan Secondary School for the period September 2005 to present. I am currently teaching Economics, Principles of Business and Social Studies.

_________________: Bachelor: BSc Economics from the University of the West Indies, Mona for the period 2005 to 2008.

__________________________:

Skills: Teaching, Microsoft Office

Interests and hobbies: Cricket, reading, volunteer work

References: Available on request

11. Match these work ethics (**i–v**) with their descriptions (**a–e**):

i) honest
ii) integrity
iii) trustworthy
iv) responsible
v) self-motivated

a) can be relied upon
b) gets things done without having to be told to do so
c) always tells the truth
d) honest in one's principles
e) behaves in a sensible manner

12. Which organisations in Jamaica help to solve workplace disputes?

Grade 9 Unit 8 Summary

People, careers and jobs

In this chapter, you have learned about:

- The effects of technology on the types of work people do
- The different ways people work and earn a living
- Some of the challenges that people face in the world of work
- The reasons people work, and how it benefits individuals, families and communities
- Types of jobs that are often available
- Jobs that have disappeared because of technological advancements
- Career opportunities in the hotel industry in Jamaica
- Education and training, and the soft skills needed to pursue specific career opportunities
- The factors to consider when choosing a career
- What a résumé is and the things to consider when writing one
- How to write a cover letter and prepare for an interview.

Problems in the workplace

In this chapter, you have learned about:

- Issues that arise in the workplace
- How to deal with sexual harassment
- The rights and responsibilities of individuals in the workplace
- The importance of laws which protect the rights and responsibilities of employees
- The importance of performance appraisals in the workplace.

Work ethics and trade unions

In this chapter, you have learned about:

- Why employers look for employees with work ethic
- The strategies workers use to show dissatisfaction in the workplace
- The ways to resolve workplace conflict
- The role of trade unions in Jamaica and how members benefit.

Checking your progress

To make good progress in understanding individuals in the workplace, check that you understand these ideas.

- Define the terms: *value, work, work ethic, job.*
- Describe at least three factors which influence personal values.
- Explain how personal values affect decision making.
- Explain the value of work and good work ethics.
- Explain how the economy benefits when a large percentage of the labour force is employed.
- Describe how you write an application letter and résumé and complete job application forms.
- Describe how you prepare for an interview.
- Name at least five rights and five responsibilities of individuals in the workplace.
- Explain the importance of trade unions in Jamaica.

SOCIAL STUDIES

Unit 9: Tourism

Objectives: You will be able to:

Tourism in Jamaica

- define relevant terms and concepts
- identify tourism sites in Jamaica.

Development of the tourist industry

- explain the natural factors that are responsible for the development of the tourist industry.

Tourism and culture

- explain the human factors that are responsible for the development of the tourist industry.

Advantages of tourism

- describe the advantages of tourism.

Cruise tourism

- describe the success of cruise tourism
- explain how cruise tourism is different from other types of tourism
- describe advantages of cruise tourism.

The impact of tourism on the environment

- discuss the impact of tourism on the environment.

Tourism in Jamaica

We are learning to:

- define relevant terms and concepts
- identify tourism sites in Jamaica.

Tourism

Tourism is the practice of visiting places for pleasure. This might be visiting different countries or areas, or visiting specific sites of interest.

Tourists enjoying the beach at Montego Bay.

One of the most important industries in Jamaica is tourism, and for many of the countries in our region, tourism is crucial.

The economy of Jamaica is heavily reliant on services, accounting for 70% of the country's GDP (Gross Domestic Product).

A **resort** is a place designed to offer visitors relaxing accommodation. A resort is usually a large hotel, or a type of complex, that offers accommodation, shops and leisure facilities such as swimming pools and restaurants. A resort town is a tourist destination that has many places to visit and stay, for example Negril, Ochos Rios or Montego Bay.

Recently there has been a focus on **ecotourism** in Jamaica, a type of tourism that allows tourists into a country or area but focuses on protecting the environment and local culture. Ecotourism means:

- travelling to undisturbed or unspoiled natural areas
- enjoying, studying or experiencing the natural environment without damaging it
- treating the environment responsibly and carefully
- benefiting local communities
- supporting conservation projects
- providing education to travellers and local communities.

Mass tourism is a type of tourism that involves tens of thousands of people going to the same resort often at similar times of the year. It is the most popular form of tourism as it is often the cheapest way to holiday, and is often sold as a 'package deal'. For example, many people visit Jamaica for the beaches such as Montego Bay, deep sea fishing at Port Antonio, caves at Cockpit County, golf courses island-wide and water sports in Montego Bay.

Ecotourism is a form of environmentally-friendly tourism which involves people visiting ecologically fragile, unspoilt areas that are usually protected. Eco-tourism is designed to be low impact and small scale. For example; bamboo rafting on the Blue Lagoon, or hiking trips in the Blue Mountains. By visiting these eco-friendly attractions, tourists are supporting sustainable tourism.

Hiking in the Blue Mountains is an example of eco tourism.

Community tourism is a type of tourism where local communities invite tourists into their communities, giving them a chance to understand their culture and daily lives. It is a form of sustainable tourism that allows travellers to connect closely to the local community they visit.

9.1

In Jamaica, the Sustainable Communities Foundation (SCF) was established to help Jamaican communities to take responsibility for their future, through education and training in business management and tourism. For example you can try making Jamaica's national dish ackee and salt fish with spicy callaloo, dumplings, bammy and fried plantain in Mandeville, Manchester, or visit Resource Village or Beeston Spring.

Tourist sites in Jamaica

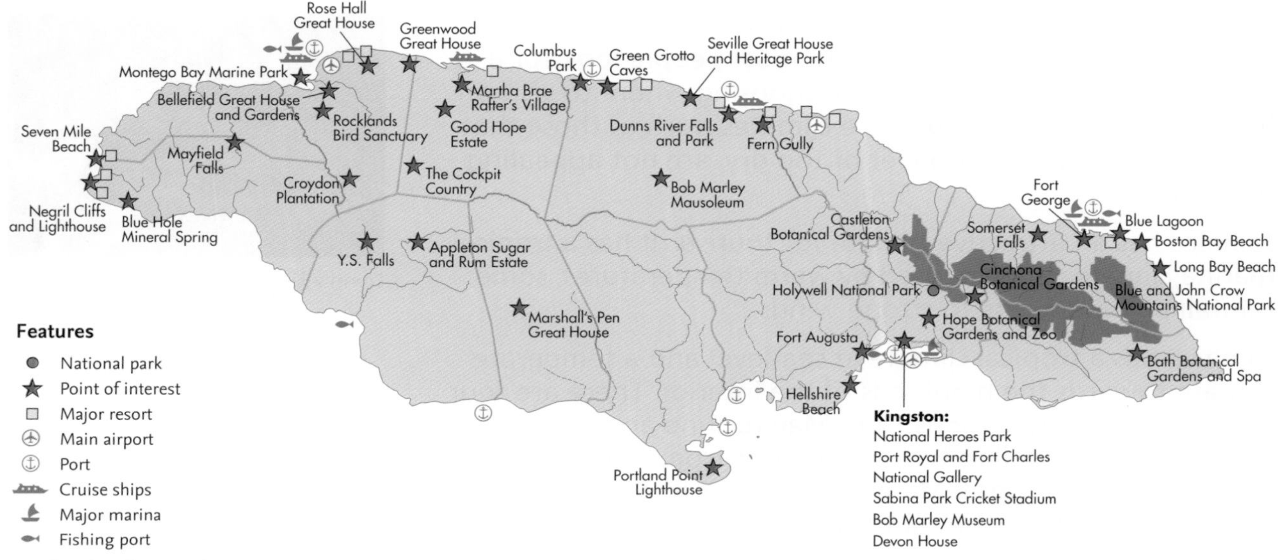

Tourist sites in Jamaica.

Project

The map above shows some of the important tourist sites in Jamaica. Draw an outline map which shows:

- **a)** a north arrow and scale
- **b)** the capital city, airport and main harbour or port
- **c)** the locations of each of the sites listed.

For each site listed, write a short paragraph describing the site. Include interesting facts like the site's history, activities that can be done or wildlife that can be found there.

Exercise

1. In your own words, define the terms: tourism, resort and ecotourism.
2. What percentage of the GDP of Jamaica is made up of tourism related activities?
3. Why is tourism important to the economies of many Caribbean countries?

Key vocabulary

ecotourism

community tourism

mass tourism

resort

Development of the tourist industry

We are learning to:

- explain the natural factors that are responsible for the development of the tourist industry.

Climate

The climate is one of the main factors affecting tourism. Depending on the type of holiday, most people look for a warm, dry climate when they are choosing where to visit on holiday. Countries with extreme climates, such as those that are too hot, too cold, too wet or too dry, are not appealing to tourists.

Jamaica has an attractive climate for tourists. It has a tropical marine climate, characterised by warm temperatures, some rainfall and moderate to strong winds.

Jamaica has a tropical climate at sea-level and a temperate climate towards the highlands of the interior. There are four seasons, two rainy seasons from May to June and September to November as well as two dry seasons from July to August and December to April. Many tourists visit to enjoy warm temperatures with little rain and to escape the cold.

Dunn's River Falls, Jamaica.

Flora

Flora refers to plants that grow in a particular region. This varies from country to country and area to area. Countries and regions that have diverse flora can be more attractive to tourists, as they produce beautiful landscapes with interesting plants and vegetation.

Jamaica has a variety of vegetation, including coastal mangroves, central rainforests and mountain forests. These ecosystems attract people to the island.

Exercise

1. Why is climate an important factor that influences tourism?
2. What characterises a tropical marine climate?
3. Describe the flora in the area where you live.

Activity

Using a mobile phone, work in groups to create a short video welcoming tourists to Jamaica.

Activity

Write a short essay explaining why tourists should visit Jamaica. Write about 100 words.

Fauna

Fauna includes all mammals, birds, amphibians, reptiles and fish that are found in a country or region. This may not be the most important factor affecting tourism. However, if a country has a large, varied fauna, it may be more appealing to tourists.

The most varied wildlife is found on volcanic islands. The chance to see, or swim with, nesting Green, Hawksbill or Leatherback sea turtles is particularly attractive to tourists. Rare bird species like the steamertail or the Jamaican Tody, and butterflies are also a main attraction on the islands. Attractive fauna also include a variety of colourful species of reef fish and coral.

> **Did you know...?**
>
> Coral reefs are called the 'rainforests of the ocean' and the Caribbean has the highest level of coral reef diversity in the Atlantic Ocean.

Natural sites

Tourists visiting a country want to see the natural sites within the country. Some countries have many natural sites, such as lakes, beaches, mountains, coral reefs and forests, and these will all be appealing to tourists.

Jamaica has an abundance of natural sites that are popular tourist destinations:

- nearly 479 square miles of coral reefs.
- lagoons such as Glistening Waters and the Blue Hole
- waterfalls such as Dunn's River Falls, YS Falls and Mayfield Falls.

Hiking is popular on the peaks of Blue and John Crow Mountains, which include hiking trails.

There are many tropical forests throughout Jamaica that have an abundance of flora and fauna. Jamaica is popular for reef diving and snorkelling.

Blue Hole Lagoon, Jamaica.

Exercise

4 What does the term 'fauna' mean?

5 What types of fauna can be found in Jamaica? Name some which you have seen in your country.

6 Countries with plenty of natural sites can be more appealing to tourists. Why is this?

Tourism and culture

We are learning to:

- explain the human factors that are responsible for the development of the tourist industry.

Natural factors make the region an attractive destination; however, human factors also attract tourists.

Social and economic stability

Jamaica is relatively stable, without social unrest or wars, so it is attractive to visitors.

Social services such as hospitals, police, sanitation and transport are also easily accessible and are run using internationally accepted standards.

Amenities such as running water, telecommunications and electricity are also well maintained.

Tourists are accustomed to certain comforts and conveniences, and the availability of these in Jamaica makes the region attractive.

Food is a cultural attraction in the Caribbean.

Heritage

Jamaica has a rich and diverse heritage created by a mix of indigenous cultures, colonial rule and African ancestry. This means that in a relatively small space, tourists can experience cultural experiences from many different parts of the world. Jamaican heritage is intriguing for tourists:

- colonial-era buildings such as forts, religious buildings and plantation houses are major attractions
- indigenous crafts and ways of life, both current and archaeological
- **Patois** – a language created by mixing different languages.

Research

Write a recipe for one of the popular dishes of Jamaica. Make sure you list the ingredients.

Food and drink

Jamaica has a culinary culture based on:

- the use of local ingredients
- differences in popularity and availability of ingredients
- preferred cooking methods and...
- ultimately, taste.

Tourists appreciate the opportunity to try something different and unique. Many islands have developed tourism products based around food, for example the Jamaican Food and Drink Festival. Tourists make it a point to try the local national dish on visit.

Festivals

Jamaican festivals of music and dance are known for featuring local musical styles such as reggae and dancehall, along with calypso and soca, and for featuring local and international artists.

Events such as Reggae Sumfest, Calabash, Accompong Maroon Festival, Bacchanal and Saint Ann Kite Festival are popular for their relaxed atmosphere, where tourists and locals alike enjoy food, dancing and entertainment.

A number of events are scheduled around these parties such as dance or reggae competitions and large outdoor markets selling local products.

People

Jamaican people are known for their hospitality, approachability and friendliness. Tourists like to visit the area because of this. Jamaican people are aware of the importance of tourism to the economy and make an even greater effort to make visitors comfortable.

Exercise

1 In your own words, describe why tourists find each of the following factors attractive in Jamaica:

- **a)** social and economic stability
- **b)** heritage
- **c)** food and drink
- **d)** festivals
- **e)** people.

2 Describe three aspects of Jamaican heritage that are present in your local community.

3 Research the development of Patois over time, explaining how it represents Jamaican culture.

Project

Write a short report on the history of one festival and one heritage site that attract tourists in Jamaica.

Key vocabulary

amenity

Patois

Advantages of tourism

We are learning to:

- describe the advantages of tourism.

Generation of income

There are many positive effects of tourism for a country or region. All countries are keen to develop their tourist industry, as it can generate lots of money for the country. This money can then be used to improve the services in the country, such as schools, hospitals, housing and communications. It also improves the standard of living of the people of the country.

If a country has a profitable tourist industry, many companies and businesses will want to invest there. When this occurs, more jobs are created – which helps with the problem of unemployment – and more wealth is produced for the country.

Around a quarter of all jobs in Jamaica are in tourism. About two million tourists visited Jamaica between January and June of 2019 and received US$2 billion in revenue from these visits. In 2018, Jamaica had a record number of arrivals totalling 4.32 million and earnings of US$3.3 billion.

An increase in tourist numbers allows more people in the country to create small businesses of their own that cater to foreign visitors. This can help to tackle unemployment within Jamaica.

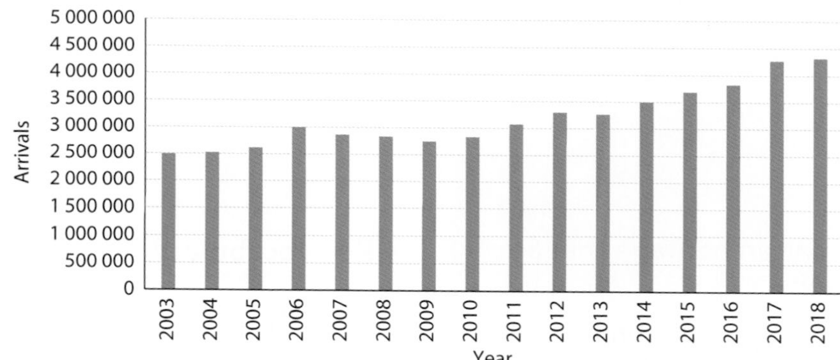

A representative graph of Jamaica's tourism levels.
Source: My Island Jamaica website

Job creation

Tourism creates jobs directly such as in hotels, restaurants, cafés, entertainment facilities and other shops and services. Jobs are also created indirectly by tourism such as tour operators, transportation service operators, taxi drivers, and craft vendors. Tourism is also linked to other industries such as agriculture, fishing and construction. This helps to tackle the high unemployment rates in the country.

Discussion

In groups, discuss the impact of tourism on the environment. Identify disadvantages as well as advantages, and then share your findings with the rest of the class.

Promotes interconnectedness

Interconnectedness is a geographical term that refers to countries being connected and is used to show how countries are connected in the world today.

Transport and Communication – Improvements in worldwide transport have made visiting foreign countries much more possible than previously. It is now possible to fly around the world in approximately 70 hours – almost three days.

Countries must make sure that there are good road, rail (where possible) and air networks in the country. Many countries now have international airports, big enough to accommodate large planes. The Jamaican tourism industry is well developed and is one of the premier tourist destinations in the world. Jamaica's airports and ports have been upgraded to allow faster processing of visitors and to accommodate more tourists. Major infrastructure developments have been carried out to improve access and travel across the island. The most recent was the construction and opening of the North-South Highway. The Caribbean Tourism Organization is working hard to promote tourism in all Caribbean regions, focusing specifically on the importance of air transport as a means of allowing and supporting tourism in these regions.

Multiplier effect – the increased income generated by businesses associated with the tourism industry creates more wealth. More people are employed in the tourist sector and unemployment is reduced. Local people then have more spending power and are able to spend money in other shops and services, making these business owners wealthier. More and more money is then injected into the economy.

Other consequences of the multiplier effect include:

- transport improvements, such as building more main roads, as well as improving existing road networks
- improvements to schools and health care
- increased employment.

Tourists have the opportunity to swim with dolphins at Dolphin Cove.

Exercise

1. What percentage of the workforce are employed in tourism, according to the graph?
2. What types of jobs are created by tourism? Can you think of any more?
3. Find a tourist site near where you live and describe the jobs that have been created as a result.
4. In your own words, define the term 'interconnectedness'.
5. Choose two advantages of tourism and state why they are so important.
6. Explain why tourism in the Caribbean is so important to the region.

Key vocabulary

interconnectedness
multiplier effect

Cruise tourism

We are learning to:

- describe the success of cruise tourism
- explain how cruise tourism is different from other types of tourism
- describe advantages of cruise tourism.

Cruise tourism development

Cruise tourism developed as a strong industry for the Caribbean in the 1980s and now the Caribbean is the most popular destination for cruise vacations. The port a cruise starts from is called a **home port** and destination ports are called **ports of call**. The busiest home ports for Jamaican cruises are Ochos Rios, Montego Bay and Port Antonio. Ships sail between ports of call at night, and during the day passengers disembark to enjoy each destination. Destinations with cruise terminals receive more cruises.

Cruise ship docked at Falmouth Pier, Jamaica.

In 2018, a floating pier system was installed at Port Royal to make it accessible to cruise ships without damaging the historic location. A new deep-water pier opened at Falmouth Pier in 2011, at a cost of nearly $200 million, which can accommodate even the largest cruise ships.

The cruise terminal at Falmouth, Jamaica.

The Caribbean has been successful in cruise tourism because:

- it is close to the USA, the main cruise market
- there are colonial links to Europe so Europeans visit to experience a part of their country's colonial past
- each island has a unique character in culture, language and landscape, so tourists get a variety of experiences on one trip
- The Caribbean has a range of islands to visit, so trips can be scheduled to visit one island every day.

Cruise vs long-stay tourists

- Cruise tourists spend one or two days while long-stay tourists usually spend a week or more.
- Cruise passengers spend less money on-shore since many of their needs, such as meals, are provided on the cruise ship. However, cruise tourists visit many islands and more islands benefit from each tourist's spending in one trip.
- Cruise tourists usually do not have enough time to participate in many different activities or see many attractions. Usually they invest in seeing one attraction and shopping, while long-stay tourists can see a variety of attractions.

Project

Write a list of cruise ships that visit Jamaica. Find out where each ship's home port is and what other destinations they visit. On a map of the Caribbean, draw a line representing each cruise. Use a different colour for each line. Add a key to your map.

- Cruise tourists prefer short tours, coastal activities and attractions close to the port or capital city, where transport back to port is easy and there is duty-free shopping. Cruise ships follow very strict schedules, and cruise tourists are always concerned about having time to shop and make it back to the ship on time.

Advantages of cruise tourism for the Caribbean

Employment and spending – cruise ships employ some Jamaican citizens, providing training and skills development, and reducing unemployment. Cruise ships form links with local tour companies so they have guaranteed customers and income. Ships may resupply at ports of call, purchasing products from local businesses. Each individual visitor may spend less, but cruise ships bring many tourists at the same time so local businesses benefit from volume spending. Sellers of handicrafts and speciality foodstuffs (local spices, seasonings and sauces) and small-scale tour guides benefit most from this type of spending.

Taxes – Caribbean governments receive **head tax**, taxes paid by cruise lines for the use of port facilities, and taxes from large and small businesses that benefit from cruises.

Marketing – cruise ships organise vibrant marketing campaigns that promote their Caribbean destinations. Cruise trips can be considered a type of window shopping for a future long-stay Caribbean holiday.

Discussion

As a class, discuss the possible disadvantages of cruise tourism to the Caribbean.

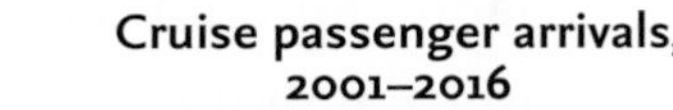

Cruise passenger arrivals, 2001–2016

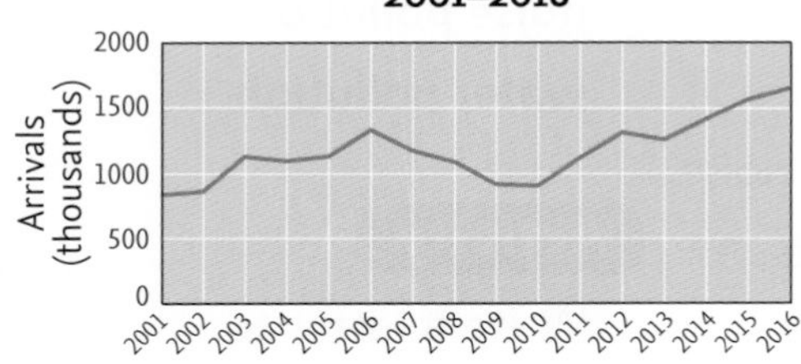

Cruise passenger arrivals by month, 2016

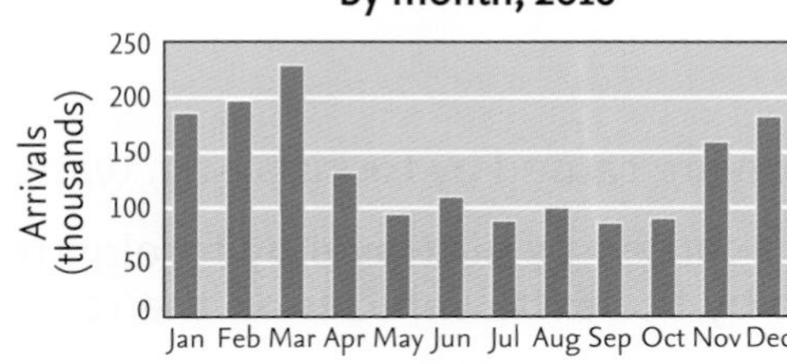

Exercise

1. Why has cruise tourism been successful in Jamaica?
2. Describe some differences between cruise and longstay tourists.
3. Explain how cruises benefit the Caribbean economy.

Key vocabulary

head tax

home port

port of call

The impact of tourism on the environment

We are learning to:

- assess the disadvantages of tourism on Jamaica's economic and social development.

Impact of tourism on the environment

Tourism can bring many benefits to a country, but it can also have some negative effects on the environment. Negative effects will occur when the number of visitors is greater than the environment's ability to cope with these people.

Water resources

If a country has limited access to fresh water, many tourists visiting the area will need plenty of water for things such as swimming pools and showers and baths. This can lead to water shortages where there are already low water levels.

Activities such as jet skiing can cause water pollution.

Land degradation

Land degradation is a process in which the quality of the land is reduced, either by extreme weather or human activities. One example is soil erosion, which can occur where there are large volumes of people walking in fragile areas. Soil erosion can occur in mountain and hilly regions, where tourists go hiking. The constant trampling over the vegetation causes it to die and the soil to wear away.

Pollution

All types of pollution are caused by tourists – air, water and noise.

- **Air pollution** is caused by air travel by foreign tourists. It is made worse by the extra vehicles on the roads.
- **Water pollution** can be caused by watersport activities on the lakes and seas, such as speedboating and jet skiing, and the disposal of sewage directly into the sea. This causes water pollution and poses a serious health risk. It also damages fragile environments like coral reefs.
- **Noise pollution** can be caused by planes and cars, as well as by recreational activities such as jet skiing.

Key vocabulary

air pollution

land degradation

noise pollution

water pollution

Activity

Write a letter to the editor of your local newspaper, either condemning or supporting the development of a new tourist resort in your community.

Exercise

1. Explain how tourism can have a negative impact on the natural resources of a country.
2. What tourist activity can cause soil erosion?
3. Describe the causes and effects of pollution in Jamaica.

Loss of land and habitats

In order to cater for tourists, large areas of land are lost to tourism:

- Farmland is replaced with large-scale holiday resorts and complexes.
- Coastal regions have hotels built on them.
- Communities may even make way for tourist facilities.

The environmental impact of this is substantial. Not only are large-scale tourist resorts and facilities unsightly, but coastal regions are often fragile environments and can be damaged by the large numbers of visitors. Wildlife and habitats may be badly affected or even lost completely.

Climate change

Climate change is a major problem associated with tourism. The biggest environmental problem caused by tourism is the method of transportation. Air transport is one of the largest generators of increased carbon dioxide in our atmosphere, leading to climate change and global warming. Some of the effects of climate change include:

- increased flooding
- more frequent and stronger hurricanes
- rising sea levels
- coastal erosion and damage to coral reefs.

Damage to historical sites

As with any fragile environment, whether it is natural or man-made, an increase in the number of people visiting that place or area puts a huge amount of pressure on the attraction in question. Quite often historical sites of interest can be damaged by increased visitor numbers.

Organisations such as the Caribbean Conservation Association work with local governments to help create a greater awareness of the value of the Caribbean's natural resources.

There are also challenges to the tourism industry. These include:

Competition – other countries in the Caribbean also attract tourists and may offer cheaper accommodation, stopovers and tours.

Global recession – where there is a slowdown in the global economy, people have less money to spend on holidays. Economic investment and development is reduced so tourist attractions may not be able to grow as strongly.

Activity

Write an open letter to the Minister of Tourism in which you acknowledge the value of tourism to Jamaica while lamenting the negative impact that tourism has on the natural environment, as well as the social and economic development. Include specific examples, and offer realistic solutions which, if implemented, could reduce the negative impact of tourism, while enhancing the country's economic development.

Exercise

4. What are the main types of pollution caused by tourism?
5. What type of land is lost to make way for tourist resorts?
6. What is the biggest contributor to increased carbon dioxide levels in the atmosphere?

Questions

See how well you have understood the topics in this unit.

1. Draw an outline map of your country and label the location of four popular tourist sites.
2. Label the map of Jamaica below with:
   a) the three main cruise ports
   b) The Blue and John Crow Mountains
   c) three tourist beaches
   d) an ecotourist site.

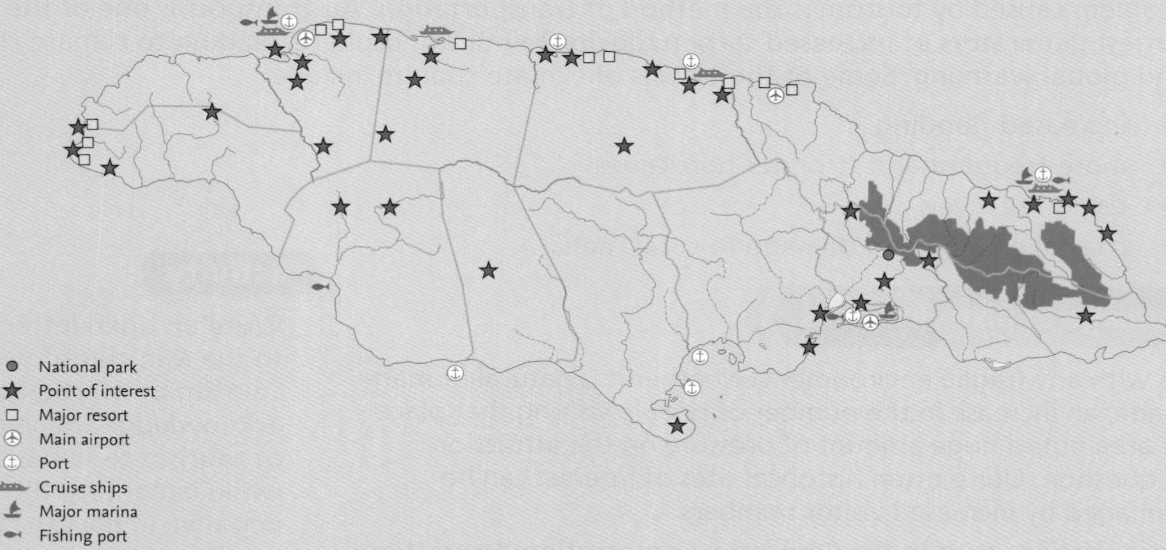

3. Describe some of the unique flora and fauna that can be found in Jamaica.
4. Explain what it means when it is said that Jamaica is known for its 'hospitality'.
5. How many jobs in Jamaica are related to tourism?
6. Write a short essay explaining how tourism promotes interconnectedness.
7. Describe the climate of Jamaica and explain why it is attractive to visitors.
8. Explain two of your favourite heritage sites of Jamaica, using images and maps.

9. Carry out some research into the most visited sites in Jamaica and offer reasons why these are so popular.
10. What can be done to ensure that tourism does not negatively affect the environment? Suggest three strategies.
11. Discuss why social and economic stability attracts tourists.
12. Why do tourists find Caribbean heritage intriguing?
13. Name two food festivals and two cultural festivals which attract tourists to Jamaica.
14. Using examples, say what is meant by a home port and a port of call.
15. Explain why cruise tourists prefer shorter tours and coastal activities.

Grade 9 Unit 9 Summary

The tourism industry in Jamaica

In this chapter, you have learned about:

- The meaning of terms such as mass tourism and community tourism
- The major tourism sites in Jamaica
- The link between climate and tourism
- The link between flora, fauna, natural sites and tourism
- How the natural environment contributes to the development of the tourism industry
- The development of cruise tourism
- How cruise tourists are different from long-stay tourists.

Tourism and culture

In this chapter, you have learned about:

- The link between tourism and social and economic stability
- Heritage, food and drink, festivals and people
- The contribution of cultural and heritage to the development of the tourism industry.

Advantages and disadvantages of tourism

In this chapter, you have learned about:

- How tourism generates income
- How tourism creates jobs
- How tourism promotes interconnectedness
- Advantages of cruise tourism
- The impact of tourism on the environment
- The effect of tourism on water resources, land degradation and pollution
- Loss of land and habitats
- How climate change and tourism are connected
- Damage to historical sites.

Checking your progress

To make good progress in understanding tourism in Jamaica, check that you understand these ideas.

- Explain and use correctly the term *tourism*.
- Describe three of the main tourist sites in Jamaica.
- Explain the impact of tourism on the local environment.

- Explain and use correctly the terms *ecotourism* and *resort*.
- Describe the main cultural attractions in Jamaica.
- Explain the role of tourism in creating employment opportunities in Jamaica.

- Explain and use correctly the term *amenities*.
- Name three reasons why people want to visit Jamaica.
- Explain the advantages of tourism.

- Explain and use correctly the term *interconnectedness*.
- Describe the role of cruise ships in the Jamaican tourism industry.
- Explain the problems that tourism can create.

End-of-term questions

Questions 1–6

See how well you have understood ideas in Unit 7.

1. Explain what is meant by:

   a) green energy **b)** green technology (giving examples of each).

2. Write a short essay on an environmental issue in Jamaica, including the key causes and possible solutions to the issue.
3. Match these definitions to the correct terms:

   a) hydroelectricity
   b) solar energy
   c) wind energy
   d) carbon footprint

   i) the amount of carbon dioxide released into the atmosphere as a result of the activities of a particular individual, organisation, or community.
   ii) Energy emitted by air flowing
   iii) Energy emitted by the sun
   iv) The generation of electricity by flowing water

4. Briefly describe the work of the Jamaican government in encouraging alternative energy solutions.
5. Suggest 5 ways of recycling in your daily life.
6. Explain how companies can reduce their waste and pollution.

Questions 7–13

See how well you have understood ideas in Unit 8.

7. Explain the difference between an employer, and an employee.
8. Provide three reasons why people work.
9. Write a description of the main factors to consider when choosing a career.
10. Imagine you are advising someone on how to write a good resume. What advice would you give them?
11. Describe the work of unions and explain why it is important to join a union when you begin a job.

12. Write an introduction to the world of work, types of work, and how people work using each of the following words at least once:

business	employment	manufacture	secondary
career	entrepreneurs	miners	self-employed
doctor	fishermen	nurse	technology
employee	jobs	primary	tertiary
employer	lifelong learning	process	

13. Match these items of information you should include on a CV to their definition:

1) a summary
2) contact information
3) experience
4) education
5) training and qualifications
6) skills and abilities
7) interests and hobbies
8) references

a) school name and qualifications
b) outlines what you can offer the employer
c) your name, address, email, phone number
d) two people who can vouch for your skills
e) previous jobs, name of employer, dates of employment and positions held
f) clubs you belong to, community activities
g) any information related to other qualifications
h) computer skills

Then, complete a CV for yourself.

Questions 14–18

See how well you have understood ideas in Unit 9.

14. Explain why Jamaica is a popular destination for tourists.

15. Why is tourism important to the economy of Jamaica? Write a short paragraph to explain.

16. Write a short essay of six paragraphs in which you explain the advantages and disadvantages of tourism in Jamaica.

17. Explain why Jamaica is an ideal destination for cruise ships.

18. Create a spidergram showing these key tourist attractions in Jamaica:

a) flora and fauna **b)** cultural heritage **c)** natural heritage sites.

Glossary

ability the quality or skill that you have which makes it possible for you to do something

accountable to be responsible for something

accountant an accountant keeps track of and records the flow of money in an organisation or business

adult suffrage the right of adults to vote in an election

agriculture farming and the methods that are used to raise and look after crops and animals

AIDS a disease which destroys the natural system of protection that the body has against other diseases; AIDS is an abbreviation for 'acquired immune deficiency syndrome'

air pollution substances found in the atmosphere that are harmful or dangerous

algae a type of plant with no stems or leaves that grows in water or on damp surfaces

ambassador an important official who lives in a foreign country and represents his or her own country's interests there

amenities things such as shopping centres or sports facilities that are provided for people's convenience, enjoyment, or comfort

anarchy when the absence of a government causes a breakdown of law and order in a society

apartheid a system in South Africa where people were kept apart on racial grounds

appraisal the official or formal assessment of the strengths and weaknesses of someone or something. Appraisal often involves observation or some kind of testing

arbitration the judging of a dispute between people or groups by someone who is not involved

arts and crafts decorative handicraft and design

associate member a member state which does not have all the benefits of full membership

Association of Caribbean States an association created to build on and improve existing links in the Caribbean and integrate the region further

aviation operation and production of aircraft

ballot a vote

ballot box a box in which ballot papers are collected

ballot paper a piece of paper on which a voter records his or her vote

bicameral two houses or chambers in a government

bilateral agreement agreements between two countries

by-laws a regulation made by a local authority or corporation

Cabinet part of the executive, consists of Prime Minister and Ministers

campaign series of events which are organised to help a candidate get elected

candidate a person who seeks election

capital money; anything that an economy needs in order to produce goods and services

capital goods goods are used to make other products

carbon emission see **carbon footprint**

carbon footprint a measure of the amount of carbon dioxide released into the atmosphere by a single endeavour or by a company, household, or individual through day-to-day activities over a given period

career a job or profession that someone works in

Caribbean Court of Justice a court which serves CARICOM member states and settles disputes between them

CARICOM The Caribbean Community

CARIFESTA Caribbean Festival of Arts

CARIFTA Caribbean Free Trade Association

CDEMA Caribbean Disaster Emergency Management Agency

characteristics the characteristics of a person or thing are the qualities or features that belong to them and make them recognisable

child abuse physical, sexual, or emotional ill-treatment or neglect of a child, esp by those responsible for its welfare

Child Protection Family Services Agency an organisation which receives reports of children who have been, are being or are likely to be abandoned, neglected, physically or sexually ill-treated, or are otherwise in need of care and protection

choice someone or something that you choose from a range of things

citizen someone who is a member of a country and who has certain rights in that country, but also has duties towards that country

climate the climate of a place is the general weather conditions that are typical of it

climate change the change of the Earth's temperature and weather patterns as a result of increased carbon dioxide in the air

coal a hard black substance that is extracted from the ground and burned as fuel

cohort a person's cohorts are their friends, supporters, or associates

collective bargaining negotiation between one or more trade unions and one or more employers

community tourism a type of tourism where local communities invite tourists into their communities, giving them a chance to understand their culture and daily lives

composition when you talk about the composition of something, you are referring to the way in which its various parts are put together and arranged

concentrated a concentrated activity is directed with great intensity in one place

constituency an area in a country where voters elect a representative to a local or national government body

constituent a person who lives in a constituency

constitution the principles and laws by which a country is governed

contract work short-term work, based on a temporary contract; contract workers are also sometimes called freelancers

conventional agriculture traditional farming used on large farms

cooperation working together

copyright if someone has copyright on a piece of writing or music, it is illegal to reproduce or perform it without their permission

coral bleaching occurs when coral polyps expel algae that live inside their tissues; caused by rising sea temperatures

coral polyp tiny, soft-bodied organisms related to sea anemones and jellyfish

creativity creative ability; artistic or intellectual inventiveness

crime an activity or offence that is against the law

CSME Caribbean Single Market and Economy

cuisine the cuisine of a country or district is the style of cooking that is characteristic of that place

cultural background the beliefs and traditions that a group of people share

cultural bonds cultural ties that bring people together

cultural diffusion the spread of cultural beliefs and social activities from one group of people to another

cultural heritage the cultural traditions that we have inherited from past generations

culture the customs, arts, shared language, history and ideas of a group

curator someone who is in charge of the objects or works of art in a museum or art gallery

curriculum the courses or subjects that are taught in schools, colleges and universities

data information that can be stored and used by a computer program

deforestation the removal of trees and vegetation to create open spaces for human activities

democracy a system of government in which a country's citizens choose their rulers by voting for them in elections

democratic based on the idea that everyone should have equal rights and should be involved in making important decisions

democratic government a government that is elected by the citizens of a country

demography the study of the changes in numbers of births, deaths, marriages, and cases of disease in a community over a period of time

dependant your dependants are the people you support financially, such as your children

dependence relying on someone or something

dependent to be dependent on something or someone means to need them in order to succeed or be able to survive

desalination the process of removing salt from sea water so that it can be used for drinking, or for watering crops

development the gradual growth or formation of something

diaspora the dispersion of people who originally came from a particular place, but now live in many different parts of the world

diplomatic someone who is careful about what they say without offending anyone

direct democracy a political system which allows citizens of legal voting age to establish rules and laws

disbanded broken up

diverse having variety and differences

domestic abuse abuse that takes place in the home, especially by one person against their partner

dreadlocks hair worn in the Rastafarian style of long matted or tightly curled strands

dress clothes worn by men or women as dress

economic development improving a country's standard of living

economic growth the increase in the inflation-adjusted market value of the goods and services produced by an economy over time

economic integration cooperation in business e.g. trading, finance

economy the system of how industry, trade and finance is organised in a country, region or worldwide to manage wealth

ecosystem a system formed by an environment and the living and non-living things within it

ecotourism tourism that does not damage or destroy the natural environment or local culture

education the act or process of acquiring knowledge, esp systematically during childhood and adolescence

election a process during voters choose candidates by voting for them

Election Day the day on which voting takes place in an election

elector a voter or person who has the right to vote in an election

electorate people who are registered to vote in an election

eligible someone who is allowed to do something, for example vote in an election

embassy the residence or place of official business of an ambassador

empathy the ability to share another person's feelings and emotions as if they were your own

employed when someone has a job

employee someone who is paid to work for someone else or company

employer a person or organisation that employs people

employment the fact of having a paid job

endangered in danger of extinction

endemic native to a particular country or region

enemy a person hostile or opposed to a policy, cause, person, or group, esp one who actively tries to do damage; opponent

entrepreneur someone who runs their own business

equals people in positions of equivalent power or responsibility

events planner someone who plans and organises events such as entertainment, parties and weddings

Executive the branch of government that makes policies and coordinates the work of different government branches

exploitation the overuse of something

femicide the killing of females because of their gender

fertiliser chemical that promotes fast plant growth

festival any occasion for celebration, esp one which commemorates an anniversary or other significant event

filter a porous substance, such as paper or sand, that allows fluid to pass but retains suspended solid particles: used to clean fluids or collect solid particles

finite natural resources a natural resource which cannot be readily replaced by natural means

first-past-the-post-system (FPPS) a way of counting votes in which the candidate with the most votes wins

floating voter voter who has not decided for whom they will vote

folklore unwritten literature of a people as expressed in folk tales, proverbs, riddles, songs, etc

formal having fixed definitions and roles

franchise authorisation granted by a manufacturing or entertainment enterprise to market its products

free and fair a free and fair election is where the parties taking part in the election do not try to persuade citizens to cast their votes in their favour by using force or intimidation

free trade trade which allows people to buy and sell goods freely, without restrictions

full-time full-time work or study involves working or studying for the whole of each normal working week rather than for part of it

gas a fossil fuel in the form of a gas, used as a source of domestic and industrial heat

gender the state of being male or female with reference to socially and culturally defined characteristics of masculinity or femininity

global warming an increase in global temperatures

Glossary

globalisation a process of making the world more connected, with goods and services being traded globally and people moving around freely

go slow when employees deliberately work slowly

goods things that are grown or manufactured

gospel music the story of Jesus Christ's life and teachings as narrated in the Gospels through music

governance the way in which an organisation, or a country, is run

government a group of people, usually elected, who have the power and authority to manage the affairs of a country

Governor-General the representative of the King

green energy power that comes from sources that do not harm the environment and are always available, such as wind and sunlight

green technology a type of technology that is considered environmentally friendly based on its production process or the way that it is supplied

grid a system for distributing electric power throughout a region

gross domestic product (GDP) the total value of all goods and services produced domestically by a nation during a year. It is equivalent to gross national product minus net investment incomes from foreign nations

gross national product (GNP) the total value of all the goods it has produced and the services it has provided in a particular year, including its income from investments in other countries

head tax a uniform tax or surcharge imposed upon every person or every adult in a specific group, as on those entering or leaving a country or using a particular service or conveyance

heritage features that belong to the culture of a society that were created in the past and have an historical importance to that society

hierarchy a system in which people are ranked according to their status or power

historical sites a place that has special historic, cultural or social value, usually protected by law in order to preserve it

HIV a virus which reduces people's resistance to illness and can cause AIDS; HIV is an abbreviation for 'human immunodeficiency virus'

Holy Piby Rastafarian's main text

home port the port where a ship is based

honest someone who tells the truth or deceives anyone

House of Representatives the lower house of Jamaica's Parliament

house-to-house canvassing people who work for political parties knock on the doors of people in the constituency to try and persuade them to vote for their party

human capital the abilities and skills of any individual, esp those acquired through investment in education and training, that enhance potential income earning

Human Development Index a statistical measurement of life expectancy, education, and per capita (per person) income indicators, which are used to rank countries into different levels of human development

human resource development employees developing their personal and professional skills, knowledge and abilities

human resources people and their knowledge, abilities, experience and talents

human trafficking the action or practice of illegally transporting people from one country or area to another, typically for the purposes of forced labour or sexual exploitation

hung parliament when no party has gained the overall majority of seats in parliament to take control and to form a government

hydroelectric power electricity generated by the pressure of falling water

identity the way you think about yourself, the way the world sees you and the characteristics that define you

inappropriate not suitable for a given context, or not acceptable to a person or place

independent candidate a person who does not belong to any political party

industrial dispute when there is a disagreement between workers and their employer

innovation something newly introduced, such as a new method or device

innuendo hint or underlying message

insecticide a chemical substance that is used to kill insects

insurance agent someone who sells insurance policies for an insurance company

insurance policy a document that gives details of the agreement between an insurer and the person who is insured

integrate involving people from all groups and cultures

integrated to be honest in your principles

integrity someone who is honest in their principles

interconnectedness a geographical term that refers to countries being connected and how countries are connected in the world today

interdependent/interdependence the state of relying on each other

inter-governmental cooperation between multiple governments

intimate relationship a close personal relationship, often a romantic or sexual relationship

investment putting money into the development of a company in the expectation of gaining a profit

involuntary something that you do not choose

Ital the word Ital comes from the English word "vital" with the initial syllable replaced by the letter "i" to signify unity with nature

Jah the Rastafari God

job a specific set of employment tasks at a particular workplace

judge a public official with authority to hear cases in a court of law and pronounce judgment upon them

judicial of or relating to the administration of justice

Judiciary the branch of government that makes sure that laws are enforced

junior younger or having less power or responsibility

jurisdiction the right or power to administer justice and to apply laws

kerosene a clear, strong-smelling liquid which is used as a fuel, for example in heaters and lamps

kinetic energy the energy that is produced when something moves

knowledge the understanding someone has about a particular subject

labour the work that people do to provide goods and services

labour force the part of the population that is able and available to work

land degradation the reduction in quality of the land either by extreme weather or by human processes

language a system for the expression of thoughts, feelings, etc, by the use of spoken sounds or conventional symbols

law and order when the majority of people in a country respect and obey the laws of the society or country in which they live

legacy something handed down or received from an ancestor or predecessor

Glossary

Legislature the branch of government that makes laws

liberalised a liberalised system is one which is designed to allow easier trading conditions

life expectancy the length of time that a person, animal or plant is normally likely to live

lifelong learning education that continues over a whole lifetime

Lion of Judah an important symbol in Rastafarianism

majority the greater number. If a party holds a majority, it has received the largest number of votes in an election or won the largest number of seats

majority rule/minority right a democratic system in which the majority should not take away the rights of the minority

manager someone who is responsible for running part of, or all of a company or business

manifesto states the views and proposed policies of candidates and political parties in an election

marketing staff a team that promotes and sells a product or brand; this may be through advertising, promotional events and offers, and through social media

martyr someone who is killed or made to suffer greatly because of their religious or political beliefs, and is admired and respected by people who share those beliefs

mass tourism a type of tourism that involves tens of thousands of people going to the same resort often at similar times of the year

maximise to make as high or great as possible; increase to a maximum

mediate to intervene (between parties or in a dispute) in order to bring about agreement

mentorship the position of a mentor

minority right see majority rule

modern states countries with modern systems of government

monocropping planting a single crop over a large area of land

monologue a long speech made by one actor in a play, film, etc, esp when alone

mulching To mulch plants means to put a mulch round them to protect them and help them to grow

multilateral of or involving more than two nations or parties

multilateral agreement an agreement between more than one country or international organisation

multinational company/corporation organisation that has business interests in more than one country

multiplier effect refers to increased spending made possible from an injection of money from a new source

municipal associated with or belonging to a town or city which has its own local government

music an art form consisting of sequences of sounds in time, esp tones of definite pitch organised melodically, harmonically, rhythmically and according to tone colour

National Identification Card an official document (card) that states who you zare

national identity a sense of who you are and that you are part of a country

natural disaster disaster that occurs in nature, like floods, storms, earthquakes and volcanoes

need something that you need to survive or for your well-being

noise pollution harmful levels of noise

nominated proposed as a candidate

nomination procedures that candidates have to follow in order to be able to stand for election

Nomination Day the day on which candidates register their intention to stand for election

non-confrontational where someone does not show aggression or is not hostile or threatening

Nyabinghi a Rastafari ritual

obscene offensively sexual or vulgar

observer status allowed to attend meetings but not to take part in the decisions made at the meetings

occupation type of job or the work a person does

Office of Children's Registry an organisation which receives reports of children who have been, are being or are likely to be abandoned, neglected, physically or sexually ill-treated, or are otherwise in need of care and protection

oil a smooth, thick liquid that is used as a fuel and for making the parts of machines move smoothly

on-the-job training training that a worker gets while they are working

opinion poll people are asked for their views about how they intend to vote. The people running the polls use this information to try to predict the outcome of the election

Parliament a law-making agency where a countries laws are decided

part-time if someone is a part-time worker or has a part-time job, they work for only part of each day or week

passion a very strong feeling about something or a strong belief in something

patent an official right to be the only person or company allowed to make or sell a new product for a certain period of time

Patois a form of a language, especially French, that is spoken in a particular area of a country

patriarchal of or having to do with a patriarch or patriarchy

Patwa see Patois

permanent going on for an indefinite or long period of time

persistence if you have persistence, you continue to do something even though it is difficult or other people are against it

pesticide chemical that kill insects, weeds and fungi that damage crops

petrochemicals chemicals that are obtained from petroleum or natural gas

physical capital a physical resource that cannot make or provide anything by itself. Physical capital refers to assets that have been made or found that we use to produce goods and services

physical environment the part of the environment made up of physical factors we can see and use, such as water, soil and mountains

physical resources resources that are made by humans through their abilities and skills, e.g. buildings, technology

physical/natural resources resources that we can see and touch/resources that occur naturally

pipeline a large pipe which is used for carrying oil or gas over a long distance, often underground

political integration when countries work together on economic and social issues and policies

polling station where people go to vote on election day. There are a number of different polling stations within each constituency

population pyramid a graph that shows the age-sex distribution of a given population

port of call a place where a ship stops during a journey

poverty being very poor, not having enough money or food

power control and authority over people and their activities

President ceremonial head of state

primary industry an industry that harvests raw materials OR involved in the extracting and developing of raw materials

Prime Minister political leader and head of the government

principle a rule or idea that explains how something works

production the process of manufacturing or growing something in large quantities

productive capable of producing goods and services that have monetary or exchange value

proportional representation (PR) a system of voting in which each political party is represented in a parliament or legislature in proportion to the number of people who vote for it in an election

qualification the qualifications you need for an activity or task are the qualities and skills that you need to be able to do it

quality the characteristic that someone or something has

quality of life measure of happiness that a person has in their life

quantity an amount that you can measure or count

quarrying the extracting of stone from a quarry

racial integration when people from different cultural groups live and work together on an equal basis

Reasoning a Rastafarian ritual

referendum a vote by the eligible voters of a country on a single law or question and accept or reject an idea or law

refinery a factory where a substance such as oil or sugar is refined

refining process the process that separates oil into different chemicals

Reggae a kind of West Indian popular music with a very strong beat

region an area of the world, e.g. the Caribbean

regional integration the joining together or working together of countries that are close together, in order to make them economically and politically more powerful

religion belief in a god or gods and the activities that are connected with this belief, such as praying or worshipping in a building such as a church or temple

repatriation the process of transporting a claimant or their body back to their own country after they have been injured or killed in a foreign country

replenish If you replenish something, you make it full or complete again

represent act or speak for someone else

representative a person who has been chosen to act or make decisions on behalf of another person or a group of people

representative democracy political system in which people elect people to represent them in government and govern the country on their behalf

resign If you resign from a job or position, you formally announce that you are leaving it

resort a place where people go on holiday

resources sources of economic wealth, esp of a country (mineral, land, labour, etc) or business enterprise (capital, equipment, personnel, etc)

responsible If someone or something is responsible for a particular event or situation, they are the cause of it or they can be blamed for it

résumé/curriculum vitae document summarising skills, education and experience

rural development social or economic activities or initiatives designed to improve the standard of living in areas far away from large towns or cities

sanitation having a clean supply of water and good sewage system

secession when a country, or a group, separates from a larger group

secondary industry an industry mostly involved in processing and manufacturing OR manufacturing industries which make products from raw materials

secret ballot a method of voting which is not visible by other people

secretariat a permanent administrative office

self-appraisal the evaluation of one's own strengths and weaknesses

self-employed providing one's own work or income, without an employer

self-esteem respect for or a favourable opinion of oneself

self-motivated motivated or driven by oneself or one's own desires, without any external agency

Senate the upper house of Parliament of Tobago's Parliament, made up of senators

Senator a government official who is a member of a Senate and is involved in making or passing laws

senior older or holding greater power or responsibility

services activities such as banking, hairdressing or tourism which are sold to consumers

settlement a place where people settle down and live

sex tourism tourism with the intention of exploiting permissive or poorly enforced local laws

sexual harassment any attention, touch or comment that has unwanted sexual content

sexually transmitted infection (STI) an infection that is spread by means of sexual intercourse or sexual contact between two people

Ska a type of West Indian pop music of the 1960s, accented on the second and fourth beats of a four-beat bar

skill the knowledge and ability that enables you to do something well

skilled to have the ability, creativity or knowledge to do something well

social integration when people of all cultural groups, sexes and ages live and work together in an area

socialisation how we interact and communicate with others and how we form relationships

standard of living the level of comfort and wealth that a person or family may have

subculture the ideas, art, and way of life of a group of people within a society, which are different from the ideas, art, and way of life of the rest of the society

succession training where the employee's skills and abilities are developed to prepare them for promotion

suggestive suggesting something without saying it explicitly

supporter person who approves of and votes for political parties

sustainable development development of a country that uses natural resources in a way that allows them to grow back or be replenished

sustainable tourism allowing tourists to visit an area, or country, with little negative impact on natural resources and the environment

sustainable/sustainability something that can be continued without destroying the resources that make it possible OR able to continue at the same level without destroying the resources it relies on

system a way of working, organising, or doing something which follows a fixed plan or set of rules. You can use system to refer to an organisation or institution that is organised in this way

Taíno a group of Amerindians who travelled to the Caribbean from Venezuela and settled mainly in the Greater Antilles

talent the natural ability to do something well

tanker ship ships which carry oil to refineries

tertiary education education, following secondary education at a school, at a college or university

tertiary industry an industry that provides services OR service industries which sell manufactured goods OR involves providing services and making goods available to customers, like banking for example

The Jamaican Court of Appeal an appeal court which also functions to mediate industrial disputes in countries which are under its mandate

thermal expansion expansion caused by heat

trade agreement an agreement between two or more countries in relation to providing goods and services

trade union an organised group of workers which protects their interests and rights

trademark a name or symbol that a company uses on its products and that cannot legally be used by another company

tradition a custom or belief that has existed for a long time

transparent when a situation is seen to be open and honest

treaty a formal agreement between countries

trustworthy to be someone who can be relied upon

tuition assistance additional training courses for employee's to build up their knowledge and skills

unemployment the state of not having work

unicameral system a system of government that has a single legislative chamber

United Nations an organisation whose role is to encourage international peace, co-operation, and friendship

United Nations Children's Fund an organisation which provides funding to many charities and organisations which protect children

unity being joined together or in agreement

unskilled workers who have no formal training, education or skill

unsolicited not invited or asked for

urban development the development or improvement of an urban area by building

variety the quality or condition of being diversified or various

vote the ballot of voting paper on which you choose your candidate in an election

voters list a list of all persons allowed to vote

wants something that you would like to have, but is not essential

water pollution substances found in water bodies such as lakes or seas that are harmful or dangerous

watershed an area of high ground which divides two or more river systems, so that all streams on one side flow into one river and those on the other side flow into a different river

wealth all goods and services with monetary, exchangeable, or productive value

West Indian Federation a group of ten Caribbean states that formed a federation from 1958 to 1962

wind energy energy produced from windmills and wind turbines

wind farm a place where windmills are used to convert the power of the wind into electricity

work ethics the rules and standards of conduct that are acceptable in the workplace

workplace relationships relationships with people that we work with

work-to-rule where workers do just enough to fulfil the requirements of their job roles, but no more

yield the amount of food produced on an area of land or by a number of animals

Index

Acknowledgements

The publishers wish to thank the following for permission to reproduce photographs. Every effort has been made to trace copyright holders and to obtain their permission for the use of copyright materials. The publishers will gladly receive any information enabling them to rectify any error or omission at the first opportunity.

p6: Photo Spirit/SS; p7: Yevgen Belich/SS; p7: JamTravels/SS; p7: Avel Shah/SS; p7: Debbie Ann Powell/SS; p8: Shelby Soblick/Getty; p9: Shelby Soblick/Getty; p9: Leonard Zhukovsky/SS; p9: PA Images/Alamy; p10: pansticks/SS; p12: magic pictures/SS; p13: Bikeworldtravel/SS; p15: Willy Barton/SS; p16: The Life Picture Collection/Getty Images; p17: Denise Andersen/SS; p17: Carsten Reisinger/SS; p17: Lucian Coman; p18: Everynight Images/Alamy; p18: Lost Mountain Studio/SS; p19: Prachaya Roekdeethaweesab/SS; p19: Michael Dwyer/Alamy; p19: David Levenson/Alamy; p20: Aleksandr Rybalko/SS; p21: Sevenstock Studio/SS; p22: Photo Spirit/SS; p22: Debbie Ann Powell/SS; p23: Yakov Oskanov/SS; p24: MarcoVector/SS; p25: nutech21; p26: Solarisys/SS; p26: darksoul72/SS; p27: Adam Shanker/SS; p27: AF archive/Alamy; p28: Julie Clopper/SS; p28: Ververidis Vasilis/SS; p30: Debbie Ann Powell/SS; p30: Karol Kozlowski Premium RM Collection/ Alamy; p31: robertharding/Alamy; p31: Photo Spirit/SS; p31: robertharding/Alamy; p31: Mark Bassett/Alamy; p32: REUTERS/Alamy; p33: Jeff Greenberg/Getty; p34: Petr Toman/SS; p35: Allstar Picture Library Ltd/Alamy; p36: Allstar Picture Library Ltd/Alamy; p37: AF archive/Alamy; p38: Jeff Greenberg/Getty; p44: Daniel Samray/SS; p44: Debbie Ann Powell/SS; p44: Associated Press/Collin Reid/Alamy; p45: Akieem Afflick/SS; p45: Daniel M Ernst/SS; p46: Rodney Legall/Alamy; p47: MANDEL NGAN/Getty; p48: yui/SS; p50: CARFITA Games; p51: Philip Wolmuth/Alamy; p52: 506 collection/Alamy; p50: Niyazz/SS; p54: OECS; p55: OECS; p56: REUTERS/Alamy; p57: Ognjen Stevanovic/Alamy; p58: anfisa focusova/SS; p59: Gareth Copley/Getty; p60: Robert Fried/Alamy; p61: Sean Sprague/Alamy; p64: Caribbean Court of Justice; p65: maxstockphoto/SS; p66: mavo/SS; p70: mangostock/Getty; p71: Massy Group; p72: orenthomasphotography/SS; p78: orenthomasphotography/SS; p78: orenthomasphotography/SS; p79: Ozphotoguy/SS; p79: Wangkun Jia/SS; p79: Tint Media/SS; p80: antoniohugo/SS; p80: Photoroyalty/SS; p80: Leszek Czerwonka/SS; p80: SpeedKingz/SS; p80: Red Confidential/SS; p81: Andrii Vodolazhskyi/SS; p82: funnybear36/SS; p82: Roberto Herrett/Alamy; p84: Jarun Ontakrai/SS; p86: Shutterstock; p87: Women's Centre Foundation of Jamaica; p88: Mohd Shahrizan Hussin/SS; p89: ricochet64/SS; p90: fizkes/SS; p91: wow.subtropica/SS; p92: vectoraart/SS; p93: Anan Kaewkhammul; p94: Horizons WWP/Alamy; p95: Tinnakorn jorruang/SS; p102: Paul Wishart/SS; p102: Bussweh/SS; p103: osemarie Mosteller/SS; p103: Luciavonu/SS; p103: ilapinto/SS; p104: Eye Ubiquitous/Alamy; p104: Debbie Ann Powell/SS; p104: Paul Wishar/SS; p104: Debbie Ann Powell/SS; p104: Debbie Ann Powell/SS; p105: Gearstd/SS; p109: Matthew Wakem/Alamy; p109: Debbie Ann Powell/SS; p109: Debbie Ann Powell/SS; p109: Debbie Ann Powell/SS; p109: Debbie Ann Powell/SS; p109: Debbie Ann Powell/SS; p110: Eye Ubiquitous/Getty; p111: Danita Delimont/SS; p112: OSTILL is Franck Camhi/SS; p114: Xtock Images/Alamy; p116: Eye Ubiquitous/Getty; p118: AshTproductions/SS; p119: fizkes/SS; p119: HEART/NSTA Trust; p121: ICW/SS; p122: Bloomberg/Getty; p124: Denys Yelmanov/Alamy; p124: Debbie Ann Powell/SS; p126: Debbie Ann Powell/SS; p127: Stock2468/SS; p128: Kjersti Joergensen/SS; p129: Danny E Hooks/SS; p130: Aratta_Artbox/SS; p130: Colin McConnell/SS; p131: Neil Cooper/Alamy; p132: Daniel M Ernst/SS; p132: Vision 2030 Jamaica; p133: Big Joe/SS; p133: Michael Dwyer/Alamy; p134: Skyward Kick Productions/SS; p134: Craig F Scott/SS; p135: Mia2you/SS; p136: Robert Fried/Alamy; p142: orenthomasphotography/SS; p142: Robert Landau/Alamy; p143: Eric James/Alamy; p143: Debbie Ann Powell/SS; p143: Globetrotter Museum/SS; p144: photka/SS; p146: REUTERS/Alamy; p148: Globetrotter Museum/SS; p149: Lisa-S/SS; p150: REUTERS/Alamy; p153: Asma Samoh/SS; p156: Tudoran Andrei/SS; p157: REUTERS/Alamy; p164: WESTOCK PRODUCTIONS/SS; p164: Associated Press/ Ramon Espinosa/Alamy; p165: 5D Media/SS; p165: Associated Press/ Ramon Espinosa/Alamy; p165: Niyazz/SS; p166: John Gomez/SS; p169: Sean Drakes/Getty; p172: Niyazz/SS; p173: jeff gynane/SS; p174: Jeff Morgan 09/Alamy; p174: Paul Fleet/SS; p175: Jeffrey Coolidge/Getty; p176: SEAN DRAKES/Alamy; p179: Office of the Political Ombudsman; p180: ANGELA WEISS/Getty; p183: Xinhua/Alamy; p192: Marcin Sylwia Ciesielski/SS; p192: Cleon Green/SS; p192: Wirestock Creators/SS; p192: Sherry Talbot/Shutterstock; p192: Luciavonu/SS; p194: Angela N Perryman/SS; p195: Meryl/SS; p196: Rich Carey/SS; p197: TR STOK/SS; p197: zhengzaishuru/SS; p198: Paul Stringer/SS; p199: Jamaican Environment Trist (JET); p201: Borys Vasylenko/SS; p202: Millenius/SS; p203: ssuaphotos/SS; p204: Debbie Ann Powell/SS; p205: Craig F Scott/SS; p205: Quote Studio/SS; p206: Bang Ucup/SS; p208: National Geographic Image Collection/Alamy; p208: Thierry Eidenweil/SS; p208: Michael Smith ITWP/SS; p208: reptiles4all/SS; p209: David G Hayes/SS; p211: Eye Ubiquitous/Alamy; p211: Jason Bleibtreu/Getty; p212: Phatranist Kerddaeng/SS; p212: Belovodchenko Anton/SS; p212: Cheng Wei/SS; p213: jeremy sutton-hibbert/Alamy; p214: Debbie Ann Powell/SS; p216: Ethan Daniels/SS; p217: Damsea/SS; p217: TheModernCanvas/SS; p222: Craig F Scott/SS; p222: Debbie Ann Powell/SS; p222: Prostock-studio/SS; p223: Roman Samborskyi/SS; p223: LightField Studios/SS; p224: Cultura RM/Alamy; p224: Shutterstock; p228: GeraldConnell/Getty; p229: MBI/Alamy; p231: Everett Collection/SS; p231: Sueddeutsche Zeitung Photo/Alamy; p232: David Gilder/SS; p233: michaeljung/SS; p237: SpeedKingz/SS; p238: ONOKY - Photononstop/Alamy; p244: Moodboard Stock Photography/Alamy; p245: Tony Tallec/Alamy; p246: Amir Ridhwan/SS; p249: Cavan Images/Getty; p250: laflor/Getty; p252: Octa corp/SS; p253: Ian Townsley/Alamy; p254: satit_srihin/SS; p254: Janine Wiedel Photolibrary/Alamy; p255: John James/Alamy; p260: Debbie Ann Powell/SS; p260: Debbie Ann Powell/SS; p260: Wangkun Jia/SS; p261: Debbie Ann Powell/SS; p261: Debbie Ann Powell/SS; p242: CO Leong/SS; p262: ajlatan/SS; p264: Stefan Herremans/SS; p265: Nzuri Photography/SS; p266: Paul_Brighton/SS; p269: M. Timothy O'Keefe/Alamy; p270: Solarisys/SS; p270: Jason Bryan/Alamy; p272: puksamran/SS.